SANCTUARY PEOPLE

Sanctuary People

Faith-Based Organizing in Latina/o Communities

Gina M. Pérez

NEW YORK UNIVERSITY PRESS

New York

NEW YORK UNIVERSITY PRESS
New York
www.nyupress.org

© 2024 by New York University
All rights reserved

Please contact the Library of Congress for Cataloging-in-Publication data.

ISBN: 9781479823901 (hardback)
ISBN: 9781479823918 (paperback)
ISBN: 9781479823956 (library ebook)
ISBN: 9781479823932 (consumer ebook)

This book is printed on acid-free paper, and its binding materials are chosen for strength and durability. We strive to use environmentally responsible suppliers and materials to the greatest extent possible in publishing our books.

Manufactured in the United States of America

10 9 8 7 6 5 4 3 2 1

Also available as an ebook

For sanctuary people everywhere

CONTENTS

Introduction

Sanctuary and Accompaniment in Moments of Danger

On September 5, 2017, Edith Espinal entered into sanctuary in the Columbus Mennonite Church in Columbus, Ohio. On that bright morning, she stood before microphones in the parking lot leading to the entrance of the Clintonville neighborhood church, surrounded by her family, faith leaders, community activists, immigrant rights advocates, and members of the Columbus Mennonite Church and other faith communities who stood with her as she publicly entered into a church that would be her home for more than three years.[1] As a longtime resident of the city, this immigrant rights activist, community member, and mother in a mixed-status household had tried unsuccessfully for years to regularize her citizenship status.[2] Her decision to publicly seek sanctuary in a church was not one she made in haste. But the urgency of the moment—the shifting immigration enforcement landscape and rising anti-immigrant and white nationalist sentiment—led her and others across the nation to embrace a centuries-old strategy of turning to sacred spaces and houses of worship for protection, and in her case specifically, to shield her from deportation. During the press conference, Pastor Joel Miller of the Columbus Mennonite Church announced, "Today, we are welcoming Edith into sanctuary in our church building."[3] As Pastor Joel continued his comments, he described Edith's long history of living and raising a family in Columbus. "Edith is a neighbor. Edith is a mother. Edith is a child of God who sought refuge in our country many years ago and now wishes to remain united with her family in this city which has become her home."[4]

By focusing on family, faith, and community, Pastor Joel was telling the story of what grounds Edith had in the local community, which also resonated with the experiences of a growing number of people seeking public sanctuary in churches across the country in 2017. Her strategy was concomitant with an increasing number of cities, counties, states, and even college campuses declaring themselves sanctuaries following the 2016 presidential election. The late Columbus-based community activist Ruben Castilla Herrera, for example, emphasized the significance of Edith's entering into sanctuary to affirm the city's commitment to immigrants when he somberly observed, "Today, Columbus, Ohio, truly became a sanctuary city, because sanctuary comes from the people." Edith and her daughter, Stephanie, emphasized the importance of keeping families together and the ways sanctuary is a collective response to a shared experience of precarity. "I'd like to thank you for being here to listen to our story," Edith somberly declared through an interpreter. "I'm fighting to keep my family united." Stephanie conveyed the grief of the moment, one shared by so many other undocumented families, when she emotionally proclaimed, "I don't want her to go or to leave us at all. It's not just us. It's more families that get separated every day. My mom means everything to me."[5]

While Edith Espinal's was one of the most visible public sanctuary cases between 2017 and 2021, her story is part of a longer history of faith-based organizing and sanctuary practices in the United States that primarily include, but are not exclusive to, undocumented migrants. As many scholars have documented, sanctuary movements in the United States have involved organizing to support conscientious objectors during the Vietnam War, Central American refugees in the United States during the 1980s, and, most recently, the New Sanctuary Movement beginning in the mid-2000s, which has focused on aiding undocumented individuals and families faced with deportation, often after residing for many years in local communities. These efforts have drawn on ancient Western traditions of sanctuary that, as anthropologist Linda Rabben has observed, have involved "social groups and individuals who mobilize to provide sanctuary often outside the law and at great risk."[6] In this way, invocations of sanctuary have emphasized appeals to a higher transcendent authority to justify the decision by communities of faith to offer refuge, safety, and protection to those who are most vulnerable to state power. Such evocations also affirm commitments to align oneself with others to challenge state power and to potentially endure state-sanctioned punishment and harm as a result.

Following the 2016 presidential election, sanctuary was clearly in the air. There were calls for sanctuary campuses, sanctuary cities, sanctuary streets, and, as the Quakers put forth succinctly and powerfully, "sanctuary everywhere." This language of offering sanctuary to people in need suffused organizing and service work across the country. In Northeast Ohio, for example, faith communities, activists, community leaders, and service providers employed the language of sanctuary to characterize their responses to what felt like unrelenting instances of family separation, displacement, and increased economic and social vulnerability due to immigrant detention, natural disasters, and economic and political crises within Latina/o communities.[7] Following Hurricane María's devastating impact in Puerto Rico in September 2017, people quickly mobilized to collect food, water, medical supplies, clothes, and money to send to the island and to help resettle hundreds of Puerto Rican families. In cities like Lorain, Ohio, just twenty-five miles west of Cleveland, Latina/o community members, faith leaders, and service workers framed their responses and support for Puerto Rican newcomers as providing refuge for displaced families facing unimaginable loss and uncertainty. These same community members mobilized, once again, in June 2018 following workplace raids at Corso's garden center in Sandusky, Ohio, where 114 workers were detained and faced deportation and family separation. In the days and weeks following the raids, faith and community leaders, activists, and service workers in Lorain organized food and clothing drives, collecting diapers and baby food, offering free legal advice about immigration, and even helping parents complete affidavits detailing instructions for care for their children in the event that they were detained by Immigration and Customs Enforcement (ICE). In press conferences, public speeches, and daily conversations, organizers and service providers framed their responses to detained migrants and their families as being similar to their approach to meeting the needs of migrants post-Hurricane María. As Victor Leandry, executive director of El Centro de Servicios Sociales in Lorain, observed about the children of detained parents, "These kids are going to need our help. . . . This is not a new problem. Yes, it's getting worse, but it is an ongoing problem. . . . Right now there are children taking care of children in Norwalk [Ohio, because their parents have been detained]. And just like we did after [Hurricane] María, [El Centro] will take care of people in need and find ways to help the community."[8]

Linking the fates of people displaced by Hurricane María with families ripped apart by immigration detention is a prescient, if grim, reminder of a shared precariousness defining the lives of many Latinas/os in Northeast Ohio. Organizations like El Centro have a long history of working with faith communities, social workers, mental health providers, and community activists to address the broad range of needs of people whose daily lives are constrained by draconian immigration policies, (un)natural disasters, economic dislocation, and punitive policing. And while, as Victor Leandry notes, these are not new problems, neither are the resources people draw on as they collectively respond to the challenges they face. Indeed, these long histories of organizing and struggle are precious resources that sustain and animate community responses today.

On the surface, organizing to relocate families fleeing natural disasters and supporting families ripped apart by deportation might not seem to fall within a shared framework of sanctuary. But drawing on my ongoing ethnographic work in Latina/o communities in Northeast Ohio—as well as reading the work of scholars, journalists, artists, community activists, and service workers—I argue that what binds these responses and experiences together is a commitment to become what Ruben Castilla Herrera referred to as "sanctuary people." In a lecture at Oberlin College in the fall of 2018, Ruben discussed the intersectional organizing work that he and his fellow activists were involved in, including supporting people like Edith Espinal in public sanctuary through organizations like the Columbus Sanctuary Collective. But his work also included efforts to address racial profiling and the impact of police violence in Black communities and other communities of color in Columbus; supporting the integration of asylum seekers in the city; working with migrant workers throughout Ohio; and organizing with others to make Columbus a sanctuary city. All of these efforts, he argued, were key to making stronger, safer, and inclusive communities, and required all of us to become sanctuary people.

This book employs Ruben Castilla Herrera's notion of sanctuary people to shed much-needed light onto myriad organizing efforts and resistance strategies that a diverse group of people employed following the 2016 presidential election. It examines the role that faith communities in Ohio have played in the development, proliferation, and strengthening of sanctuary practices and other forms of organizing connected to Latina/o communities and Latin American migrants. By focusing on efforts to help those affected by immigrant detention and Puerto Ricans displaced in the wake of Hurricane María, this book reveals the ways faith communities, activists, and community leaders are creating new strategies to address the increasingly precarious contexts in which Latina/o people live, and how they are imagining and enacting new forms of solidarity. It also analyzes the distinct alliances, relationships, and ways of knowing and being that faith-based activists have employed to create places of safety. In doing so, this book seeks to center the role of faith-based organizing in these communities, contributes to a growing scholarly literature documenting these efforts, and reveals what Puerto Rican journalist Mari Mari Narváez describes as the need to "build a more horizontal society, a place for everyone to live and work and love in."[9]

Based on four years of ethnographic work, this book documents how for many, immigrant detention, natural disasters, and race-based violence are often viewed as intertwined experiences. In this context, practices of offering sanctuary and refuge bind up the diverse yet overlapping experiences of Puerto Rican, Mexican, and Central American families in moments of precarity, uncertainty, and vulnerability, and also point to the ways their shared precarity is connected to African American and other communities facing state-based violence and exclusion. By focusing on these seemingly disparate experiences, I argue that becoming sanctuary people requires building meaningful relationships and coalitions across differences of class, race, ethnicity, gender, language, religion, education, and citizenship status to strengthen and support Latina/o communities in a moment of uncertainty, danger, and hopeful possibilities.

Theorizing Sanctuary, Faith-Based Organizing, and Accompaniment in Latina/o Studies

Sanctuary People foregrounds the experiences and organizing efforts of Latina/o communities in Northeast Ohio and locates them within a larger context of faith-based organizing that is multiethnic, cross-racial, and multi-issue. Notably, these efforts are informed by gendered ideas of family, kinship, and belonging. My analysis of formal interview data, news reports, and participant observation from rallies, protests, organizational meetings, prayer vigils, and countless conversations and informal interviews is grounded in three scholarly areas broadly defined:

research on sanctuary movements in the United States; burgeoning scholarly attention to faith-based organizing in Latina/o communities; and engagement with the notion of accompaniment as liberatory praxis. In what follows, I demonstrate the ways my research builds on the insights of other scholars and writers, with a particular emphasis on the debates and lines of inquiry within Latina/o studies that inform my understanding of the ways the people whose experiences I document here embody what it means to be sanctuary people.

Sanctuary Movements, Past and Present

Sanctuary is a capacious concept. According to Rachel Buff, sanctuary "can denote both broad aspiration and specific practices; it draws on religious roots as well as internationalist imaginings."[10] With its roots in ancient traditions, sanctuary—the idea of providing refuge, safety, and protection in sacred spaces—involves specific practices governed by specific rules. Indeed, as anthropologist Linda Rabben argues, "Almost every major religious tradition includes concepts and rules governing sanctuary."[11] From ancient Egyptian shrines and Greek temples, groves, and altars dedicated to gods, to Hebrew cities of refuge, sanctuaries were well known to fugitives, slaves, refugees, and exiles in the ancient world who sought safety and protection in them. Sanctuary was also "one of the most powerful and important medieval institutions," used to resolve conflicts and sometimes to avoid punishment and retribution, and serving an important function of "defining the boundaries of the law and the sacred meaning of justice."[12] Scholars like Aimee Villarreal have argued for an understanding of sanctuary in the Americas "as a dynamic autochthonous tradition and Indigenous survival strategy cultivated (and continuously remade) in regions of refuge and rebellion."[13] Naomi Paik, Jason Ruiz, and Rebecca Schreiber offer yet another definition of sanctuary: "At its core, [sanctuary] provided an alternative, and ultimate source of authority, rooted in the divine. . . . Put differently, the existence of sanctuary practices and spaces stood as a reminder that the nation-state does not have exclusive sovereign control over what happens in its territories."[14] Understanding sanctuary in this way draws our attention to a range of examples in US history where people have appealed to a higher transcendent authority to challenge the power of the state, including nineteenth-century abolitionists defying the Fugitive Slave Act, conscientious objectors to the Vietnam War, and, of course, challenges to restrictive immigration policy and the consequences of US-fueled war and military support in Central America and beyond.

Research on contemporary sanctuary movements in the United States and internationally is quite vast.[15] This is particularly the case when we broaden our understanding of sanctuary to include what Rachel Buff describes as "not only a specific place in a church or other building but a set of practices by which people come into relations of accompaniment and solidarity."[16] Susan Coutin and Hilary Cunningham, for example, document the important history of the sanctuary movement of the 1980s and the ways it connected faith communities in the United States with refugees fleeing US-fueled wars in Central America. Others have noted the gendered dimensions of sanctuary, with the focus on women faith leaders and workers who played a pivotal role in the 1980s, an important corrective given scholarly and popular attention to the efforts of men like Reverend John Fife and Jim Corbett in the 1980s sanctuary movement that often elided the critical role women played.[17] Yet others, like María Cristina García, have offered a broader hemispheric lens for understanding the sanctuary movement of the 1980s to see the ways that migrants from Central American countries like Guatemala, Nicaragua, and El Salvador connect to Mexico, the United States, and Canada through a long history of war, displacement, and migration.[18]

The New Sanctuary Movement (NSM), which emerged in the mid-2000s, has a much different but related history to that of the 1980s. As Paik, Ruiz, and Schreiber note, the NSM developed as a response to the need to "defend immigrants, particularly long-term residents, from the escalating deportation regimes instigated by the post-9/11 creation of the Department of Homeland Security (DHS), Immigration and Customs Enforcement (ICE), and Customs and Border Protection (CBP)."[19] With the rising number of deportations under President Obama, immigrant rights activists like Elvira Arrellano in Chicago turned to the ancient yet temporally adjacent strategy of sanctuary not to seek refuge across borders, but rather to remain in a place where she and so many others had built family, community, and home. Sanctuary, in this way, is more than seeking refuge and safety. It is also about laying claim to home and belonging. As Villarreal has eloquently argued, "Sanctuary is fundamentally about the search for a home and the making of homeplaces in often hostile territory."[20] Recent studies on sanctuary have foregrounded this notion of home-making and belonging in the context of state-fueled deportation policies, family separation, and punitive immigration enforcement and have drawn attention to the different organizing strategies as well as alliances that emerge in these struggles. Amalia Pallares, for example, provides a detailed discussion of the struggles of Elvira Arrellano and Flor Crisóstomo, two women in Chicago who employed distinct strategies to fight deportation orders and remain with their communities and families, and the ways that gender, race, ethnicity, and family framed both the strategies and the backlash to their public sanctuary cases.[21] Similarly, Lloyd Barba and Tatyana Castillo-Ramos explore how within the growing New Sanctuary Movement beginning in late 2016, "sanctuary seekers, workers, and leaders have enacted various kinds of sacred resistance to respond to the shifting contexts of immigration crises."[22] This was particularly evident during the explosive family separation policies at the US-Mexico border beginning in 2018 and the ways they emboldened a range of faith-based activists and leaders across faith traditions to publicly stand with migrants and denounce family separation immigration policies, including deportation.

Within activist and scholarly circles, there have also been ongoing debates about the efficacy of sanctuary as a political strategy, including critiques of the limitations of sanctuary practices that rely on distinctions between deserving and undeserving migrants. Indeed, as Naomi Paik has cogently argued, "sanctuary must become more expansive if it is to be effective." She has called for "an abolitionist approach to sanctuary, one that works on multiple, simultaneous fronts of struggle against capitalist exploitation, borders, policing, caging, and patriarchal power, among others whose connections may not always be so obvious. An abolitionist sanctuary cannot focus solely on the foreign-born, or race and immigration status, but must undo the structures through which people become targeted."[23] This observation is supported by many activists who have argued for a broader approach to organizing that seeks to understand the multiple factors that both produce social inequality and shape imagined liberatory futures. According to historian Barbara Ransby, it is precisely this kind of intersectional approach to organizing, grounded in a long history of Black feminist praxis, that has bolstered contemporary freedom struggles such as the Black Lives Matter movement and the Movement for Black Lives and that offer an important model for other freedom struggles. Like the Black radical feminist thinkers who authored the foundational Combahee River Collective Statement of 1977, Ransby calls for an approach to organizing with "more national campaigns that bring activists from various sectors together with focused strategic purpose. We can think of the ongoing national coalition-building and united-front work as a wheel with spokes rather than a hierarchical, top-down pyramid. But the wheel has to have a hub and center to connect the spokes (i.e., local and issue-specific struggles). And there needs to be more serious and rigorous political education, in terms of both history and theory."[24] Contemporary sanctuary practices are part of a larger landscape of organizing and activism to address familiar and new mechanisms of power that both produce and affect individuals and communities.

Despite disagreements and concerns about sanctuary's scope and efficacy, there seem to be several important areas of consensus among those who study and work with sanctuary movements: First, as Rabben has argued, "sanctuary has remained a morally and religiously based obligation that often takes place outside or against the law."[25] Second, the sanctuary movements of the twenty-first century have deep roots in the Central American solidarity and sanctuary movements of the 1980s, which, according to Sergio M. González, "stretched national borders," and whose transnational scope "grew out of a confluence of armed conflict in Central America, concurrent mass displacement, and a growing anger among Americans concerning their country's intervention in the region."[26] Faith-based activists responded to these events in ways that often brought them into broader coalitions with anti-imperialist organizing, LGBT liberation movements, and critiques of US militarization and counterinsurgency in Central America and the Caribbean.[27] Finally, and perhaps most importantly, the contemporary movement represents a form of what political scientist Amalia Pallares refers to as "family activism," a complex political strategy by immigrant rights activists as they construct, reinforce, challenge, and redefine notions of family to fight deportation and family separation.[28]

This book's focus on public sanctuary in Ohio builds on this scholarship to demonstrate the enduring power of sanctuary as a faith-based strategy of resistance; the ways many people committed to contemporary sanctuary work often come to it through decades-long faith-based organizing and service; and the continued reliance on family activism to challenge family separation and deportation. By understanding sanctuary in this way—as a strategy building on long histories of community organizing and self-defense—I not only explore the locally specific ways sanctuary practices are deployed and embraced by activists, but also highlight the ways sanctuary "provides an expansive archive of social movements that we might not otherwise see as being connected."[29]

Latinas/os and Faith-Based Organizing

As a number of scholars have noted, Latina/o studies is relatively late in addressing the role of religion within the field.[30] This elision reflects the field's foundational attention to colonialism, US imperialism, labor, migration, and racial exclusion in Puerto Rican, Chicana/o, and later Latina/o studies. The role of religion and religious institutions in each of these areas, however, has always been an important part of understanding these processes, even when scholars fail to see or acknowledge their significance.[31] From the role of the Catholic Church in colonial governance and the ways Protestant missionaries shaped migration practices between sending and receiving communities, to the importance of priests, nuns, ministers, and pastors in labor struggles of farmworkers, urban youth social movements, and faith-based organizing, secular and religious concerns within Latina/o studies clearly infuse one another. Although the study of religion and religious practices was never entirely absent from early Chicana/o and Puerto Rican scholarship and through the 1980s, beginning in the early 2000s "a new generation of scholars emerged determined to cross disciplinary borders and bring religious history into conversation with fields such as ethnic and cultural studies."[32] One of the many emerging areas of focus includes attention to religion, politics, and faith-based organizing both past and present. Burgeoning scholarship in Latina/o history and ethnography that explores what Felipe Hinojosa, Maggie Elmore, and Sergio González refer to as "Latino religious politics" provides an important corrective to approaches that narrowly defined what constitutes Latina/o religious practices, beliefs, and spirituality and how they inform political practices. They also remind us that not only have Latina/o communities "drawn from their faith and spirituality to build networks of mutual aid" for more than half a century, they have done so often through progressive, faith-based social movements "centered around questions of justice, human dignity, and the common good."[33]

Historical accounts of the relationship between faith, religion, and politics have drawn our attention to the civil rights era to deepen our understanding of the role of religion, politics, race, ethnicity, gender, and social movements in Latina/o communities in both rural and urban settings. Latina/o Mennonites, for example, were active participants in the Chicana/o, Puerto Rican, and Black freedom struggles, which led them to develop meaningful organizations and spaces within the church to address issues of gender, race, and ethnic belonging, as well as intertwine their faith, religion, and the civil rights struggles in ways that "fostered an eclectic mix of religious activists in unexpected places."[34] Some of these unexpected places and eclectic mix of activists were found in rural communities in Central California, where agricultural workers and key leaders in the farmworkers' movement, like César Chávez and Reies López Tijerina, were deeply influenced by both Catholicism and Pentecostalism and drew on "religious tactics, imagery, and symbols" in their organizing efforts.[35] Some of the most iconic visual images of the United Farm Workers (UFW) protests include marchers carrying banners of La Virgen de Guadalupe and other Catholic religious symbols. But they also drew on Pentecostal affective practices—such as Mexican Pentecostalism's use of corridos and much livelier musical selections in their worship services than in the Catholic mass—as both an organizing strategy and a mode of resistance. As Lloyd D. Barba observes, "In contrast to Catholic visual religious stimuli, Pentecostals wielded the power of the sonic, to such a degree that a group of twelve could exhibit 'more spirit' than two hundred in a mass."[36] Church occupations by Chicana/o and Puerto Rican activists in the 1960s were also steeped in religious symbolism, such as unfurling a banner hanging from the second floor of the First Spanish United Methodist Church in East Harlem to proclaim it "La Iglesia de la Gente, the People's Church." Recalling some of the most iconic moments of the Young Lords and the Chicano movement organizing, Jorge Juan Rodríguez V calls for an analysis of these struggles that "takes seriously the history of the occupied church and the role of religion within the occupation."[37] Doing so reveals how struggles around faith, religion, and politics are often simultaneously *intra-Latina/o* struggles and ones that, in the case of the church occupation in East Harlem by the Young Lords, were "arbitrated through religious language, embodiment, and space."[38] Excavating these histories of Latina/o faith, religion, and politics is absolutely critical to our contemporary understanding of these relationships and underscore Rodríguez V's prescient observation: "Latinx religious politics has always been about making meaning in community as people wrestle with the sacred."[39]

Ethnographic studies of faith-based organizing, religion, and politics help to document the various ways communities "wrestle with the sacred." From Latina/o communities organizing marches with Catholic symbols to both contest the proliferation of anti-immigrant legislation in 2006 and lay claim to multiethnic belonging in the Midwest, to Latina/o Saints in the Mormon Church working to ensure that their church "publicly defend them as part and parcel of the Mormon deseret," Sujey Vega's work, for example, reveals the complexity of religious identity and politics in local communities as they grapple with restrictionist immigration legislation at the federal and state level.[40] Research on Pentecostal addiction ministries and organizing efforts by and with formerly incarcerated people to expand political and social rights underscore a variety of religious traditions, histories, and practices people draw on in efforts to redeem, rehabilitate, and remake themselves and their communities.[41] Ethnographers have also documented the important role of religion, spirituality, and ritual kinship ties for women of color activists, organizers, and community workers as a mode of both self-care and spiritual sustenance as they respond to political forces undermining their safety in neighborhoods and communities. This activism also has long ties with reproductive justice, labor, LGBTQ, and immigrant rights organizing.[42] Such insights highlight the ways that "the spiritual is political," but also draw our attention to the gendered dimensions of lived religion, political practice, and faith-based organizing.[43]

This book builds on this growing scholarly body of writings by exploring the ways various communities in Ohio wrestled with the sacred during a time of great upheaval, uncertainty, and precarity for Latina/o residents in the state.[44] By focusing on the central role that churches, faith-based workers, secular activists, and service providers played in responding to what often felt like recurring moments of crisis, I hope to contribute to efforts in Latina/o studies to excavate the "vital component of faith and religiosity" in Latina/o organizing. I also seek to build on scholarship that calls for a more capacious approach to studying Latina/o religious politics.[45] Moreover, my focus on the ways Latinas/os in Northeast Ohio worked across differences of class, education, race, ethnicity, language, religious denominations, and faith-traditions also responds to the need for more research that is comparative across Latina/o groups and examines the challenges and opportunities of multiethnic and cross-racial faith communities. By centering the activities, oral histories, and experiences of faith-based practitioners across race, class, ethnic, and linguistic difference as well as legal status, I demonstrate how a commitment to being sanctuary people animates, connects, and sustains people from vastly different social locations to a shared sense of divine purpose.

Accompaniment in Theory and Practice

Throughout my research and writing about sanctuary, I found myself reflecting quite often on the relationship between sanctuary and accompaniment. I have been particularly interested in theorizing accompaniment as a practice and its relationship to solidarity. In these endeavors, I am not alone. Indeed, the concept of accompaniment has been clarifying and useful for not only my own analysis, but for other scholars as well. In a 2013 *American Quarterly* article, Barbara Tomlinson and George Lipsitz write powerfully about the urgency for American studies scholarship to interrogate the dangerous moment in which the United States increasingly "seems to be unraveling at the seams." Class polarization, race-based surveillance and mass incarceration, environmental degradation, a permanent warfare state, and the social, economic, and political consequences of decades of "neoliberal dispossession, displacement and disciplinary subordination" characterize the conditions in which people struggle to work and live meaningful lives.[46] They continue,

> These conditions do not represent simply one more episode in the nation's long history of periodic economic downturns and intermittent social ruptures. This is the chaotic breakdown and systemic disintegration of an en-

> tire way of life. The people in power cannot fix the things they have broken. They cannot repair the damage they have done to the planet and its people. . . . It is no longer a question of whether there will be radical changes but rather a matter of which changes will be made and whose interests they will serve. As things fall apart, it will matter who tries to put them together again, whose voices are heard, and which interests are represented.[47]

While Tomlinson and Lipsitz clearly want to draw attention to the crisis of neoliberal global capitalism, they are also unsparing in their critique of the academy, urging scholars to see the ways we reproduce and participate in neoliberal hegemony through destructive academic practices. Powerfully, they exhort us to do the difficult work of reflecting on "*the work we want our work to do.*"[48] The future of American studies, they argue, depends on this reflection, as well as on our "taking responsibility for the world we are creating through our endeavors, for the ways of being in the world that we are modeling and promoting." One way to approach the work we do as scholars, therefore, is to be guided by the notion of accompaniment, which they describe as "a disposition, a sensibility, and a pattern of behavior."[49]

Drawing on a rich history of Latin American liberation theology, accompaniment is guided by a commitment to solidarity and fellowship. Its "potential to be a transformative experience" has rightfully captured the imagination of scholars concerned with neoliberal political-economic forces constraining people's daily lives, the ways universities and other institutions operate and increasingly organize themselves, as well the culture of knowledge production itself that increasingly rewards individual achievement.[50] In short, a politics grounded in accompaniment provides a much-needed corrective to neoliberal thinking and resonates with scholars, activists, and community workers alike. Latina/o ethnographers, for example, have theorized how accompaniment guides the actions and commitments of the communities and people they work with, as well as their own approach to research that defines accompaniment as a "principle informing ways of being and knowing grounded in a post–Vatican II commitment to preferential option for the poor, as well as for people and communities politically and socially marginalized."[51] This understanding resonates with the insights of Paul Farmer, anthropologist, medical doctor, and human rights activist, who describes accompaniment as a process deeply grounded in humility, discernment, careful listening, and most importantly, proximity. He writes, "To accompany someone is . . . to go somewhere with him or her, to break bread together, to be present on a journey with a beginning and an end. The process is humbling, since there is always an element of temporal and experiential mystery, of openness, in accompaniment."[52] By emphasizing the inherent value of being close, present, walking, and sharing with others, accompaniment invites people into deep relationships, which is a precondition for developing the skills necessary for understanding social suffering and marginalization as a form of structural violence that all people are required to see, witness, and remedy. According to liberation theologian Father Gustavo Gutiérrez, one of the central tenets of liberation theology is "to accompany, to be close, and to mitigate the suffering of individuals. This is an expression of love, with the intention being to show that you are relevant for me. This kind of theology is not pragmatic theology, it is practical theology."[53]

This commitment to binding up the lives of people from distinct social locations is precisely the practice of accompaniment and/or practical theology that guides the work of social justice activists who work for racial justice through Black Lives Matter, immigrant rights activists, international solidarity organizations, healthcare providers, social workers, and those committed to working with prison reentry programs and challenging the carceral state.[54] This practical theology also informs the work of faith-based activists, service workers, and others in Northeast Ohio as people made decisions, organized, developed programming, collected resources, and offered support to Latina/o communities in a moment of profound need, uncertainty, and precarity. Sergio M. González's notion of religiopolitical accompaniment that captures "a mode of understanding and developing solidarity and movement building across borders, be they national, denominational, ethnic or otherwise," is particularly useful for understanding the various efforts of people who believed that they had a moral obligation to offer support and care in the face of powerful punitive forces at the local, regional, and national levels.[55] This book documents these efforts and locates them in longer histories of place-based organizing and community building that connect contemporary struggles of primarily Latina/o and immigrant communities to other marginalized communities throughout Ohio.

Latinas/os in Ohio

This research is based on four years of ethnographic work primarily in Northeast Ohio as well as the work of faith-based activists and community organizers in Columbus, Ohio, about two hours south of Oberlin, where I live and work. According to the 2021 American Community Survey, more than 505,000 residents in Ohio are Latina/o, a number that has doubled since 2000.[56] Ohio's Latina/o population is approximately 4.2 percent, a number that is far lower than the percentage nationally (18.8 percent). Approximately 20 percent of Ohio Latinas/os were born outside the United States, while the majority are US-born. Forty-two percent of Ohio Latinas/os are of Mexican ancestry, with the majority being born in the United States. The number of Mexicans and Mexican Americans more than doubled in size since 2000, and they account for much of the growth of Ohio's Latina/o population. Puerto Ricans make up nearly a third of Ohio Latinas/os and, like Mexican Americans, have long roots within Ohio. Finally, approximately 10 percent of Ohio Latinas/os hail from Central America, in particular from El Salvador and Guatemala, the majority of whom were born abroad.

Ohio Latinas/os are largely urban, with approximately a third living in the four major cities of Columbus, Cleveland, Lorain, and Toledo. The rural areas in the northern and northwestern areas of the state, however, have a surprisingly large number of Latina/o residents, reflecting local political economies that rely heavily on agricultural laborers in gardening, nursery, and dairy industries. Lorain County and the city of Lorain index the highest percentage of Latinas/os in the state (10 percent and approximately 28 percent, respectively). And as is the case nationally, Ohio Latinas/os are younger than the overall population, with their median age being 26.5 years, compared to 39.6 overall. With a median household income of $52,100 compared to $62,300 for all Ohioans, Latinas/os in the state experience higher poverty rates than the population overall. With 7.9 percent of Latinas/os unemployed, approximately 20 percent of Latinas/os in Ohio live below the poverty line. The educational attainment of Latinas/os in Ohio lags behind the state overall as well, with approximately 20 percent of adults not having a high school diploma and 31 percent having a postsecondary degree, compared to 40 percent across the state. These data provide important context for understanding the economic and social conditions of the majority of Ohio Latinas/os.

Starting with migrant labor circuits of Mexican and Mexican American families in the early twentieth century and then postwar Puerto Rican migration to work in expanding industrial sectors of the economy, the settlement experiences of Latinas/os in Northeast Ohio share a great deal with those in other midwestern cities, including Chicago. In the city of Lorain, the recruitment of Puerto Ricans to work for companies like US Steel and United Tube Company in the late 1940s helped plant the seeds for further growth. Oral history accounts of the postwar era emphasize the important role that a smaller Mexican community played in helping to provide housing and a sense of community to Puerto Rican newcomers, who quickly outnumbered Mexican residents in the city and began establishing important civic, religious, and service organizations. In addition to El Hogar Puertorriqueño and Mexican Mutual, organizations like El Centro de Servicios Sociales were established to meet the needs of a community that faced economic, social, and political marginalization. Historian Eugene Rivera also notes the important role churches played in the development of Latina/o Lorain, including the founding of La Capilla del Sagrado Corazon in 1952, the first Hispanic church in the state of Ohio, and El Templo Bethel, a Pentecostal church, faith communities that still serve a growing and diversifying Latina/o population in Lorain today.[57]

Lorain's Latina/o communities are among many that comprise the International City, a moniker that residents proudly embrace. Every year, the city celebrates its diverse and im/migrant history with an international festival, complete with multicultural princesses representing immigrants from Hungary, Slovenia, Mexico, Puerto Rico, Poland, and the Czech Republic as well as African American residents with their own migration history. Lorain's diversity and race politics serve as the backdrop and inspiration for writings by Nobel- and Pulitzer Prize-winning novelist Toni Morrison, a Lorain native. And the city is also home to strong labor unions and organizing that connects the struggles of white, African American, and Latina/o working-class residents. The history of Latina/o activism and organizing in Lorain and Northeast Ohio includes its active involvement with the UFW in the 1960s and 1970s and its support of the grape boycott and organizing efforts to convince local grocery stores to participate in these efforts. In 1972 local community activists such as José and Felisitas Mendiola welcomed UFW leader César Chávez and hosted a meeting with him and the community at Sacred Heart Chapel, an event that brought together Mexican, Mexican American, and Puerto Rican residents to hear him speak of the UFW's efforts to organize farmworkers in both California and Ohio.[58] Similarly, Puerto Ricans in Lorain used their work in El Hogar Puertorriqueño not only to challenge urban renewal policies that decimated the once thriving Latina/o commercial area of Vine Avenue, but also to address the lack of affordable housing for Puerto Rican and Mexican residents in South Lorain, where the majority of Latinas/os continue to reside.[59] These local efforts operated simultaneously with transnational organizing that included inviting Puerto Rican activists and leaders from the island as well as cities like Chicago and New York, an approach that affirms a diasporic and transnational approach to understanding the challenges in Lorain.

This history of organizing, activism, and advocacy established a solid foundation for the development of new strategies responding to the changing needs of Latina/o residents in Lorain and throughout Northeast Ohio in the twenty-first century. In 2014 community members in Lorain established LOIRA, the Lorain Ohio Immigrant Rights Association, and since that time have been actively involved in developing relationships with local law enforcement, city councils, churches, colleges and universities, and other civic organizations throughout Northeast Ohio to create networks of support to respond to increased immigration enforcement that has made undocumented immigrants increasingly vulnerable. For immigrant rights activist Anabel Barrón Sánchez, her work with LOIRA was not something she anticipated doing. In fact, in oral histories, public lectures, and community conversations, she consistently shares the story of how her own detention and deportation order politicized her and led her to the immigrant rights activism that now defines much of the work she does in the community. As increased immigrant surveillance and detention impacted local community members, people responded in a variety of ways. And while many of these responses intensified in the wake of the 2016 presidential election, people drew on a variety of tools honed in past struggles that offered opportunities for people to imagine and actively create radically resistive futures.

Book Overview

The pages that follow take up the following questions: What does it mean to be a sanctuary people? Why has Ohio indexed some of the highest numbers of public sanctuary cases in the nation? What are the strategies organizers use to address the disparate needs of increasingly diverse Latina/o communities in Ohio? How do they frame and analyze the work they do? When do they embrace sanctuary as a political strategy and spiritual practice and when do they deploy other vocabularies/frames to capture the work they do? And finally, what are the efficacy and limits of sanctuary as a political movement and faith-based strategy? *Sanctuary People* explores these important questions and builds on a burgeoning scholarly literature on sanctuary movements, faith-based organizing, and Latina/o community building.[60] It also addresses an important elision in the literature by locating contemporary sanctuary practices within broader organizing efforts in order to explain why sanctuary has become one of the most visible, contentious, and least understood political strategies today.

In chapter 1, "Sanctuary Cities, Streets, and Campuses," I locate current debates about sanctuary—sanctuary cities, sanctuary streets, sanctuary campuses, public sanctuary—within a broader historical context. While sanctuary practices are certainly not new, I argue that since 2016, discourses and practices of sanctuary reveal novel political and economic shifts and social movements that connect sanctuary to broader social justice concerns. Based on interviews with sanctuary leaders in Tucson and the Bay Area in Northern California, this chapter explores the ways activists, faith-based organizers, and scholars on a national scale understand the work of sanctuary, past and present. This chapter provides national context for the Ohio-based ethnographic chapters that follow.

Chapter 2, "Hay Una Vida fuera de Santuario—There Is Life outside of Sanctuary," focuses on public sanctuary in Ohio, and in particular the experiences of Edith Espinal as well as others who sought public sanctuary in houses of worship between 2017 and 2021. Using a feminist lens, I explore what living in sanctuary means for those who seek it, explore the gendered dimensions of sanctuary practices, and answer important questions such as, Where does sanctuary derive its power? Under what conditions is it an effective strategy to challenge deportation orders? And what are the goals of sanctuary practices?

Chapter 3, "¡No Estás Solo!," continues the previous chapter's discussion of sanctuary to explore the different ways Latina/o leaders, activists, and service providers respond to experiences of extreme vulnerability produced by the state. This chapter focuses on two seemingly disparate experiences—the workplace raids at Corso's garden center in Sandusky, Ohio, in 2018 and the relocation of Puerto Rican migrants to Northeast Ohio in the aftermath of Hurricane María in 2017—to explore the ways activists and faith leaders regarded them as inextricably linked. In Ohio, the notion of sanctuary everywhere gestures toward an intersectional approach to organizing that binds up the consequences of migrant detention and deportation to what some scholars refer to as the "coloniality of disaster" that set in motion the largest exodus of Puerto Rican migrants since the postwar era.

Chapter 4, "Becoming Sanctuary People," focuses specifically on the ways that for many of the faith-based activists, their current work is grounded in years of organizing and resistance across struggles for racial justice, LGBTQ rights, immigration reform, anti-police violence, and critiques of US interventionist foreign policy. This chapter foregrounds the oral histories of these activists and explores the ways that their activism is deeply rooted in religious epistemologies. Drawing from the insights of community activist Ruben Castilla Herrera, I argue that the long, rich, and varied activist histories of faith-based organizing reflect what he described as the power of and possibility of sanctuary people to create safe and nurturing communities.

In the conclusion, "The Spiritual Power and Political Uses of Sanctuary," I take up the allure and power of sanctuary as a political strategy, including the ways the political right has adopted/co-opted this language in its efforts to support anti-abortion legislation (sanctuary cities for the unborn) and resist challenges to the Second Amendment (Second Amendment sanctuary jurisdictions). What allows for sanctuary's enduring power in a moment of both increased secularization and an invigorated and increasingly powerful white Christian nationalist political right? What are the possibilities and cautionary tales for progressives who have embraced sanctuary as a way to challenge the political, economic, and military power of the state? What is the future of sanctuary practices for communities who have relied on them in moments of danger? What does it mean to be a sanctuary people?

1

Sanctuary Cities, Streets, and Campuses

Sanctuary in the Trump Years

When I type the words "sanctuary definition" into Google, the first result that appears is "a place of refuge and safety."[1] And while this is neither surprising nor particularly profound, it does offer a space to consider why writing about sanctuary in the years between 2016 and 2020 was both challenging and urgent. For although the dangerous, precarious, and uncertain conditions that characterized much of those years for immigrants, communities of color, LGBTQ people, Muslims, Jews, and so many others were, sadly, not new, it was also clear that Latinas/os in a range of different places and in a range of different ways were in great need of places of safety and refuge.

Between 2017 and 2021, Ohio was home to five people who publicly sought sanctuary in a church, making the state home to one of the largest number of public sanctuary cases in the country. According to a Church World Service report from 2018, thirty-seven people entered into public sanctuary in 2017, a 65 percent increase from the previous year, defining this time as one when "more people [were] taking Sanctuary in congregations than at any time since the 1980's."[2] The dramatic rise in public sanctuary cases was concomitant with the proliferation of faith communities developing or joining existing sanctuary coalitions, declaring themselves sanctuaries for immigrants, and organizing with other groups to "prophetically confront the administration's immoral and unjust deportation policies."[3] By January 2018, more than 1,100 houses of worship and 40 coalitions were engaged in actions that demonstrated the enduring ways that "faith resistance continues to grow against harsh and inhumane immigration policies."[4] This activity occurred not only in places with long histories of immigrant organizing and vibrant immigrant communities, such as Chicago, Los Angeles, and New York, but also in rural and urban communities in states like North

Carolina and Ohio that witnessed relatively recent growth in immigrant populations. In short, the growth of "sanctuary in the age of Trump" built on older histories of migrant advocacy and inspired new forms of immigrant activism.

This chapter focuses on global, national, state-level, and local events and political-economic realities that provide important context for the ethnographic chapters that follow. Ohio offers valuable insight into the mundane and profound ways sanctuary practices emerged, proliferated, and were contested and subsequently modified. Until recently, Ohio was considered an important swing state whose importance often seems limited to the four-year cycle of presidential elections. Moreover, like much of the Midwest, Ohio is also home to heterogeneous, long-standing, growing, and young Latina/o communities. In order to understand the myriad ways social movements in Ohio responded to intensified attacks on various communities during the Trump administration, we need to pay careful attention to the long histories of struggle, resistance, and organizing that have allowed Latinas/os in Ohio to persevere, thrive, and inspire new ways of knowing and being. In advancing this argument, I build on the insights of Paik, Ruiz, and Schreiber, who observe, "Thus, while some have been galvanized into social justice work for the first time in response to the Trump regime, foundations for the energized sanctuary movements were built not only on a few past cases but also on longue durée histories of community self-defense and on already existing organizing by multiple affected communities."[5] This chapter documents these foundations nationally and locally and the creative responses and new relationships they engender. By focusing on public sanctuary, efforts to support sanctuary cities and campuses, and the creation of welcoming spaces for those fleeing the consequences of (un)natural disasters, and drawing on the power of place to ground sanctuary practices, I document the new kinds of sanctuary spaces in Northeast Ohio that are created and those whose collective efforts make those spaces possible.

The Roots and Routes of Public Sanctuary

Faith leaders, activists, scholars, and immigrant rights advocates all regard the sanctuary movement of the 1980s as the foundation for today's faith-based organizing around issues of immigration and the rise of the New Sanctuary Movement (NSM) beginning in 2007. And while the activities of the 1980s spanned geopolitical borders from Mexico to Canada and connected a broad network of places, Tucson and the North American borderlands hold a particularly meaningful place in the development of the US sanctuary movement. A long-standing tradition of immigrant advocacy that involved "regional, national and even transnational developments" included the sheltering of refugees from El Salvador and Guatemala, clergy and lay organizing that featured public testimonies by migrants fleeing death squads and state-led violence, and the role of migrants in educating the American public about US-fueled wars in Central America.[6] US imperial and military involvement in Central America was certainly not new in the 1980s. Indeed, Cold War anxieties around communism, Latin American liberation struggles, and revolutionary movements defined US foreign policy in the region in the postwar era. These interventions were almost exclusively focused on providing military, economic, and political support to repressive regimes that would "crush the revolutionary movement in El Salvador" and preserve the US anti-communist policies in the region.[7] As the Reagan administration spent billions of dollars supporting repressive governments in El Salvador and Guatemala and the Contras fighting against the Sandinista government in Nicaragua, thousands of people fled this US-fueled violence, seeking safety throughout Central America, Mexico, and the United States. Despite well-documented experiences with death squads, persecution, and the killings of civilians, nuns, priests, and humanitarian workers, Salvadoran and Guatemalan refugees were consistently denied political asylum in the US immigration courts, which regarded them as economic rather than political refugees.[8]

This refusal to provide asylum to Central American refugees, the increasing number of migrants who risked their lives crossing through the Sonoran Desert and elsewhere to seek refuge, and the crackdown on undocumented migrants by the Immigration and Naturalization Services compelled people like Jim Corbett, a Quaker and rancher in the Tucson area, to act. Working with Presbyterian minister John Fife as well as migrant advocacy groups in Tucson, such as the Tucson Ecumenical Council, local immigrant rights groups, and clergy on both side of the US-Mexico border, Corbett and others covertly facilitated the safe passage of Central American migrants to Mexico, the United States, and even Canada.[9] These clandestine efforts shifted on March 24, 1980, the second anniversary of the assassination of Monsignor Óscar Romero in El Salvador, when Reverend Fife, who was the pastor of Southside Presbyterian Church in Tucson, declared the church a sanctuary, a declaration that was accompanied by five other Bay Area churches as well.[10] The decision to publicly declare Southside Presbyterian and other sacred spaces sanctuaries was motivated by a belief that faith compelled people to act and "assert our God-given right to aid." But it was also motivated by a belief that going public would compel others to join in their cause and change US foreign policy. This public, faith-based resistance was an inspiring and powerful motivator. Indeed, by 1983, forty-five churches and synagogues declared themselves sanctuaries, and six hundred sanctuary groups had developed throughout the nation.[11] But this resistance also led to FBI surveillance, infiltration, arrest, and a highly visible public trial where Reverend Fife, Corbett, and six others were convicted for "running a modern-day underground railroad." This history, according to Naomi Paik, not only "emboldened the movement," but also inspired faith-based activism in the years that followed, providing an example of "the work accomplices can achieve when they willingly assume the risks that affected communities are forced to live with."[12]

The late twentieth-century and early twenty-first-century sanctuary movements are deeply rooted in an understanding of the value of sacred resistance. But how people conceptualize what sanctuary entails has evolved in meaningful ways since the 1980s. In those years, the biblical basis for sanctuary work was primarily grounded in religious and spiritual commitments to welcome the stranger. In contrast, the New Sanctuary Movement, emerging in 2007, rooted itself in the values of protecting family, community, and people's sense of belonging in a post-9/11 world that witnessed a dramatic restructuring of the immigration control and border security apparatus and an equally dramatic rise of anti-immigrant sentiment. The ascendance of what Alfonso Gonzales refers to as "the homeland security state" resulted in draconian migration control policies and increased numbers of immigrant detention and deportation, and undermined myriad efforts to pass comprehensive immigration reform, under both President Bush and, subsequently, President Obama.[13] One of the most extreme examples of these legislative efforts was the 2005 Border Protection, Anti-Terrorism, and Illegal Immigration Control Act, or the Sensenbrenner Bill (named after Wisconsin congressman Jim Sensenbrenner), which included expansion and fortification of the US-Mexican border, increased penalties for immigrant documentation fraud, employer sanctions for hiring undocumented workers, and, most notoriously, penalties "to any person or group providing aid to undocumented migrants."[14] Although the Sensenbrenner Bill failed in the Senate, it was an important piece of what Gonzales refers to as "anti-migrant hegemony" that defined the moment and informed state and local legislation that negatively impacted immigrants. Most notorious of this legal and social hegemony was Arizona's SB 1070, also known as the "show me your papers" act, which allowed law enforcement to ask for proof of legal immigration status during routine traffic stops.[15] These sentiments and policies certainly affected all migrants; however, their impacts were experienced differently by Latinas/os, who were increasingly enmeshed in what anthropologist Leo Chavez refers to as the "Latino threat narrative," which justified immigrant detention, deportation, and family separation.[16]

This is the context that gave rise to the New Sanctuary Movement. As Myrna Orozco and Noel Anderson observe, "As immigration raids in neighborhoods and work places escalated in a climate of political paralysis for immigration reform, [congregations across the United States] opened their doors to provide refuge to those facing deportation. This new model of providing Sanctuary adjusted to the new times—no longer were congregations only receiving arriving refugees, but instead fought alongside neighbors who had been in the US for decades and built their lives here."[17] The case of Elvira Arrellano exemplifies this new model for sanctuary work and faith-based activism. In August 2006, Arrellano and her young son, Saúl, entered into sanctuary in the Adalberto United Methodist Church in the Humboldt Park neighborhood of Chicago. This decision followed years of Arrellano's efforts to avoid several deportation orders following her detention in a workplace raid at Chicago's O'Hare Airport in 2002, as well as her involvement with immigrant rights organizations like Centro Sin Fronteras. While in sanctuary for more than a year, Arrellano had a visibility in polarized public debates that was significant for a number of reasons. First, her fight to remain in Chicago with her US-born son represents what political scientist Amalia

Pallares refers to as "family activism," a complex political strategy by immigrant rights activists as they construct, reinforce, challenge, and redefine notions of family to challenge deportation and family separation.[18] In press conferences, prayer vigils, and public presentations, Arrellano and others emphasized her role as a mother as the basis for remaining in the United States.[19] This gendered strategy is one that would emerge again, particularly between 2016 and 2020, when the number of people entering into public sanctuary rose dramatically. Arrellano's case was also significant because, as Barba and Castillo-Ramos demonstrate, it "set a tone for the NSM in that it would almost exclusively take on the cases of immigrants whose deportation would result in family separation. In this move, sanctuary activists, who are generally left-of-center politically, sought to seize control of the robust family discourse the conservatives had built up and deployed effectively since the late 1970s with the rise of groups such as Focus on the Family, the Christian Right, and the Moral Majority."[20]

By embracing the central tenet of the family values rhetoric of the political right—the distinctive spiritual role of motherhood valued by evangelical Christians committed to gender complementarianism—Arrellano and NSM activists hoped to lay bare the contradictions at the heart of the family values rhetoric espoused by political and religious adherents who also supported family separation for immigrants.[21] Finally, Arrellano's case was a reminder of the enduring importance of sacred space and physical sanctuary as a way to challenge state power. Many faith leaders embraced this point to justify sanctuary as one of many tools to resist state power, but they also understood the unique power of public sanctuary in sacred spaces to advance certain struggles when those who are often charged with protecting the most vulnerable, such as migrants, fail to do so. Reverend John Fife, for example, reflected in the following way: "What we've seen is the rise of sanctuary again in faith communities to not only provide protection with the failure of nation-states to do that, but also to reinstitute a recognition of faith communities as the place we may need to go back to with the failure of secular nation-states."[22]

Anti-immigrant sentiments, policies, and practices leading to family separations, therefore, were not new when President Trump was elected to office in 2016. In fact, the groundwork established under the Bush administration enabled the continuation of the "deportation regime" under President Obama, earning him the moniker "deporter in chief," as a result of millions of people deported in the early years of his administration. Immigrant rights activists—and in particular undocumented immigrant youth organizers—responded in sustained, creative, and increasingly confrontational ways. Most importantly, their activism was grounded in a commitment to understanding social justice struggles as deeply intersectional. In other words, their efforts as immigrant rights activists were informed by an analysis of how race, gender, sexuality, and legal status together constrained their lives legally, economically, socially, and politically. According to Kevin Escudero, activists' intersectional movement identities enabled them to confront the legal limitations they faced as well as "build coalitions with members of other similarly situated communities."[23]

For example, while many undocumented youth activists had supported legislative efforts to pass the DREAM (Development, Relief and Education for Alien Minors) Act, which would offer protections for undocumented youth, the repeated failures to do so at the federal level led activists to question the narratives that legislators, immigrant advocates, and others used to built support for DREAM Act legislation. Dreamers were characterized as innocent children who did not *choose* to immigrate illegally, and whose work ethic and demonstrated ability to assimilate and strive/dream for a better future merited legal protections. This narrative, which pitted "good" Dreamer children against their allegedly "bad" immigrant parents, was not only harmful for immigrant communities, it failed to gain the necessary political traction to pass the DREAM Act or any kind of meaningful immigration legislation. This repeated failure mobilized Dreamers to respond in bold and creative ways, which included rejecting narratives that reproduced the categories of bad/good immigrant and borrowing from other social movement strategies. As Cristina Beltrán shows, undocumented youth activists were "inspired by and appropriated the gay rights movement's strategies of visibility. Often LGBT youth themselves, DREAM activists who choose to 'come out' and openly declare their undocumented status emphasize the linkages that connect sexuality and migration."[24] This new approach to immigrant rights activism, which rejected "secrecy in favor of more aggressive forms of nonconformist visibility, voice and protest," played a significant role in pressuring the Obama administration to shift its immigration focus and also reflected additional emerging social justice movements that were intersectional, coalitional, and deeply grounded in local and national communities.[25] On June 15, 2012, President Obama issued an executive action establishing the Deferred Action for Childhood Arrivals (DACA) program, offering temporary relief from deportation and work authorization for unauthorized migrants who arrived before the age of sixteen, lived in the United States continuously for at least five years, and met other specific requirements.[26] On November 20, 2014, Obama issued another executive action—Deferred Action for Parents of Americans (DAPA), which would allow for parents of DACA recipients to remain legally in the United States.[27] Although DAPA was quickly rolled back after repeated legal challenges, DACA survived similar attempts by anti-immigrant elected leaders and actors and consistently enjoys broad popular support in national polling. These small but significant victories were the result of decades of immigrant organizing and reflect long histories of immigrants rights activism that laid important groundwork for a variety of sanctuary practices following the 2016 presidential election.

Reverend Deborah Lee, executive director of the Oakland-based Interfaith Movement for Human Integrity, for example, traces her work in 2018 back to organizing efforts in 1994 to oppose Proposition 187, which sought to restrict undocumented immigrants from accessing California's public services such as healthcare and public education. That work not only provided a strong foundation for sanctuary practices in the Trump years, but also pushed the movement to be more capacious in its approach, since a broader framing has always defined the work of many social justice organizers. She explains,

> We started using sanctuary as the frame for the work on immigrant justice we were already doing, which involved advocacy. . . . Our organization [Interfaith Movement for Human Integrity] had a different name in the 1990s, called Interfaith Coalition for Immigrant Rights. It started on the heels of the sanctuary movement [of the 1980s] because after the sanctuary movement in California [there was] Prop. 187 in 1994. . . . Our organization started because all this pushback started happening, the backlash. And so the real focus was not on housing people and refugee

status, but literally how do we protect the rights of people to go to school, ... to have food stamps at that time? You know, basic survival things. So we defined sanctuary as advocacy, accompaniment, networks of protection, and housing hospitality.[28]

This capacious understanding of sanctuary—of advocacy, accompaniment, networks of protection, and housing hospitality—is probably one of sanctuary's greatest strengths. Not only does a broader framing of sanctuary allow organizations to conceptualize how overlapping concerns are interrelated and develop strategies to address them, but this capaciousness also fosters flexibility to respond differently in distinct contexts. In Northeast Ohio, for example, organizers and faith-based groups have framed the resettlement of newcomers from Puerto Rico following Hurricane María as offering sanctuary, safety, and refuge in ways similar to the efforts to support migrant families devastated by workplace immigrant raids, detention, and deportation. It also is reflected in the coalitions that protest both police violence and criminalization of African American youth as well as immigrant family separation in cities like Columbus. In this way, these more capacious understandings of sanctuary embody what Paik refers to as "abolitionist sanctuary"—an approach that "combines the community defense that is needed right now with the deep envisioning and building of a new society where we welcome all our neighbors. It is guided less by creating a space of safety for a select few; instead it seeks to build communities that not only fight systemic oppression but also advance shared liberation."[29]

This is certainly a sentiment shared by many faith leaders. Like Reverend Lee, Reverend Alison Harrington, pastor of Southside Presbyterian Church in Tucson, argues for broadening our understanding of sanctuary:

I think that the future of sanctuary has to be expanded. I think we have to go beyond the four walls of congregations because we don't want people to be living within a church. We don't want people to be stuck here ... so I'm hoping that what happens is this movement of congregations who have said they would physically house someone, whoever they may be, to protect them from persecution. But that they're also really committed to being church in a different way, in a way that reaches out to those who are directly affected to find out how we can walk with you, how we can support you. . . . How does mass incarceration, how do broken windows policies, how all of these criminal justice policies [create] a net in which people are trapped in. . . . The work of sanctuary can't just be to protect immigrants, but has to challenge mass incarceration, criminalization of poor people and people of color. . . . It has to be an expansive kind of movement. So that's . . . what I see for the hope and future of [sanctuary].[30]

Pastor Jeff Johnson of University Lutheran Chapel in Berkeley, made a similar point, explaining that "sanctuary means everything from . . . physical sanctuary to . . . post-detention release, . . . housing for asylees or legal accompaniment, . . . packing the courts when someone's hearing has come. It means all those things."[31]

Cultivating a broader understanding of sanctuary, however, requires a great deal of work. For some, this involves a delicate balance between acknowledging the power of offering physical sanctuary in a congregation's house of worship and challenging congregations to see the limitations of this strategy. Reverend Lee, for example, explained how sometimes you have to "change people's minds" about physical sanctuary, especially when religious communities have a physical space ready to house someone. Sanctuary isn't just about housing, she explains to congregations. "There are so many other things people need. . . . It's nice for them to know there is a room. . . . But nobody really—it's not a great option if you've been living here. . . . So in fact we told congregations that had created spaces like [Pastor Jeff's], you can modify how you're thinking of that space and it can be used for a new arrival or someone who just got out of detention or someone who needs a place to settle for three months to figure out how to get going again."[32]

Pastor Harrington concurs:

One of the things we're trying to deal with is that the congregations are saying, "It's all about sanctuary, physical sanctuary." And so they'll go through the process and they'll declare sanctuary and then they'll just kind of wait to see who's going to knock on the door. If nobody does, they're kind of like, "Well, why isn't anybody coming?" And so we've tried to help people see that sanctuary is not the goal of the work. Ending deportations is! Sanctuary is one tactic that we use to stop deportations, but it's not the goal. And so if someone isn't coming into sanctuary, that's a good thing! And you need to maybe refocus your efforts and go into the community, work with those who are directly affected in order to make it so nobody has to go into sanctuary. That *their home* is a sanctuary. Their schools are sanctuary. Their workplaces are sanctuary.[33]

By emphasizing that sanctuary is a tactic and not a goal in itself, Pastor Harrington not only emphasizes the need to redirect some people's valuable and well-meaning efforts, but also identifies concrete ways in which they can do so, drawing on the many economic, social, class, and educational resources that many mostly white, mainline Protestant communities have that immigrant communities often do not. Reverend Pablo Morataya, pastor of Iglesia Presbiteriana Hispana in Oakland, California, made a similar point when he described the challenges of building support among well-meaning and well-resourced faith-based activists in the Bay Area for programs like Nueva Esperanza, a refugee resettlement program run out of his church that connects volunteers from other churches with newly arrived families from Central America to accompany them during the initial critical months of transition and settlement. He explains,

> There is a family living in the city of Alameda, a woman who came with her young child, although her husband already lived here. When she arrived, one of these other teams that normally belongs to another church and to another religious denomination, they also gave her shelter for an entire year in their house in Alameda while they settled themselves here. They offered a lot of help, including mental health counseling for the child, who was eight years old—now the child is nine—and for the woman, who arrived traumatized as a result of her journey. So they also provided emotional support. This is a good example, in my opinion, because they are also taking her once a week so she can learn, little by little, English and feel more secure by the time she leaves and finds a job. . . . The changes that we have seen now compared to traditional sanctuary that is about housing someone and having them inside, now we have broadened [our understanding and practice of sanctuary].[34]

As a parish with limited economic resources, Iglesia Presbiteriana Hispana can draw on support from other faith-based volunteers to help congregants as well as other community members in need. Indeed, as he and other Bay Area faith leaders noted, new migrants, primarily Central Americans, many of whom are Indigenous, are well aware of Pastor Pablo's church and it is often one of the first institutions newcomers turn to once they arrive. This expanded notion of sanctuary, therefore, has concrete and material consequences to provide support—economic, social, educational, and political—to those who most need it.

Pastor Pablo described yet another dimension of the work involved in cultivating a broader understanding of sanctuary, namely, faith communities (particularly Latina/o religious congregations) that are compelled by their beliefs to help others, but who fear the legal consequences. Under President Trump, this was no small consideration. As with the 2005 Sensenbrenner Bill, the Trump administration threatened significant sanctions, punishments, and retribution to a broad range of institutions, organizations, and people involved in sanctuary work. For Pastor Pablo, whose work includes collaborations with other Latina/o faith communities, including politically conservative evangelical churches, this work is critical since those congregants often empathize with the needs of migrants whose experiences are often similar to their own, but who might not be ready to commit to the radical work of sanctuary.

> Nevertheless, I believe that we have to take risks, and right now what we are trying to do is tell other pastors, we are inviting them—and Deborah Lee is witness to this—we are always trying to invite people [to join us in this work]. With the broadening and modified notion of sanctuary, a church doesn't need to necessarily declare itself a sanctuary in the sense of receiving someone who is facing an order of deportation, because now there are other ways of helping. And I think that has helped, especially with those faith groups who have said, OK, our church . . . we're not even ready to begin this dialogue about becoming a sanctuary or not. But we are ready to help, to form a group of accompaniment. This has helped us a lot, because those groups of accompaniment have been very effective in the work they do. They are very good at what they do. Some Hispanic churches are able to do this work too, but that requires us to do a little more work with them.[35]

These sentiments are echoed by Reverend Lee, who described congregations who "want to do something," but were either still in the process of discernment and not ready to vote or, for other reasons, were reluctant to commit to the work. Quoting a sanctuary worker from the 1980s, she remarked that "there's a thousand ways to do sanctuary. . . . I've been trying to tell people that sanctuary is an invitation to a commitment, to a covenant, to a relationship with a community that is under attack. It could be the Muslim community [or the] undocumented community. . . . It's a commitment to walk with them and do what's needed and support them. And we won't know what's needed because this thing changes every day."[36] Her role as a pastor and faith leader is to "organize the faith sector and people of shared values . . . because if you're not a faith person, it's very hard to get a faith community to do anything. You have to know how to approach them and how to do it." An essential element of this work involves not judging those who hold different religious or political positions and to, instead, share stories, listen, and welcome people into the movement. Pastor Harrington explains, "I think it was Toni Cade Bambara who said it's the artist's job to make the revolution irresistible. So I feel like it's the progressive Christian church's job to make this revolution look irresistible. And so that as people are having a crisis of faith, that we are people who are welcoming and who say, 'Sure, you weren't with us last year, but you are here and we want to welcome you.'"[37]

Finally, this broader conceptualization of sanctuary has to confront what Reverend Lee refers to as "the criminalization narrative." From border crossings, juvenile involvement with gangs, and DUIs, to underground economic activity, there are myriad ways that the daily activities and constrained decisions of immigrants and low-income communities of color are criminalized, with young men of color in particular enmeshed in what sociologist Victor Rios refers to as "the youth control complex."[38] Years of punitive governance, zero tolerance in schools, mass incarceration, and political gain for being tough on crime and securing the nation's borders against gangs, drugs, and other illegal activities have enabled the circulation of a criminalization narrative that is pervasive, persistent, and difficult to dislodge. Indeed, as many scholars have noted, such narratives are deeply implicated in the social death of communities that are unable to meet a standard of deservingness of dignity.[39] Pastor Jeff shared the difficulty in challenging the criminalization narrative in sanctuary work:

[A] lot of people in our community buy into the criminalization frame. So, for example, there was a man who was in the process of taking up sanctuary at our church who had a record. And we deliberately allied ourselves with him *because* he had a record and because we didn't want that to be a determining factor because we—and Reverend Deborah Lee has been very good about promoting previously incarcerated, undocumented persons among the coalition as people that we need to be in close proximity to and in solidarity. And that causes all kinds of anxiety for people because on some level they buy into the idea of the good migrant. . . . How can we have a felon in sanctuary? But I think Deborah's contention is, and I completely agree, that we have to push really hard against the criminalization frame. And the way to do that is to be in solidarity with those who have been targeted and labeled to try to break those things open.[40]

Both Pastor Harrington and Reverend Lee described similar challenges and the different strategies they have used to try to undermine them. Reverend Lee, for example, helped develop the Migrant Voices in the Pulpit series, "where we train speakers to tell their stories that would fall into the exception category, who haven't had convictions," and others who have committed serious crimes, sometimes as juveniles, and who have tried to turn their lives around. These stories and the encounters and conversations the Migrant Voices in the Pulpit series facilitates are key to disrupting the criminalization narrative. In this way, they are part of many sanctuary practices that include physical sanctuary, but also exceed it. Pastor Jeff observed, "While the term 'sanctuary' has taken on new meanings, the tried-and-true practice of harboring is yet again being tested. Sanctuary today, though largely expanded in practice and in the demographics of its seekers, is still firmly grounded in the acts of sacred resistance that began with Central American sanctuary seekers and North American sanctuary workers."[41] And while these acts of sacred resistance are roots and routes of recent sanctuary movements, what faith leaders, activists, and scholars have demonstrated is the need for an approach to sanctuary that affirms and supports all.

Sanctuary Cities, Sanctuary Campuses

Immediately following his inauguration, President Trump issued three executive orders, including Executive Order 13768, "Enhancing Public Safety in the Interior of the United States," which strengthened immigration enforcement priorities to focus on the interior United States, reinstated federal and state agreements such as 287(g) that had been abandoned during the Obama administration, and penalized sanctuary cities. The executive order states,

> Interior enforcement of our Nation's immigration laws is critically important to the national security and public safety of the United States. Many aliens who illegally enter the United States and those who overstay or otherwise violate the terms of their visas present a significant threat to national security and public safety. This is particularly so for aliens who engage in criminal conduct in the United States. Sanctuary jurisdictions across the United States willfully violate Federal law in an attempt to shield aliens from removal from the United States. These jurisdictions have caused immeasurable harm to the American people and to the very fabric of our Republic.

Providing more detail about the punishments that would be meted out to sanctuary jurisdictions, the executive order outlined the following:

> Section 9: *Sanctuary Jurisdictions*. It is the policy of the executive branch to ensure, to the fullest extent of the law, that a State, or a political subdivision of a State, shall comply with 8 U.S.C. 1373.
>
> (a) In furtherance of this policy, the Attorney General and the Secretary, in their discretion and to the extent consistent with law, shall ensure that jurisdictions that willfully refuse to comply with 8 U.S.C. 1373 (sanctuary jurisdictions) are not eligible to receive Federal grants, except as deemed necessary for law enforcement purposes by the Attorney General or the Secretary. The Secretary has the authority to designate, in his discretion and to the extent consistent with law, a jurisdiction as a sanctuary jurisdiction. The Attorney General shall take appropriate enforcement action against any entity that violates 8 U.S.C. 1373, or which has in effect a statute, policy, or practice that prevents or hinders the enforcement of Federal law.

(b) To better inform the public regarding the public safety threats associated with sanctuary jurisdictions, the Secretary shall utilize the Declined Detainer Outcome Report or its equivalent and, on a weekly basis, make public a comprehensive list of criminal actions committed by aliens and any jurisdiction that ignored or otherwise failed to honor any detainers with respect to such aliens.

(c) The Director of the Office of Management and Budget is directed to obtain and provide relevant and responsive information on all Federal grant money that currently is received by any sanctuary jurisdiction.[42]

Together with the two other executive orders implementing the Muslim travel ban and the construction of the border wall, the new administration's intention to intensify interior enforcement and the punishment for sanctuary jurisdictions that dared to defy immigration enforcement practices reverberated throughout immigrant communities and their allies. Latina/o communities in Ohio, with its northern border along Lake Erie and in proximity to Canada and therefore within the one-hundred-mile border enforcement zone, were particularly concerned. Immigrant rights organizations, advocacy groups, and activists redoubled their efforts to fortify the networks of support and protection that they had built over the years, including expanding sanctuary spaces. Indeed, as Reverend Pablo Morataya, Reverend Deborah Lee, Reverend Alison Harrington, Reverend Jeff Johnson, and Reverend John Fife all underscored in their interviews with me, "immigrants have already been providing sanctuary—they're already sanctuary to each other."[43]

Supporting the development and growth of sanctuary cities, counties, states, and other jurisdictions is certainly one of many ways immigrant rights activists have been providing sanctuary to each other. How they have done so is as varied as the meanings of sanctuary cities themselves. As Loren Collingwood and Benjamin Gonzalez O'Brien observe, "There is no concrete definition of just how exactly a sanctuary city should be defined," although broadly speaking, sanctuary policies are ones that "limit local cooperation in federal enforcement to varying degrees."[44] As with physical sanctuary, the 1980s are an important point of departure for understanding the rise and debates around sanctuary cities. The city council of Madison, Wisconsin, for example, passed a resolution "commending churches in the city that were offering sanctuary to Central

American refugees" on June 7, 1983, and then declared itself a sanctuary city on March 5, 1985.[45] Many other cities passed resolutions during this time, such as Berkeley's and Seattle's "city of refuge" resolutions on February 19, 1985, and January 13, 1986, respectively, with "more than two hundred locations nationwide [passing] similar laws limiting the participation of local officials in the enforcement of federal immigration law" between 1985 and 2018.[46]

Both then and now, public support for sanctuary cities has waxed and waned and has been informed by a number of factors, including local and national media coverage and politicians' opinions, as well as local traditions and ideological commitments. Moreover, the sanctuary resolutions of the 1980s were an important foundation for policies in the years to come. In fact, as Collingwood and Gonzalez O'Brien demonstrate, many sanctuary policies established in the 1980s remained in place years later, but "they also began to evolve into something different" as the focus of these policies was to protect undocumented migrants, many of whom had long histories living in the United States, rather than refugees.[47] This was particularly true post-September 11, as increased immigration enforcement, resurging anti-immigrant sentiment, and the proliferation of state-level resolutions targeting immigrants led immigrant advocates to develop new and revise older sanctuary resolutions.[48] Thus, "sanctuary policies during the 1990s and 2000s were . . . both an ideological statement of opposition to anti-immigrant legislation and were meant to foster greater trust between immigrant communities and local government."[49] Although these policies vary among jurisdictions, some shared features include forbidding local officials from inquiring into an individual's immigration status; prohibiting law enforcement from holding undocumented immigrants on ICE detainers if they have not been charged with a violent crime; and preventing participation in federal programs like 287(g) (deputizing selected state and local law enforcement officers to enforce federal immigration law) and Secure Communities (information sharing among law enforcement and ICE about deportable immigrants). In short, these resolutions fostered trust with local institutions by ensuring access to local resources regardless of immigration status, support from law enforcement, and networks to strengthen immigrant incorporation in the broader community.[50]

While some jurisdictions opted for formal declarations as sanctuary cities, others opted for an informal approach, implementing specific practices, such as declining to honor ICE detainers or refraining from asking about immigration status for city services or during traffic stops, for example. Cities like Boston, Chicago, Cleveland, and Winston-Salem, North Carolina, have adopted terms like "welcoming cities," while others have embraced the label "immigrant-friendly" cities. In each instance, localities weighed the risk of losing federal funding by declaring themselves sanctuary cities and the risk of not doing so. In other words, as Melvin Delgado argues, designations like "welcoming" might not have "the same political significance as 'sanctuary,' although it functions in much the same manner, and this may be an attempt to depoliticize a term with strong political connotation."[51] These debates were particularly visible in Ohio following the 2016 presidential election and offer insight into the ways history, place, and ideology inform local designations.

Ohio is home to cities and counties that have long histories of formal and informal sanctuary policies and practices. By mid-November 2016, local news reports identified at least eight "sanctuary locations" in the state and various efforts to expand and challenge them.[52] On February 21, 2017, the city of Oberlin passed a resolution to "reaffirm and extend Oberlin's welcoming commitments to persons and families of all backgrounds and nationalities, including those who have entered the United States as refugees fleeing war and terror in other countries."[53] This resolution built on the city's 2009 public declaration to support immigrants in the wake of a local workplace raid in 2008 that resulted in the detention and deportation of several restaurant workers in the city, but it was also grounded in more than a century's worth of activism, organizing, and resistance by the city and Oberlin College that includes challenging the 1850 Fugitive Slave Act, welcoming Japanese American students during the period of Japanese internment during World War II, welcoming students, faculty, and staff from Kent State University following the killing of four students protesting the Vietnam War in May 1970, and support for the 1980s sanctuary movement.

In the city of Lorain the police chief, Celestino Rivera, put in place specific practices that are often regarded as sanctuary policies, but without formal municipal resolutions. As a city with a large Latina/o population (primarily Puerto Rican and Mexican, although with increasing numbers of Central American residents), a growing number of immigrant families, and a distinguished history of Latina/o leadership and community organizing, Lorain was not immune to the immigration enforcement policies that led to family separation. According to Celestino, who led the Lorain police department for twenty-five years, when he decided to instruct his officers not to inquire about the immigration status of people reporting crimes, people who are stopped due to minor traffic violations, or people who have other minor offenses, and not to notify ICE when Lorain police detained someone who is undocumented, his decision was the result of faith-based organizing that held him to account. He explains,

[In 2013] I got a call from Father Bill [Thaden, of Sacred Heart Chapel in Lorain] and he asked me to come to a meeting, an HOLA meeting. I hadn't heard of HOLA, but he wanted me to come to the meeting, so maybe egotistically I said, "OK, Father, what do you want me to talk about?" And he said, "Well, we don't want you to talk. They don't want you to talk, Cel. They want you to listen. They want to hold you accountable." I said, "For what?" and he said, "For separating families." I said, "Father, we don't do that." "Yeah, you do, actually." I said, "OK, we don't, but I'll be at the meeting." And when I walk in they had protestors and signs. And I listened to about eleven or twelve testimonials, including Anabel Barrón Sánchez. That's when I met Anabel. And there were others. And they were all crying, and they had their children with them, and they were crying and talking about being stopped for the most trivial offenses. It was all women. . . . They didn't have any of the men there. They were talking about their husbands being stopped. The only woman that actually got stopped herself was Anabel. It was their husbands. [There was one woman], it just broke my heart. She was a young girl, maybe about twenty-six or twenty-seven. And she said [to] the police officer [who took her husband], "How can you do this? Don't do this to us. We've got three kids. Don't do this to us. Don't take their father." And she actually knelt down . . . and his response was, "You know what? You better get up before I take you too." I found that so offensive. I really did. And to find out that my police officers were doing that. . . . As a result of that [meeting], we put out a policy.[54]

Celestino's emphasis on the critical role women like Anabel and others play in bringing attention to these issues and setting in motion concrete policy changes highlights the visible, consistent, and sometimes underappreciated interventions women, mothers, and gender play in social movements. Their interventions, however, are often met with resistance. Thus, when Celestino spoke with his officers about the new policy, there was significant pushback since some officers believed that they were merely enforcing the law. Celestino continued, "Do you think this is good police work? . . . There are state laws, federal laws, there are wildlife laws. There are all kinds of laws. You became a *city* police officer, and we need the respect, the support of the people that we work with. We need them to report crime. We can't have a group of people who are victimized because they're too afraid."

While Celestino Rivera implemented these policies in 2013 to some debate, it wasn't until 2017 that he and other police departments and city governments began to feel the impact of the executive orders to punish sanctuary cities. In meetings with city officials and the law director, Celestino had to defend his departmental policy and his commitment to "be responsive to the community" and not to what he believed was overreach by the president. His ability to receive grants for initiatives like gang prevention required that the city law director sign an affidavit affirming that the city didn't have any policies that could be regarded as being aligned with sanctuary city policies. He described the difficult choice he had to make: "We've got to make a decision. My first impulse is to say, 'You know what? Keep your fifty-five thousand dollars.' But that will not come across [well] because we are having these kids killed [from gang violence] and [the grant] also deals with officer safety. And it's like I'm putting my politics—I guess that is the way they've put it—ahead of my officers' safety and community safety. So I'm going to have to make a decision . . . that's going to be a tough one."[55] Celestino, however, was not alone. Like law enforcement across the country, he joined lawsuits, attended conferences, and was part of national discussions and strategizing by law enforcement and prosecutors to challenge the Trump administration's attempts to "entangle local police with federal immigration enforcement, saying it threatens community trust and endangers public safety."[56]

Federal efforts to punish sanctuary cities and organizations were matched by state and local initiatives throughout Ohio. In 2017 state treasurer Josh Mandel was particularly vocal in his support of legislation put forth by Republican state representative Candice Keller that would punish municipalities and individuals who stand with sanctuary cities by holding them criminally liable for crimes committed by undocumented immigrants.[57] This proposal was dropped but revived two years later when state representatives Niraj Antani and Candice Keller proposed yet another bill, House Bill 169, to punish not only cities but also school districts that embraced sanctuary policies. According to the *Dayton Daily News*, the bill was in response to the Dayton School Board's declaration as a "'Safe and Welcoming School District' that 'shall do everything in its lawful power to . . . ensure that our students' learning environments are not disrupted by immigration enforcement actions.'"[58] And although both bills failed, they reflect legislative efforts at the state level in Ohio that mirrored national trends. In 2019, for example, the National Conference of State Legislatures published a report detailing the number of states where sanctuary bills had been proposed. By April 2019, ten states had "enacted legislation in favor of sanctuary policies," twelve passed legislation prohibiting sanctuary jurisdictions, and approximately a dozen more had legislation that was pending.[59] The fear of losing federal funding for valuable programming, often to help those most in need of resources and support, certainly prevented some jurisdictions from formally declaring themselves sanctuary sites, but it also emboldened others who believed that taking a principled stand against the administration was warranted and necessary.

This is certainly what informed the dynamic sanctuary campus initiatives that emerged almost immediately following the 2016 presidential election. Like sanctuary cities and physical sanctuary, colleges and universities have a history of creating and defending protected spaces on campuses. In 1987, for example, sixteen universities were included in the list of national sanctuary sites.[60] Melvin Delgado argues that understanding the reach of sanctuary as a concept and practice requires recognizing the existence of "sanctuary organizations" such as schools, hospitals, health clinics, libraries, even restaurants that provide precious resources to people in their daily lives and that typically fall outside the politicized sanctuary debates.[61] In this way, the rapid growth of sanctuary campuses beginning in November 2016 is not surprising. Indeed, students, faculty, and administrators organized petitions, marches, and teach-ins and expanded campus-wide trainings to demand that their colleges and universities declare themselves sanctuary campuses. Within weeks, "undocumented students and allies at 100+ universities and high schools nationwide launched #SanctuaryCampus protests demanding universities provide sanctuary to immigrants. With support from community members, professors and allies, they staged walkouts, sit-ins and other actions at campuses in red and blue states—including Michigan, Wisconsin, Pennsylvania, Minnesota, Florida, New Jersey, and more— and launched calls for campuses, churches, and other social institutions to declare sanctuary as well."[62]

Students, faculty, and staff at the University of California and the California State University systems sought to expand existing resources for undocumented students on their campuses—including Dream Resource Centers and other offices focused on supporting vulnerable students— and, in the case of UC Berkeley, demanded that the administration declare the campus a sanctuary or Fourth Amendment campus. "We do not write to you, the administration and the University community at large, in search of sympathy or symbolic support. Instead, we urgently demand that you directly support our undocumented students at the College and in graduate programs by declaring the Berkeley campus to be a Sanctuary Campus or Fourth Amendment Campus."[63] Colleges like Lewis and Clark in Portland, Oregon, also pushed for a sanctuary campus declaration, but they used the moment to strengthen relationships between the campus and the city of Portland and created a semester-long workshop on the history and practice of civil disobedience. And at Oberlin College, students, staff, faculty, and administrators drew strength and inspiration from the organizing efforts of Pomona College and Yale University—some of the first to compile a list of sanctuary campus resolutions that was shared widely and that facilitated sharing resources nationally to bolster local support—to push for a sanctuary campus statement that drew on the college's and town's unique history challenging unjust laws and providing refuge to victims of state power.[64]

Oberlin's sanctuary campus statement was the result of weeks of sometimes tense meetings in which students made a compelling case for a strong statement from the administration that would be unequivocal in its support for its undocumented students and to do so by using the term "sanctuary campus" as a way to signal solidarity with the national movement that was quickly growing and gaining visibility. On November 14, 2016, Oberlin faculty and staff sent a petition signed by more than 2,400 students, staff, faculty, and alumni to Oberlin College president Marvin Krislov calling on the college to "stand with other colleges and universities and investigate how to make Oberlin a sanctuary campus that will protect our community members from intimidation, unfair investigation, and deportation."[65] While it was clear that Oberlin's administration supported these efforts and was willing to put out a statement affirming its commitment to protect its students, it also expressed concerns similar to those detailed by historian Elliott Young from Lewis and Clark College, which included the fear that "declaring a sanctuary [campus] made a false promise to protect students since the college could not really prevent ICE from arresting students if they possessed a legal warrant."[66] On December 1, 2016, Krislov issued a formal statement that affirmed the college's commitment to protect its students and addressed the broader issue of power and challenges that the concept of sanctuary entails:

> I know many of you, reckoning with your own uncertainty and anxiety about possible changes in the Federal government, signed the petition calling on Oberlin "to join other colleges and universities and investigate how to make Oberlin a sanctuary campus that will protect our community members from intimidation, unfair investigation, and deportation." . . . The term "sanctuary" in this context is not well defined. But it does convey Oberlin's long-standing values of respect for diversity, inclusion and human rights. So as I embrace the spirit of the "sanctuary campus" movement, I also want to outline practical measures Oberlin is taking to protect those who may be at risk during this challenging time.[67]

Some of the practical measures included affirming the college's prior commitments and policies regarding undocumented students, which were also the result of student organizing by groups such as Obies for Undocumented Inclusion, as well as new initiatives, including expanded UndocuAlly training sessions across the college.

The sanctuary campus movement, like church-based sanctuaries and sanctuary cities, reflects a commitment to ensure that concrete policies and measures are put in place to protect students. But the movement also served an equally important role of taking a principled stand against the Trump administration, which had demonstrated contempt for programs, policies, and practices to protect immigrants and sought to both eliminate such programs and punish those who dared to defy their new orders. Indeed, as Shelley Lee, professor of comparative American studies and history at Oberlin College, maintained, "We wanted to take a moral stand on this issue very quickly and to urge the administration to take the steps to make a meaningful institutional response to this very uncertain situation in which very vulnerable members of our college and university community could potentially be targeted."[68] Powerful statements such as these reflect the multiple ways sanctuary functions in our contemporary political landscape: they establish clear policies designed to protect immigrants; they lay bare the specific roles of federal, state, and local officials in immigration enforcement; and they raise the question of whether schools—universities and colleges, in this case—are required to cooperate with immigration officials to enforce immigration policies.[69]

Conclusion

Sanctuary practices do not occur in a vacuum. They are deeply informed by local histories as well as regional, national, and global dynamics. They emerge in specific moments, modify to new contexts, and inspire and challenge those around them, but they also endure across space and time. As Aimee Villarreal eloquently reminds us, "Sanctuary is capricious and often conditional, precarious and temporary, but it has a sublime staying potential. Its staying power is a combination of human agency, divine intervention, a tenacious will to survive, collective actions and sacrifices that create and sustain home-making projects."[70] In the chapters that follow, I offer insight into the conditional, precarious, temporary, and tenacious ways people engage in sanctuary practices in Ohio that nurture Latinas/os' feelings of belonging. For some, these efforts are grounded in longer histories of home-making in the Midwest; for others, political-economic shifts, natural disasters, and dramatic political and social upheaval impel new beginnings. What unites such disparate experiences is the surprising way that the capaciousness of sanctuary offers a framework for holding, understanding, and responding to uncertainty and danger by providing a sense of safety and refuge for those most in need.

2

"Hay Una Vida fuera de Santuario—There Is Life outside of Sanctuary"

Physical Sanctuary in Ohio

"Sanctuary is one of the only active forms of resistance we have now," explains Ruben Castilla Herrera. It is a Saturday morning in November 2017, and a small group of us is gathered in a quiet meeting room in the Columbus Mennonite Church on the city's north side to meet Edith Espinal, who had recently entered into sanctuary at the church for a second time. As I discussed earlier, Edith first entered into sanctuary following an emotional press conference on September 5, 2017, the day attorney general Jeff Sessions announced the end of DACA. She made the decision to leave when she believed that she could apply for a stay of removal that would protect her from being deported and separated from her family. When she learned on September 25 that her stay of removal was denied, she entered into sanctuary once again on October 2, where she remained until February 18, 2021.[1] As Edith described her decision to seek sanctuary in the Columbus Mennonite Church, she consistently referred to her family, especially her three children, and how being able to remain near them compelled her to make such a dramatic decision. "I am fighting my deportation," she explained. "And thanks to [Pastor] Joel and Ruben, I feel even stronger in this struggle." Edith spoke resolutely and clearly about the circumstances that led her to turn to sanctuary; she also exuded a kind of cautious optimism forged in a history of immigrant rights organizing that would soon be tested throughout her more than three years living in the Columbus Mennonite Church. It is hard to imagine, however, that any of us that day anticipated that she would remain in the church for forty months. Indeed, throughout the meeting, Edith, Ruben, and Pastor Joel Miller all shared details about the relationships they had built to support Edith and her family, the advice given by lawyers and local community activists, and how Edith was one of many across the state and country to seek public sanctuary in the wake of the 2016 presidential election. All of these actions reflected the increased concern among immigrants—particularly undocumented migrants—with how the new administration's policies would adversely affect them and the vigorous responses that communities deployed to challenge, defy, and resist such measures. Physical sanctuary, as Ruben noted, was one of these acts of resistance and a critical feature of what Reverend John Fife described as a "layered strategy" that binds up faith communities with secular institutions to offer protection to people facing state power.

This chapter examines the distinctive role physical sanctuary plays in a layered strategy of resistance in Ohio. As a state with one of the highest numbers of people seeking public physical sanctuary from 2017 to 2021, Ohio offers insight into the enduring power of faith-based physical sanctuary and its reach that extends far beyond the sacred walls housing those seeking protection. In what follows, I offer an analysis of sanctuary as a gendered strategy of resistance that mobilizes notions of motherhood and family as a way for "sanctuary leaders" to lay claim to local and national belonging and to their right to remain with and raise their families. While living in a church is one way to resist deportation and family separation across geopolitical borders, this strategy exacts an incredible toll on the mental health and emotional well-being of those immediately involved. "Hay una vida fuera del santuario—there is a life outside of sanctuary," Edith soberly shared with me two years into the more than three years she lived at Columbus Mennonite Church.[2] This life outside of sanctuary is both what motivated her to continue to fight to remain and what she found nearly impossible to endure as her family members navigated their complicated lives without her daily presence. Indeed, there is a life outside of sanctuary, but it is a life forever transformed for sanctuary leaders and the sanctuary networks, families, and communities that accompany them.

Sanctuary Leaders

When I met with Edith on October 23, 2019, she had been living in the Columbus Mennonite Church for a little more than two years, and it was clear that her time in sanctuary was taking a significant toll on her emotional well-being. Just that month alone, Edith had met with Democratic presidential candidate Julián Castro, who was in Columbus for a Democratic primary debate in nearby Westerville and who pledged to help her and implement more humane immigration policies if he were elected president. She and her sanctuary team frequently reached out to political candidates and regarded the Democratic primary debates as a special opportunity to reach out to all the Democratic presidential candidates, including Elizabeth Warren and Bernie Sanders, to seek support for her case. At the same time that members of Edith's sanctuary team engaged in this outreach, her lawyers were involved in a months-long battle with the Department of Homeland Security, which had recently notified her that she was being fined nearly $500,000 for defying her deportation order, a tactic the Trump administration employed against Edith and others in public sanctuary.[3] On the day of my visit with Edith, a Spanish-language television reporter and crew were also there to interview her about the news that ICE was dropping the fines levied against her and others in sanctuary. She was happy to talk with the media, something she had become incredibly good at doing in both English and Spanish and which she believed would help advance her case. And while ICE dropping its fine was a significant victory, it offered only some relief for Edith, who returned to her room on the second floor of the church with her little white dog, Bella, by her side to share her thoughts about her life in sanctuary.

> I can tell you that since I have been living in sanctuary, my life has been very difficult. Apart from the stress involved, I have also been depressed. Sometimes the loneliness is overpowering, and as I say to so many people, it's not just living in sanctuary [that is hard], I have my family and my children. There is a life outside of sanctuary. When I entered into sanctuary, the only thing I thought about and I talked with Ruben about was that we had to have an emergency plan just in case something happened to me and I get sick and need to see a doctor. And then a couple of days later, my son got sick with appendicitis and he had to be hospitalized. And it was in that moment that I said I also have to think about my family and the fact that I couldn't be with my son when he was in the hospital. That was in June of 2018. . . . And just now, in 2019, my daughter graduated from high school and I couldn't be at her graduation. These are things that this administration has deprived me of. Because there are

other options to regularize my migration status, but they still want to deport me. This administration has made everything so difficult for all Hispanics and refugees, and I believe what they are doing is unjust and it makes living day to day very hard. There are days I am just so alone.[4]

Life had, indeed, been very hard for Edith and her family. As she lived in the church, her husband and one of her sons had their own immigration proceedings, including ICE check-ins and court dates. Edith's daughter and younger son, as US citizens, did not face the uncertainty of their own deportation, but as part of a mixed-status family with a mother whose case drew national and international attention, they, too, experienced what Leo Chavez has referred to as "diminished citizenship."[5] Researchers have amply documented the impact these experiences have on the mental and emotional well-being of immigrant families, particularly in the context of broader anti-immigrant narratives and policies characterizing immigrants as a threat to the nation. In this regard, Edith and her family shared experiences with many others equally enmeshed in the stigmatizing discourses that had such a dramatic impact on her family.

What is distinctive, however, is Edith's role as a sanctuary leader. In media interviews, press conferences, workshops at the local and national level, and strategizing meetings, people living in physical sanctuary were constantly referred to as sanctuary leaders. This framing conveys a number of important features of contemporary sanctuary practices. First, it centers the voices, lived experiences, and insights of people who are often invisible or mischaracterized in public debates about sanctuary and immigration specifically. The value of centering sanctuary leaders' voices was particularly visible when hundreds of people convened at Columbus Mennonite Church on January 16, 2018, to be a part of the first-ever video-conference that brought together Edith and four others—Hilda Ramírez, Eliseo Jiménez, Samuel Oliver Bruno, and Carmela Hernández—living in public sanctuary in Austin, Texas, Raleigh and Durham, North Carolina, and Philadelphia, respectively.[6] As Pastor Joel welcomed everyone to this event, intentionally scheduled on Martin Luther King Day to both honor the civil rights leader and frame racial, economic, and migrant justice as being of the same struggle for freedom, he began by offering a special welcome to the sanctuary leaders and noted that we were all participating in something that had never been done before:

We will be hearing from five sanctuary leaders tonight. . . . Sanctuary, first and foremost, is about people and families. . . . If you are here, consider yourself a sanctuary person. Sanctuary is also about community and about ending unjust deportations. It is a movement of people increasingly energized to challenge a cruel and unjust immigration system. . . . God is our sanctuary. Grant us and our neighbors near and far, courage in our hearts, peace in our homes, and justice in our streets.

Ruben Castilla Herrera translated Pastor Joel's welcome into Spanish and invited each of the sanctuary leaders to share their stories. They did so, offering insight into why they made the decision to enter into sanctuary, their experiences since entering, and their hopes for the movement. "For me, sanctuary is a movement that has changed my life completely," Edith began, setting the tone for the comments that followed. "I am a stronger woman, and my children are stronger too. . . . Today I am sharing my story with everyone to show this administration that united we are stronger. We cannot give up. We are going to win this fight because this fight is for our children and families. We have a right to move forward and improve our families. . . . I want to thank all of my *compañeros del santuario*. Together we will fight, and God is with us in our struggle."

When Hilda, Eliseo, Carmela, and Samuel spoke, they offered similar stories of hope, defiance, gratitude, and sense of purpose. Some, like Edith, were explicit in their condemnation of the Trump administration and the negative impact its policies and practices had on their families. Carmela, for example, criticized the president for his lack of compassion and his criminalization of migrants. "The president says he is kicking out people who do bad things in this country. The only criminal here is the president himself because he doesn't show compassion and doesn't realize people have families and want to be in a safe space. This administration is unjust." Others focused more on their families both as the motivation and biggest challenge of living in sanctuary. Samuel, who, like Edith, had lived in the United States for more than twenty years, ended his comments by saying, "I am here [in sanctuary] because my family needs me. Thank you for asking how we are feeling, and thanks to all of you who nourish the sanctuary movement."[7] Others shared stories that revealed how distant undocumented migrants feel from non-Latinas/os and the lack of empathy this can engender. Eliseo, for example, described his gratitude to people who surprised him with their kindness and commitment to the sanctuary movement since he expected very little from others. "I want to give thanks to so many people who have helped me. As undocumented people, we think that Americans and white people won't help, but they will. When you enter into sanctuary, you realize that so many people care for you. They listen to you. They help you and they help your family."[8] Carmela focused on the ways her sanctuary in the Church of the Advocate, a historically Black church in Philadelphia, built important bridges between African Americans and undocumented Latinas/os and how the daily pain, difficulty, and indignity of wearing an ankle monitor engendered empathy with those who wear it as a result of their criminalization and location within the carceral system.[9] "The ankle bracelet I wear is the same as other people of color wear. It is a similar process of criminalization."[10] By focusing on the daily struggles with ankle monitors, the pain of being separated from family, and new perceptions of non-Latinas/os as well as their indictment of the Trump administration, sanctuary leaders were able to fashion and center their own stories, offering inspiration and instruction to others on how they can be part of the movement. As Noel Anderson from the Church World Service observed during the event, "Any movement for freedom and liberation has to be from the voices of the people impacted. They are the ones who have to lead the movement."

An emphasis on sanctuary leaders also affirms the unique role those in sanctuary play in making decisions about their case both legally and in public media, highlighting their agency, power, and authority in extremely constrained circumstances. While Edith was one of at least five public sanctuary cases in Ohio between 2017 and 2021, hers garnered the most public attention in the state. This was largely due to her decision to take a very public position about her case and to the strategies she embraced to draw attention not only to her own circumstances, but to the broader sanctuary movement. Edith gave public lectures at the church and via social media and videoconferences; she was interviewed by local, national, and international media; she met regularly with others in sanctuary through videoconference to discuss strategies on the local and national levels; she participated in workshops; and she frequently attended meetings with her legal and local sanctuary teams to discuss strategies for her to leave sanctuary. In all instances, she worked collaboratively with others who were largely volunteers donating their time and energy to support her, something she repeatedly expressed gratitude for. "I didn't know everyone who is a part of my sanctuary team before I entered into sanctuary. But they all decided to help me. . . . I believe there is a reason God put them in my journey and I am grateful to them for always having time for me and my family. They always come to the meetings and for the phone calls. They give their time—they give their time to me. And I think that is really important. At every event there are people donating their time . . . to listen to my story, to hear what we need, and to learn how they can help. All of this gives me even more strength to continue."[11]

Collaborations with a wide range of people strengthened sanctuary leaders' authority, power, and political efficacy. This also underscored that exercising agency is a process. Pastor Joel Miller emphasized this point when he reflected on the ways Edith, whom he described as "a natural leader," had grown during her first two years in sanctuary.

> Edith—she's become a leader of her own. She's the leader. There are some really committed team members and leaders, but this second year especially, she has been the leader of her own case. . . . I think part of it was being in a place long enough . . . the comfort and knowing people. . . . When she came in, she didn't know us. We didn't know her. She was very deferential. . . . Her English has gotten better, and most of us [on her team] are not bilingual. . . . I think she comes across as very quiet and unassuming. But when she's comfortable, I think she is a natural leader. She's become more settled in her role.[12]

One of the most revealing examples of Edith's leadership style was in her long campaign to get US congressional representative Joyce Beatty to sponsor a private bill on her behalf.[13] During the first two years in sanctuary, Edith and her team lobbied various political leaders—Columbus mayor Andrew Ginter, US senator Rob Portman, US senator Sherrod Brown, among others—to visit her in sanctuary and to advocate for a stay of removal. They sent letters, made phone calls, and publicly offered invitations to them to visit and talk about her case, but these efforts were often met by tepid or no responses at all. While this process was frustrating and "le gasta uno mucho la energía," she persisted while in constant conversation with her lawyer and sanctuary team.

Sometimes you just lose the energy [to fight] and then you wonder, How am I going to find the energy? How are we going to do this? . . . My lawyer has helped me a lot figuring out how to organize my case. She has been a good lawyer and has been incredibly helpful. . . . I share ideas with her and she tells me some strategies that we can use to push [forward]. If I tell her, "This is what I'm thinking," she says, "OK, let me think about how we can do this." . . . Just like how we finally got a private bill [introduced] because Joyce Beatty did it when she saw that Morgan Harper, who was running against her, spoke with my lawyer, who asked her to submit a stay [of removal to ICE] and she said she would. . . . Joyce Beatty then came to visit me . . . and told me she would introduce a private bill. . . . I think that [reaching out to Morgan Harper] helped to push [Beatty] to make that decision. . . . Even though Congress was in session, Joyce Beatty did what she told us she would do.

Succeeding in getting Representative Beatty to introduce the private bill HR 4224, "For the Relief of Edith Espinal Moreno," on August 30, 2019, was significant and a testament to the different approaches Edith employed.[14] But these various approaches also reflect very different strategies people in sanctuary take—from the very public campaigns like Edith's, which involved national organizations, local leaders, and even her children advocating on her behalf privately and publicly, to more muted approaches that seek to resolve their immigration status that are less visible and public.

As Amalia Pallares documents in her research exploring the different experiences and outcomes of the sanctuary cases of Elvira Arrellano and Flor Crisóstomo, the strategies sanctuary leaders take reflect their distinct lived experiences and circumstances; they also can result in dramatically different outcomes, even when the cases appear to be quite similar. Elvira Arrellano was very public, focusing on a family rights discourse concerned with keeping her together with her young son, Saúl. Flor Crisóstomo, on the other hand, had difficulty getting publicity for her case, which focused less on family unity and more on her rights as an Indigenous woman who wanted to care for her transnational family that she was already separated from as a result of immigration policies. These strategies also reflect distinctive approaches to faith-based organizing that, as Edward Orozco Flores documents, can range from political lobbying and organizing that draws on more combative tactics grounded in Saul Alinsky-inspired organizing to tactics based in relationship building. According to Orozco, insurgent and pastoral approaches to faith-based organizing are rooted in different religious traditions—African American Protestant faith traditions and practices versus Latin American liberation theology traditions, for example—and they also reflect specific local histories of organizing that are deeply informed by race, ethnicity, and class.[15] Some of the different strategies sanctuary leaders in Ohio used also reflected how specific local histories, relationships, and faith traditions informed their efforts. Notably, however, gender, family, and kinship play an even more significant role in explaining different approaches to sanctuary strategies.

When Miriam Vargas entered into sanctuary on July 2, 2018, at the First English Lutheran Church (FELC) in Columbus, she stood beside faith leaders, community activists, and supporters in a ritual increasingly familiar to participants and observers of the growing sanctuary movement. As Ruben Castilla Herrera welcomed people on that warm summer morning, he began reminding everyone that this was a challenging day, especially for Miriam.

> But we do not despair. . . . What we do is listen to the people. We listen to the cry of the people. To the laugh of the people. To the voice of the people. And then we move, nos movemos, no? And that's what we are doing. . . . Thank you for coming. . . . I'm going to ask that everyone, que tenemos respeto sobre el caso de Miriam. I just ask that we have respect for Miriam and her family. She is new to this, and she has stepped up. She's a sanctuary leader. She decided, "I'm going to lead my case, but I'm also going to lead the case and fight . . . what's happening, . . . the inhumanity of this administration." She's got children and she's got a family, so please be respectful for that.

Ruben's comments highlighting Miriam's agency and what compelled her to make the decision to enter into sanctuary were followed by statements from other religious leaders, who emphasized how their faith compelled them to act as well. The FELC pastor, Reverend Sally Padgett, for example, offered a moving explanation of why her church made the decision to offer sanctuary to Miriam and her family:

> This is a sanctuary space now. . . . In this space . . . we believe that all are welcome here. . . . [Miriam] has been welcomed and will continue to be welcomed by this community. People have . . . recently been asking, "How did this congregation decide to do this so quickly?" And for this congregation, I have to say it was an easy decision. The question was more: How can we not do this? In Matthew 25 . . . Jesus tells us to welcome the stranger, so following our Lord's call, that is what we did as a congregation. All Christians are called to love their neighbors as themselves. I ask you . . . to love Miriam. Love her and love her children as you would yourself. Help her get the legal help she needs. And help her to stay united with her family. Can you make a donation? Can you provide food? Can you be supportive of this issue and help make sure she stays safe? That is what we are asking.

Such sentiments were echoed by Bishop Suzanne Dillahunt when she praised the FELC for "taking seriously the gospel and putting it into action as they feel called to do. We continue to pray for separated families, leaders, and congregations as we strive to live out this calling to do justice, love kindness, and to humbly walk with our God."

Throughout the press conference and in the months that followed as Miriam remained in sanctuary, preserving families and specifically keeping Miriam with her daughters were recurring themes. As Miriam herself noted that morning, her only desire was to remain with her US-born daughters:

> I want to thank everyone for being here and for your warm welcome and the support you have given me. The only thing I want is not to be separated from my family. . . . My greatest desire is to remain with my daughters. . . . I also have a message for the president. I would like to ask him . . . to think about his family and what he would do to prevent being separated from his children. How would he feel? And how would he feel if he were being persecuted not for a crime or anything he had done wrong? Everyone here has welcomed me and my daughters and all my family and I am so grateful to the church community, the community of Columbus, and I give thanks to all of you, and may God bless you all.

Miriam's decision to enter into sanctuary with her young daughters, ages five and nine, was significant and also distinguished her experience from that of Edith. While Edith struggled knowing her family lived without her outside sanctuary, visiting her regularly at the Mennonite Church, Miriam chose to live in the church with her daughters. She, Ruben, and others worried about protecting their privacy, especially since the girls attended local public schools. This was in contrast, again, with Edith, whose adult children, especially her daughter Stephanie, were actively involved in her campaign. Stephanie met with elected officials, attended rallies, led protests and press conferences, and also was in conversations with her mother and her legal and sanctuary teams. Edith's decision to have a highly public campaign about her case rested in large part on her daughter's participation, while Miriam chose a less public route, in part to protect her young children. Ruben emphasized this point during the press conference: "[Miriam's children] are here with her. And that's something I want to say from the Columbus Sanctuary Collective, is to respect the young children. We are concerned about their safety, but also the fact that they will have to return to school and what that might do. So we are honoring her wish to have them protected and not shown at the moment."

The role of young children in physical sanctuary cases has elicited strong reactions. Elvira Arrellano, for example, was excoriated in the media for the visible role her son, Saúl, played in her case. It was also one of the reasons why her case was met with incredible empathy as well. When Leonor García entered into sanctuary in the Forest Hills Presbyterian Church in Cleveland Heights in September 2017, she was holding her youngest son throughout the press conference, as she tearfully shared her decision to enter into sanctuary. Sanctuary leaders consistently appeared with their children surrounding them as they publicly entered into sanctuary. Religious leaders wearing garments and symbols of their distinctive faith traditions enveloped sanctuary families during these solemn and deeply emotional moments as they entered into a sacred space to seek protection. These rituals sanctifying the centrality of family evoked familiar visual references to the Holy Family and were a reminder that when religious communities welcomed sanctuary leaders, they were welcoming in their families and especially children as well. The presence of faith leaders who traveled to convene in a sacred place as witnesses was also a reminder of the shared experiences of exile, displacement, and repressive state power that lead people to seek refuge and protection from others.

While each person in sanctuary made different decisions about how their cases should proceed, they were in conversation with each other throughout the process. Just before Miriam entered into sanctuary at the FELC, for instance, she reached out to Edith, who shared some of her struggles, strategies, and ideas about how to best approach such a monumental decision. She also described conversations with Leonor García, who entered into sanctuary about the same time Edith had, as well as with Angelica, who left sanctuary after living in a church in Mentor, Ohio, for several months. According to Edith, these conversations were not only moments to "darse ánimo—lift each others' spirits," but they also included sharing ideas about what strategies have worked and which ones have not. What was clear is that each person ultimately made their own decisions, even while being connected to one another and even while their strategies diverged significantly from each other.

Finally, a focus on sanctuary leaders that centers their voices and affirms their agency is critical in mitigating against the hierarchies of difference that largely define those who seek public sanctuary and those who are able to offer it. In other words, by taking the leadership of those in sanctuary seriously and being guided by their decisions and strategies, those who offer sanctuary actively work against the kind of paternalism that often characterizes interaction between people whose differences based on citizenship, education, class, race, and ethnicity are significant. In each of the cases in Ohio, people taking sanctuary were doing so in churches whose congregations were significantly different based on race, ethnicity, class, education, and language. The people in sanctuary, as well as the pastors, sanctuary teams, and other volunteers, were, obviously, acutely aware of these differences and worked actively to affirm the autonomy, dignity, and agency of sanctuary leaders given how asymmetrical these power differences were. They did so, in part, by carefully cultivating networks of support that were crucial for the day-to-day care of people like Edith and Leonor, but that would also be critical to the ultimate goal of getting people out of sanctuary.

Sanctuary Networks

On June 5, 2018, nearly a hundred people convened at the Columbus Mennonite Church for a workshop titled "Sanctuary as Resistance."

The evening included sharing a modest meal, presentations, and small group discussions that included Edith, the Columbus Sanctuary Collective, faith-based activists, and college students, as well as activists not affiliated with churches but whose organizations had collaborated with the growing sanctuary movement in Columbus and beyond. Notably, there were people who drove long distances from Northeast Ohio to attend the evening's events, including members of Leonor García's sanctuary team from Cleveland Heights and people from congregations who either had declared themselves sanctuaries or were in the discernment process to do so, including a group from First Church in Oberlin. This group, like the others I had been a part of over the years, was diverse in terms of age and race, with young Muslim community organizers speaking alongside older white nuns and LGBTQ activists of color. All eagerly shared their understandings and hopes about sanctuary in small breakout groups and listened to local and national leadership provide a national context for their local sanctuary efforts. These events offer a window into the broad, flexible, and dynamic sanctuary networks that supported, sustained, and nurtured sanctuary practices in Ohio.

On this particular Tuesday evening, the workshop began with a representative from the local International Socialist Organization welcoming everyone and reminding us that what brought us together was our support of Edith and of the work of solidarity and sanctuary. "The goal is not to have sanctuary. The goal is for [Edith to be home]. Solidarity is important for Edith and others fighting to stay and standing with people whose struggles are different from [our own]. We need to publicly stand with people. *Everyone* in Columbus needs to be safe." These comments set the tone for the evening—they were inclusive, defiant, hopeful, and explicit about what our obligations were to each other and to those who couldn't be with us, but who were part of a shared precarity. A young Muslim immigrant rights organizer, for example, spoke about the need to preserve DACA and create support networks to nurture leadership among those most affected by the Muslim ban, anti-immigrant policies and enforcement, and police violence in Black, Latina/o, and poor communities. "Sanctuary is a safety net to fight back and we need to recognize the stories and voices of those in sanctuary so they can lead. . . . [We also] need to be open-minded about what sanctuary means. It might not always be living in a church." Another young activist, Amber Evans, from the People's Justice Project made a similar point, stating succinctly, "Police and ICE in Columbus are the same thing." This observation was built on one she shared at the sanctuary teleconference at Columbus Mennonite Church just six months earlier in January, when she made an explicit connection between incarceration and immigrant detention:

> The ankle monitors that those in sanctuary wear are similar to those that African Americans [and others in the criminal justice system] wear. At the People's Justice Project, intersectionality is incredibly important. Police are ICE and ICE are police. "La migra, la policía, la misma porquería!" [*chanting to applause*]. We are stronger together fighting against criminalization of our families and communities. It is destroying our families, even those addicted to drugs. What does sanctuary mean for all? Brown, Black, poor, and working-class people coming together. Because at the end of the day none of us will be free until we are all free. Like Martin Luther King said, "Nadie está libre hasta que todos estemos libres."

The explicit mention of an intersectional approach to the work of sanctuary and making connections among incarceration, immigrant detention, and the criminalization of communities of color and other vulnerable populations guided these different gatherings as the movement and its networks expanded in important and sometimes unexpected ways.

When Edith spoke near the close of the June workshop, she returned to recurring themes in all of her public presentations: her gratitude for people's support; her love for her family and her longing to be with them; and also her continued journey of trying to discern what her role in this larger movement is. "These have been the hardest eight months of my life," she shared soberly. "It is difficult for my children, especially my daughter who is in high school. I don't want to be separated from my kids and my family. But if I need to spend more time here, I will. . . . I will do everything I need to do for my family. And this is not just about me. It's about immigrants around the world. It's about opening doors for others, so I can help others. I often ask myself why God put me in this situation. I'm learning so much [through this experience]. This is my story. Thank you for everything you do for my family. I will never forget you." Edith's insistence that there is a larger purpose to what she and others are doing and her desire to help others point to the central organizing principle of sanctuary networks: the role of sanctuary leaders themselves in providing support to each other and helping to build the distinctive kinds of networks each person needs as they strategize and make decisions about their own sanctuary campaigns.

During the July press conference when Miriam entered into sanctuary the following month, Ruben made a number of important observations, including the ways that the sanctuary movement "is a movement of the people" and is sustained by people power. But he also emphasized the way this "people power" is grounded in the people in sanctuary themselves. Before making the decision to go into sanctuary, Ruben explained, Miriam reached out to Edith. "The first contact Miriam had was actually with Edith. Edith spoke to her about her experience, and the decision of entering sanctuary is not easy. After that we [the Columbus Sanctuary Collective] were able to speak with Miriam. But Edith has played a big part of the process as well. The challenge is that [Edith] cannot be here. . . . Our point is to have these people in sanctuary to be able to return home. As soon as they get in, our goal is to get them back out." The truism that the goal of sanctuary is to get people out suffused every conversation, workshop, meeting, lecture, seminar, interview, prayer vigil, and protest I attended in Ohio, Tucson, the California Bay Area, and beyond. Building networks and fortifying "people power" were key to the strategies of moving people out of sanctuary. These networks looked very different in each case, with some overlapping similarities. But they always began with the sanctuary leaders themselves.

In my conversation with Leonor García's sanctuary team in Cleveland Heights, they described their collaboration with HOLA, a nonprofit organization located in Painesville near Cleveland's east side that serves Latinas/os, and the ways the organization both put them in touch with Leonor and continued to support Leonor while in sanctuary.[16] Like Edith, Leonor participated in the weekly sanctuary calls that connected people across sanctuary spaces nationally. But those conversations were often challenging since it was a moment in which the different strategies were evident and sometimes at odds with each other. While some, like Edith, had chosen a more activist and highly public approach to organizing, Leonor and HOLA sought a different pathway through sanctuary, emphasizing the relationships that they could build to support Leonor's case. These distinct approaches are reminiscent of what Edward Orozco Flores describes as insurgent versus pastoral prophetic redemptive approaches to faith-based organizing among the formerly incarcerated to expand their political, social, and economic rights. In both cases, these collaborations draw our attention to the political empowerment of "those furthest on the margins—the undocumented, the disenfranchised, the formerly incarcerated" as well as the transformation of the broader society.[17]

Sanctuary networks are as diverse as the people they support. From sanctuary leaders with long histories of organizing who create a public platform to advocate on their own behalf as well as for a more just immigration system, to those who build relationships and strategize quietly, the variety of sanctuary practices often reflects the organizing infrastructure that exists locally, as well as the distinct personalities of those involved. While there might be diverging approaches, sanctuary networks play an indispensable role supporting those in sanctuary as well as broader efforts to transform the political, social, and cultural landscape. These efforts go hand in hand and reflect Reverend John Fife's understanding of sanctuary as a layered strategy. Sanctuary under President Trump, according to Reverend Fife, was distinctive from the 1980s and even from the years when millions were deported under the Obama administration because of the policies Trump put in place and because of the rhetoric he used, embraced, and fomented about immigrants. Such policies and discourses foreclosed legal avenues for immigrants to remain in the United States.

> There's no legal relief that is possible. So sanctuary is going to take a very different form now because there is no legal avenue to pursue. . . . During the 1980s, the sanctuary city or the sanctuary campus designation was pretty simple. . . . Solidarity with the sanctuary movement. *Now*, it's really layered. . . . There are sanctuary states, there are sanctuary cities, there are sanctuary counties, there are sanctuary colleges and universities. And then there's faith-based sanctuary. . . . All those lines of public resistance in states and cities and counties and colleges and universities are going to preoccupy the federal [government], particularly the Department of Justice and DHS. So faith communities have time to figure out—and we're going to need time because there's no option for people going into sanctuary and then getting some resolution to their case, right? Sanctuary in a church or a synagogue or a mosque is not sustainable over a long period of time. So we're already thinking about . . . what do we do then?

These strategies are clearly informed by the prevailing political environment, but they are also guided by the decisions of sanctuary leaders as they weigh the needs and demands of parenting children and supporting their own families. Just as sanctuary leaders are diverse in terms of their needs, approaches, and experiences in sanctuary, so too are their families. What binds them together across these differences is the distinctive and important role families play both materially and ideologically in sanctuary struggles.

Sanctuary Families

Sanctuary struggles are deeply gendered strategies of resistance and refusal. Of the dozens of people living in public sanctuary in the United States, the majority are women, a trend reflected in Ohio as well. Sanctuary is also a form of what Amalia Pallares refers to as "family activism." Key elements of family activism are motherhood and the ways that mothers make "claims of belonging that are based on or strengthened by their motherhood."[18] The emphasis on preserving family unity, according to Pallares, recognizes the legal basis of family reunification in immigration policy and is mobilized by "community, political and religious leaders" as part of immigration activist and reformist efforts.[19] Edith, Miriam, Leonor, and others engaged in family activism advanced their role as mothers to challenge efforts by the state to separate them from their families.

Edith consistently invoked her family, the close relationship everyone shared, and her distinctive role as a mother when she explained why she made the dramatic decision to enter into sanctuary: "We very much need each other. I'm the one that guides the family and makes sure the kids are doing what they should be, that they're not getting into trouble."[20] This was a consistent theme in every talk, interview, media appearance, and conversation with Edith. She worried about her son's own immigration case, as well as her husband's, and was emotional when she talked about the way the congregation and other members of her sanctuary team offered them support and physically accompanied them for court appearances when she could not:

[My relationship with the people in this congregation] has been really good and positive. I never imagined they would be this supportive. When

I go downstairs to attend [Sunday] service, they always ask me—and my husband too, since he goes with me downstairs for service—they always ask about my children. "How is your daughter? How are your sons?" They have accompanied my husband to court. My son too. . . . They have helped so much and I am so happy because of their help. . . . I never thought [I would be here so long]. I thought maybe a few months, a year at the most. But two years? No. And now I will probably be here for another year. I am hoping, praying that, God willing, we have a change in administration and that the next president will do something good, that something positive will happen, that he will stop the deportations. And if he does that, I think I will be able to leave sanctuary. I really don't want to be here another year and a half . . . but I have to believe that is possible, that I will be here for another year. . . . [The alternative is being] separated from my family. And as you know, my children—we do even the impossible to be with our children. That is the kind of person I am. And I also believe that this country offers them opportunities . . . and that we should never stop dreaming. We always have to dream and know that this is a country that offers us opportunities and security and safety. Mexico is a place with so much violencia del narcotráfico. I believe that is one of the reasons why people emigrate to come here. I still have my dreams for a better life. . . . We can never stop dreaming.[21]

Families are a source of hope. They are the reason why Edith, Miriam, Leonor, and their families make life-changing decisions to leave their countries of origin—Mexico, Honduras, and elsewhere—to live in the United States. And it is their children in particular who lead them to seek sanctuary, even when that means that they are sometimes separated from family and unable to do the things that they want to do to be good mothers, wives, and community members. Edith, for example, came to the United States from Mexico with her father when she was sixteen years old and, as one news report explained, it was the loss of Edith's mother when she was very young that deeply informed her decision to do everything possible to remain with her children, even at great sacrifice to herself.[22] These experiences and decisions and the attendant sacrifices families make have been amply documented by scholars, including sociologist Leisy Abrego, who questions the morality of an immigration system that continually requires migrants to sacrifice families in order to pursue a better life for them in the United States. "When will we stop sacrificing families?" she asks.[23]

Edith's observations also highlight another important element of sanctuary families, namely, the ways they are supported by congregations and sanctuary networks in surprising ways. While this is certainly one of the many ways sanctuary congregations are indelibly transformed as a result of their work, it is also a reminder of the role families play in connecting those in sanctuary with people and networks beyond. Sanctuary families are highly visible, even when their material, emotional, legal, and social needs are not always apparent. One of the ways they are visible is in the ritual that accompanies people entering into public sanctuary, which often includes having family members, especially children, appear with the parent in front of the church with clergy and congregation members by their side. When Leonor García entered into sanctuary at the Forest Hills Presbyterian Church on September 12, 2017, for example, she was surrounded by her four US-born children and was emotional when she explained why she was doing so: "I want to stay here with my family. I want to fight [the deportation order] because I love my family. I don't [have anything] in Mexico, only here."[24]

While public sanctuary rituals tend to be powerful and emotional moments marking a symbolic and material transition from living outside to moving inside a sacred space, it is often the moment of being physically separated from families and "la vida fuera de santuario" that elicits particular turmoil. For Leonor, moving into the Forest Hills Presbyterian Church in Cleveland Heights meant being separated from the daily routines of being physically present and caring for her four children, who remained in Akron (nearly forty miles away), and her oldest daughter suddenly took on the responsibility of daily care for her younger siblings. According to one news report, this has had an incredible toll on Leonor as well as her daughter:

> Leonor looks forward to Friday night when her oldest daughter, Margaret, 19, brings her two youngest children, Luis (6) and Adan (4) to stay with her for the weekend. Margaret and her oldest son, Eric, 13, visit, but usually return to their Akron home. "That's the hardest part, not seeing my children. . . . Margaret was going to go to college but instead she takes care of the children. My baby (Adan) is sick with a cold and cries for his

mother, and I cannot be there to make him feel better. . . . I want to take my children to school. . . . I want to take them to the doctor. I want to go shopping and cook dinner for them. I want what I used to have."[25]

The sadness of missing out on the daily routines, caretaking tasks, and responsibilities of mothering is compounded by being unable to attend precious rituals and celebrations like high school graduations and enduring the disappointment of seeing children delaying their own aspirations and plans. This, as Abrego notes, is a kind of trauma that adversely impacts the emotional well-being of transnational families, particularly the children separated from parents and especially their mothers. And while sanctuary produces a different kind of distance between families than crossing geopolitical borders does, it operates in a similar way, inhibiting quotidian sharing and daily interactions, support, and sustenance that engender the intimacy of familial and household bonds. In their absence, parents in sanctuary—like Leonor, Edith, and Miriam—rely on others to support their families and their lives beyond sanctuary. These relationships are also a continuous source of angst, worry, and guilt for parents as they remain indefinitely in sanctuary.

Edith, for example, talked at great length about guilt, admiration, and the ways she relied on her daughter, Stephanie, to help advance her case with elected officials and others. Stephanie, for example, traveled to Washington, DC, to meet with congressional representatives, and attended rallies, workshops, and prayer vigils throughout the three years Edith was in sanctuary and as Stephanie herself finished high school. These experiences taught Stephanie a great deal, but as Edith noted, they also were incredibly challenging for her:

> She has definitely been learning a lot. But believe me, making the decision to help my case has also been really hard for her. She has had to take a break from her studies. She had the opportunity to go to college, but she decided not to go so she could help me. That was a really hard decision for her to make, but she did it for me. She knows how important it is for her to be able to help me. And she understands that she is the voice that can make people understand that it's not just me and my suffering that's important. Rather, it is the children who are suffering too. . . . I tell her that she is an important example for so many other children who are in the same situation.

Drawing attention to children's suffering has long been a political strategy in immigrant rights organizing. Indeed, the foundational narratives supporting legislative efforts like the DREAM Act rest largely on the idea that undocumented youth who arrived as young children should not be punished for the allegedly illegal actions of their parents. DREAM activists reject this narrative, making the important critique of the ways that it criminalizes their parents in order to promote their children's innocence. They have advanced, instead, a robust defense of families' rights to remain together. Edith's comments about her daughter's role in her case resonates with this, but also turns it on its head by drawing attention to the ways that US-born children carry the burden of an immigration system that threatens to disrupt families. The weight of shouldering these responsibilities also has the same material consequences of illegality and is an example of diminished citizenship: children may delay schooling, postpone opportunities for meaningful employment, and assume significant adult responsibilities, often at the cost of their own well-being. This is also a deeply gendered dynamic whereby young girls—and more specifically daughters—take on the critical reproductive labor of caring for family that is unpaid and often underappreciated, even while their actions can be incredibly empowering.

This, of course, takes a significant toll on children of sanctuary leaders. During Miriam Vargas's sanctuary press conference, Ruben Castilla Herrera praised Stephanie for her role in her mother's case, but also reminded people that she is a teenager with extraordinary expectations before her:

> Stephanie, who is the daughter of Edith, was scheduled to be here today. She is a sixteen-year-old on summer vacation, and she wasn't able to be here. She called at the last minute and isn't here. I want for all of us [to see] how that exemplifies the movement and the resistance of sanctuary and immigrant justice, that this is a movement that is led by the people who are impacted. And we have to listen to that voice. And when they say, "I can't make it," that's fine. Stephanie has been speaking—she spoke at the rally the other day and she's been out [doing this work]. So that's OK. . . . Edith has played a big part of this process as well. The challenge is that she cannot be here [with us here today]. Our point is to have . . . people in sanctuary to be able to return home. As soon as they get in, our goal is to get them back out.

Daughters like Stephanie play a unique and important role in their mothers' cases. Like Leonor's daughter, Margaret, they postpone college, care for siblings and family members, and take on public roles advocating for their mothers' ability to return home to their families. These actions, of course, engendered incredible gratitude and admiration. But Edith, like other mothers, also struggled with deep guilt about missing out on doing the kinds of things that she, as a mother, would like to do for her daughter and being there for the little things that carry significant meaning. In her interview with me, she discussed these feelings at length, as well as the depression and stress she feels and the ways she has tried to cope with all of the loss she has felt while in sanctuary.

> All I want is to give my children a normal life. . . . It's been really hard. Sometimes I take medicine, like sleeping pills, to help me sleep. But then I don't want to take medication, to depend on it all the time. My relationship with my daughter has been really hard, and it's even more complicated because I didn't have my mother with me while I was growing up. I never wanted my daughter to be away from me. I always feel badly for her. My poor daughter, I feel so bad that I can't go with her to the store to buy her clothes—her underwear and bras, to give her advice. Sometimes when she is here, we can talk, but it's not the same. . . . She says she doesn't like it here, that she feels imprisoned, that just being here with me makes her feel depressed. Sometimes I tell her to imagine how I feel. But when she says that to me, I feel badly because I can't be there for her one hundred percent. . . . My middle son says the same thing to me when he visits. When he got sick and had his car accident, he came to stay with me for only a few days and then he said, "I have to leave, I'm going. I feel imprisoned here, like I'm suffocating." And I understand how they feel. They're young. And I can't make them come and stay with me, but I still feel badly, not being able to be with my daughter when she needs me. To give her my opinions when she is buying clothes or makeup, you know what I mean? For me, that has been the hardest relationship because we used to be really close. And now we have lost so much. I tell her, I tell all of them that they are learning to be strong and we will get through this together. This all will pass, we will get through it. But we aren't sure *how*.[26]

The guilt, sadness, and loss are debilitating for parents in sanctuary who are aware of the irony of being physically and emotionally distant from the children who motivated them to enter into sanctuary in the first place. In other words, making the decision to enter into sanctuary requires separation in order to fight the separation that deportation would bring. This irony is similar to the paradox observed by the anthropologist Gilberto Rosas in his experiences as an expert witness for asylum cases: The key to a successful asylum case is to render an asylee's country of origin unlivable in order to justify their petition to seek refuge in the United States. In other words, his role is to make people's former communities and homeplaces dead in order for them to live their lives elsewhere.[27]

Mothering in sanctuary takes on a particular urgency and power and is part of broader organizing efforts to use motherhood as a way to elicit sympathy and support and to draw attention to broader structural forces that render families vulnerable and fractured beyond immigration policies. This is precisely what animated local activists to produce the short and powerful video *Tres Madres*. In May 2018, the Columbus Sanctuary Collective released the short film *Tres Madres: Three Mothers Fighting for Justice*, featuring Edith as well as two other women, Adrienne Hood and Jaqueline Kifuko, who "came together this Mother's Day to share their story with the world and ask you to join the fight for the families that cannot be together."[28] The video focuses on their stories and links them up as a struggle to preserve families, the rights of mothers to remain in the United States and protect their children, and the broader policies preventing them from doing so. By emphasizing their roles as mothers to challenge state power, Edith, Leonor, Miriam, Adrienne, and Jaqueline engage in gendered political strategies rooted in histories of struggle that connect them to social movements and freedom struggles in Latin America, Africa, and beyond. Thus, while sanctuary families work to make it possible for Miriam, Edith, and Leonor to remain with their families and to return to their homes, these actions are part of broader organizing efforts that use the language of hospitality and safety to address issues of structural violence that include not only immigrant deportation, but also limitations in asylum law and police violence in communities of color. By focusing on structural forces that render families vulnerable and fractured, these efforts embody a broader approach to sanctuary work that Naomi Paik refers to as imagining "abolitionist futures" and involves strategies such as teleconferences, listening sessions, Mother's Day celebrations, public protests of police violence, and political organizing that serve as a reminder of the centrality of mothering and motherhood as a radical act.

Living in sanctuary is hard. It takes a significant toll on people—on those who live in the church, sometimes with their children, but often apart from them, as well as the family members and communities that support them. It is often a strategy of last resort and is, as Pastor Alison Harrington from Southside Presbyterian Church stated, a tactic, not the goal. Reverend John Fife made a similar observation, based on his many decades of working in sanctuary movements and with an astute understanding of its political efficacy as well as its limitations: "Public sanctuary is critically important to build the movement and legitimize it in the communities as well as nationally. But on the other hand, there's no way you can sustain public sanctuary. . . . It's not good for the immigrant, it's not good for the refugee, it's not good for the church or synagogue or mosque. It's just not sustainable over a long period of time. So if you do public sanctuary, then you've got to start the conversation immediately: 'How do we move this person to a safer place, eventually?' And that's safer emotionally, physically, spiritually."[29] These are the questions that face not only those in sanctuary, but also those who are part of the communities supporting them.

Sanctuary Communities

Throughout this chapter, we have seen sanctuary leaders, networks, and families engaged in the work of sanctuary. Yet another invaluable element of public sanctuary is the sanctuary communities themselves. By "sanctuary communities," I refer to the religious congregations that house people as well as the broader community that offers time, money, and emotional and spiritual support for those in public sanctuary. The religious leaders of faith communities that welcome people into their spaces play a pivotal role in articulating the spiritual foundations that justify such decisions and guide the actions of their congregations to commit to public sanctuary. For many faith communities, there is a discernment process that involves formal meetings and conversations, sharing and reading of materials about the history of sanctuary and specific examples and circumstances, and sometimes guest speakers and lecturers to answer questions and guide people to make an informed decision. Sometimes this discernment process happens well before a specific sanctuary case presents itself and often is a result of national faith-based organizing and social movements that encourage religious groups to join the broader sanctuary movement. This was clearly the case for the more than 1,100 houses of worship that, according to the Church World Service, in the months following the 2016 presidential election "signed up to prophetically confront the administration's immoral and unjust deportation policies, . . . showing that faith resistance continues to grow against harsh and inhumane immigration policies."[30] While the vast majority of these houses of worship did not house anyone in public sanctuary, they aligned themselves with the national sanctuary movement and were involved in ongoing conversations and reflection about what this participation meant to them as a faith community. For other religious communities, however, the decision-making process is accelerated because of an immediate local need that requires a swift response. While congregations may still engage in a discernment process and discussion, the urgency of a person actively seeking sanctuary highlights the commitment involved in housing someone indefinitely and brings concerns about safety, legality, and sustainability to the fore. This was the case with the Columbus Mennonite Church when congregants invited Edith to enter into sanctuary and were profoundly and indelibly transformed as a result.

In August 2017, as Edith was considering going into sanctuary, Ruben Castilla Herrera reached out to various church leaders in the Columbus area, including Pastor Joel Miller, who brought the idea to his congregation. According to Pastor Joel, he expected that there might be reluctance and that people might respond by saying, "This is moving way too fast," expressing concerns not just about the legal questions but about the fact that entering into this commitment could last for a very long time. Pastor Joel explained that money was not an issue for his largely white and middle- and upper-class congregation. But there were concerns about legal matters and the consequences they might face. These concerns were intensified in the context of the extremely visible and vitriolic national debates and President Trump's threats to punish sanctuary cities and others who support the sanctuary movement. A journalist from the *New Republic* described CMC's discernment process in the following way:

> On a warm Sunday [in August], about 70 members of Columbus Mennonite gathered after church to decide whether to give Espinal sanctuary. Columbus Mennonite calls itself an "inclusive congregation seeking to follow Jesus's teachings of love to all, justice for all, and fellowship with all." To the members of the church, the biblical message was clear: Jesus would support sanctuary. But where would Espinal live? How would her day-to-day needs be met? Where would she take a shower? And would hosting her put a target on the church's back? . . . Three days later, the congregants met again. This time, Espinal was there, wearing her ankle monitor. During their discussion of sanctuary, Espinal turned on loud music on her phone and stuffed it into her sock, in case the monitor contained a listening device. After meeting Espinal, the congregants of Columbus Mennonite voted overwhelmingly in favor of taking her in.[31]

While CMC didn't engage in a longer discernment process that some congregations have, the serendipitous convergence of Ruben reaching out to Pastor Joel, the social, cultural, and economic capital of many of the members of CMC, and the fifty-fifth anniversary celebration of the congregation that invited people to reflect on the history of the Mennonite Church served as fertile ground for welcoming Edith into sanctuary.

According to the Columbus Mennonite Church website, seeking sanctuary from violence is foundational to the church's American origins. Not only is sanctuary central to how "Mennonites tell our history," it forms the moral and spiritual framework that compels them to respond:

> In light of this calling, we have welcomed Edith Espinal into sanctuary in our church building. Edith is a neighbor. Edith is a mother. Edith is a child of God who fled violence and sought refuge in our country many years ago and wishes to stay united with her family in this city that has become her home. . . . We as a congregation have heard Edith's story. We've been inspired by her courage. We are compelled to offer our church

building as a place of safety and support where she can stay united with her three children and her husband.[32]

For Pastor Joel, family, faith, and seeking refuge provide the spiritual and theological basis for providing sanctuary to Edith. In my interview with Pastor Joel two years after Edith entered into sanctuary, he reflected further on the significance of Mennonites' history of displacement in offering spiritual grounding for his congregation's support of Edith. "We knew [welcoming Edith] was the right thing to do as a congregation," he explained. "And it also raised important questions and points of reflection: How do we talk about what we're doing? How does this fit into the broader mission of the church? And just finding the language and connecting this experience to our own history. Mennonites have a history of migration and movement away from persecution, towards refuge, towards sanctuary. So it's been really good to relearn our history in light of what we're doing. . . . I think ethics can spring from memory, when you remember things in the right way. You know, like we were once in that position even though we're quite a bit removed from that now."[33] This relationship between ethics and memory is a powerful one that many faith communities turned to as they worked through their discernment process and as their relationship with those in sanctuary developed. Indeed, in the case of the Columbus Mennonite Church, a memory of seeking sanctuary and refuge clearly informed their decision to welcome Edith into sanctuary in 2017. But it was also what guided the congregation's decision to make similar choices during the sanctuary movement of the 1980s. According to Pastor Joel, both this history of being what he calls "sanctuary people" and the congregation's experiences with the Central American solidarity movement of the 1980s laid the foundation for inviting Edith into sanctuary. Indeed, in the 1980s, the Columbus Mennonite Church already played a supportive role in the sanctuary movement while not actually providing physical sanctuary to anyone at that time.

Reverend Dr. John Lentz offered similar insight about the ways his congregation welcomed Leonor into sanctuary. In July 2017, HOLA, the local Latina/o advocacy organization in nearby Painesville, reached out to Forest Hills through the work of one of the members of its congregation to inquire about housing Leonor when it was increasingly clear that she would be deported. Forest Hills had already been focused on the ways they as a congregation could respond to the increasingly hostile anti-immigrant sentiment and policies, and in particular to the Muslim/ travel ban in January 2017 and, as Reverend Lentz explained, how they could act in ways that would be a "witness to our faith." Their Lenten program in the spring of 2017, "US Together," focused on supporting refugee programs and how they might welcome migrants, immigrants, and refugees in this particular political moment. They formed committees, had meetings, and, as the sanctuary group lightheartedly admitted, were preparing "in true Presbyterian fashion" to declare themselves a sanctuary church in January 2018 after a longer discernment process when HOLA approached them seeking immediate support. Given that Leonor was scheduled to be deported on September 15, 2017, the Forest Hills congregation had to move quickly to facilitate conversation and discussion and gain the support of its members. "We had to be of one mind on this," Reverend Lentz recalls telling church members one afternoon after Sunday worship services. After hearing about Leonor's case, the congregation offered unanimous support and quickly formed a small group to get a living space ready and to do the fundraising necessary to cover the costs to create a comfortable space to accommodate Leonor and her family. They were able to raise the money in less than two hours.[34]

On the day before Leonor entered into sanctuary, Reverend Lentz wrote a pastoral letter explaining their decision and also posted the following on the church's website:

> We are here today to announce that Forest Hills church has invited Leonor to live here at this church in sanctuary until such time that she is able to return to her home in Akron, to her work, to her community, and most of all to her family. . . . Separating a mother from her children is not what we do as a people of faith. It is not what Americans should do either. Rather, giving women shelter is what we do. Showing hospitality to those in need is what defines us. Standing with all of God's children everywhere is who we are. Being the beloved community is what we will be.[35]

Like Pastor Joel, Reverend Lentz emphasizes the centrality of preserving families as central to his faith community's deepest beliefs and links these values to those of the nation, holding Americans to a higher moral order by giving "women shelter" and "showing hospitality." Moreover, by emphasizing the religious basis of hospitality, both pastors draw on ancient traditions of sanctuary that not only are rooted in welcoming the stranger, the biblical basis that was often embraced in the first sanctuary movement of the 1980s, but also guide how one treats one's neighbor and those in need. This embrace of extending hospitality to neighbors rather than strangers represents an important shift in how faith communities framed their sanctuary practices in Ohio and nationally. Both Leonor and Edith have deep roots in Ohio, and their role as neighbors, coworkers, mothers, and long-standing community members is also an important reminder that Latina/o communities have long histories in the state.

"Sanctuary has been a gift and has transformed us," Pastor Joel observed in my first meeting with him, Edith, Ruben, and a small group of others visiting in November 2017. "It has been beautiful," Ruben added. "ICE and others didn't want Edith in sanctuary because there is power in this kind of resistance." Edith concurred, explaining how her desires were at odds with her lawyer at the time: "My lawyer didn't think sanctuary was a good option. She wanted me to return to Mexico and didn't like [the idea of sanctuary]." A recurring theme throughout my research was that sanctuary is a gift that transforms the immediate communities involved and has the power to transform and radicalize others. When I asked Pastor Joel, for example, to describe what the two years of providing sanctuary had been like for him and his congregation, he explained how his understanding of immigration had grown dramatically and how much more visible he and his congregation had become over the years. This has been positive because it has helped to strengthen relationships across divisions. "[We're more public now] because Edith has chosen to tell her story publicly and we're connected with Edith. She's caught up in the broken politics and policy, and this propels us into action through her, through a friend, through someone who has become a friend, not just theoretically. But we're actually sharing a life together with her. So I feel like faith communities, churches, congregations, mosques, synagogues stand in *that place*, where the personal and the political really meet together in a really human way." Later in the interview, he returned to the question about how he and his congregation had been transformed through this process: "There have been multiple people who have said to me, 'In the beginning, I wasn't so sure about this. But now that I know Edith, there's no doubt in my mind that this is something—that this is God's work.' It's definitely a personal journey. . . . But everybody's a little bit of an ambassador for the work, which is really good." What Pastor Joel conveys here—"*that place*" where the personal and the political converge and the ways a personal journey is also like being an ambassador—resonates deeply with the observations of others about the ways sanctuary transforms the communities that support it. This happens at the level of the church-based sanctuary teams supporting people like Edith and Leonor when they sign up for meal trains; when they take walks up and down the stairs in the church building to help Edith stay physically and emotionally strong; when they share meals and praise Edith and Leonor's excellent cooking skills; when they agree to have at least one person spend the night in the church with Leonor because she fears being alone; and when they offer friendship, companionship, and spend time talking, listening and comforting women whose decisions have resulted in significant immediate and short-term pain and suffering for what they hope will be long-term and enduring family solace and unity.

Ruben and others who are part of the broader sanctuary communities repeatedly affirm the way sanctuary transforms a broader community of people, including activists and elected officials. Near the end of the July 2018 press conference on the stone steps of the First English Lutheran Church, Ruben emphasized that "the sanctuary movement is a faith-based movement" that is ecumenical and involves people across faith traditions and non-faith traditions. And it is precisely this coming together of people—the "people power," as he and others consistently highlighted—that grounds sanctuary practices and is a critical source of its power and political efficacy. "This city [of Columbus] has been declared somewhat of a sanctuary city by the mayor. But *we the people and the sanctuary leaders* are making this a sanctuary city. Our faith is making this a sanctuary city. And that's how it's going to happen. Right now at 1015 East Main Street, we declare the city of Columbus a sanctuary city."

These words speak to Reverend John Fife's understanding of sanctuary as a layered strategy. Indeed, people who have been transformed and whose actions support ongoing sanctuary efforts have the power to create sanctuary spaces. These efforts put pressure on elected officials to set in place specific policies, directives, and approaches that, whether in name or in practice, provide protection to those most vulnerable. And these municipal policies, in turn, bolster the ongoing and much-needed organizing efforts that can invite diverse groups of people to learn, question, and engage in acts of resistance that affirm the dignity and value of people—immigrants, the criminalized, victims of racialized police violence—who are often at the margins of society and most vulnerable to illegitimate state power.

While people power certainly facilitates sanctuary practices, sanctuary derives its enduring power from the transcendent. When I asked people the question, "Where does sanctuary derive its power?," the answers were revealing of a shared understanding of how the quotidian and the transcendent meet. Sanctuary communities, for example, were deeply involved in the day-to-day, ordinary work of caring and supporting others that forever transformed them. They also understood the call and mandate to do this work as emanating from something far greater and more powerful than themselves. Pastor Joel explained,

> [With sanctuary] there's some underlying moral power that's going on. Someone commented once—we were talking about the sensitive locations memo—so hospitals, schools, churches . . . what's sensitive or sacred about these [places] is *what happens* in these buildings. Learning, healing and community worship. There's still something in our human consciousness that recognizes those things as sacred or at least as special. . . . [Sanctuary] is about claiming power, where we can say, "We're going to take care of each other." . . . Hopefully sanctuary can be an ongoing commitment, a commitment to a long, long story of people who have oriented their lives to a certain authority that supersedes, that enables one to call out poor policy. This is way bigger than just [Edith]. It's brought out so much of the best in this neighborhood and here in our city. It reminds people of our humanity.[36]

Reverend Lee in Oakland made a similar observation of sanctuary, likening its commitment to that of marriage: "[In marriage] you have a space based on the commitment of love. And it's the same thing with sanctuary. We are asking you to enter into this commitment of love, of neighborly love with this community at risk. You can make decisions later—you know, 'I can do this. I can't do that.' But you're still in a committed relationship." What distinguishes this relationship from others, however, and what offers sanctuary its power, is its relationship to the sacred. And this relationship with the sacred is profoundly transformative for the individual as well as the collective.

The metaphor of marriage to understand the complexity of sanctuary is a useful one, not only because it highlights an ongoing commitment that is rooted in the sacred, but also because it tempers our tendency to overly romanticize. In other words, in order for marriage and sanctuary to work, one must be committed to active love rather than love in dreams.[37] Sanctuary, like all relationships, requires work. It also requires recognizing moments of power imbalances not as reasons to avoid engagement, but as opportunities for clarity. Pastor Harrington in Tucson provided a clear example of how romanticizing sanctuary obscures another's pain:

> Refocus your efforts and go into the community working with those who are directly affected in order to make it so nobody has to go into sanctuary. That their home is sanctuary. Their schools are sanctuary. Their workplaces are sanctuary. And so we're trying to do a little bit of a course correction and refocus. . . .
>
> There was one church that I knew of where the church was welcoming a family into sanctuary. The church was celebrating it. And they were just like singing and joyful and, "Welcome into sanctuary." *And the family's weeping.* Because it's a horrible thing to go into sanctuary. But it's a *beautiful* thing for a church to offer it. So you have this clashing. And so there is a great power in it. But there also needs to be—there needs to be kind of this shift, like it's not about *us*. It's not about *our* own agency and *our* own brave resolve in this moment to stand against empire. But it's more about how are we really working in *collaboration* and in *solidarity* with our neighbors? And how are we following *their* leadership and really responding to *their* needs?[38]

Following Miriam's public announcement about entering into sanctuary on July 2, 2018, people attending the press conference continued to talk about the morning's events, what they hoped and feared for the days and months to come, and in one of these conversations with someone from Edith's sanctuary team, they reflected on the significance of the moment and their role in this movement. "The goal of sanctuary is to get out. We are learning to hold on to hope and what it means to be a sanctuary space. Sanctuary is an identity that you cultivate over time, not just a one-time decision." Thinking of sanctuary as an identity is profoundly resonant. It is also deeply challenging and reflects the reality of those who make incredible sacrifices to remain with families and in communities as well as the broader network of people who are indelibly transformed through the work of sanctuary.

Conclusion

Sanctuary is a layered strategy. It involves sanctuary leaders, networks, families, and communities. And it also requires an understanding of different axes of power and authority and how one engages with them. Today's sanctuary movement, as before, is built on a constellation of actors across differences of religion, race, age, class, citizenship status, language, and education. But at its core is the unique role public sanctuary plays, as well as the way its power is derived from faith in God or other higher power. In conversations with people involved in the sanctuary movement, some have raised concern about the secularization of sanctuary, meaning the ways that civic and nonreligious institutions have used the language of sanctuary to frame their resistance and political practice. If sanctuary derives its power from the sacred, this line of questioning goes, do we lose something when we stray too far from sanctuary's religious roots? Many have answered this question with a resounding no, which has created an opening for nuanced responses that insist on acknowledging the distinctive gifts and power of religious epistemologies. Near the end of my interview with Reverend Fife, for example, he made the following prescient, if uncomfortable, observation about the difference between secular and faith-based organizing efforts and sanctuary practices:

> We're all in the same struggle and we're all in a resistance movement to basic violations of human rights. You use secular terms. You use human

rights, felonies, law, all those kinds of arguments. *We're here* out of *faith.* *We're here* because of our *faith* in our tradition and our mandate to remain faithful. And we have certain advantages because of that, culturally and traditionally, and we're gonna use that in the struggle. But we need you to use secular strategies and institutions like courts and cities, colleges and universities the same way. And we'll be glad to talk to you about why we're here and what motivates us and what sustains the movement. I make the argument there hasn't been a significant movement for social change in this country without a *spiritual context* in the base. And I keep saying to them, you don't have any songs, you don't have any rituals, you don't have anything that has sustained movements for a long, long time. So you better pay attention. And that's a legitimate conversation. So that's my side of the conversation.[39]

There is, indeed, a life outside of sanctuary, but it is a life that has been fundamentally transformed. For some, this change involves a political awakening or affirming one's political commitments or perhaps even expanding them to include what Naomi Paik and others refer to as an abolitionist sanctuary movement. For others, their lives are forever transformed because of an encounter with the sacred and the divine. It is precisely this belief in transcendent power that connects today's sanctuary practices with those of ancient times. By grounding today's sanctuary in ancient practices, we acknowledge a transcendent power to challenge injustice, exclusion, and immoral treatment of others of this world.

3

"¡No Estás Solo!"

(Un)Natural Disasters, Workplace Raids, and Spaces of Refuge

On the morning of June 5, 2018, undercover ICE agents entered the employee break room at Corso's Flower and Garden Center in Sandusky, Ohio, and offered workers free donuts. As coworkers indulged in what is a not unfamiliar gesture of workplace collegiality, more than 200 ICE agents surrounded the garden center and detained 114 workers. Many of those detained were longtime residents of Northeast Ohio—some having lived there for more than fifteen years—and some of them were US citizens mistaken for undocumented workers. Thousands of family and community members were devastated by the sudden removal of loved ones. Activists, community workers, and religious leaders struggled to meet the needs of children whose parents were detained in undisclosed locations, as well as providing support for the communities affected by this sudden loss. Others immediately began to organize rallies and prayer vigils, write op-eds, and call on elected officials to denounce the raids and, in the words of Ohio senator Sherrod Brown, the broader "immoral" and "insane policies" that include the separation of thousands of migrant children from their parents.[1] The raid at Corso's garden center was soon followed by workplace raids at several meat supplier locations in the cities of Canton, Massillon, and Salem, Ohio. More than 140 employees were detained, giving Ohio the distinction of being home to the largest workplace raids in recent history.[2]

In the days and weeks following the Corso's raid, local churches and service organizations like El Centro de Servicios Sociales, based in the nearby city of Lorain, played an indispensable role meeting the broad needs of those affected by the raids. Centro staff went door to door distributing food and diapers and offering help to locate missing family members as well as to connect people with legal assistance. According to Victor Leandry, executive director of El Centro, caseworkers were in the towns of Sandusky, Norwalk, and Willard, trying to reach out to those who were affected by the raids, many of whom were too terrified to open their doors. "No one wants to open their doors," Victor explained at a press conference two days following the raid. "Our caseworkers say it's like a ghost town, and they have partnered with a local pastor to get people to open their doors" and receive assistance. After twelve hours going door to door, Centro staff were able to reach nine families who, according to one caseworker, were "in panic mode." "People don't know what to do," the caseworker explained over the phone during the press conference. "One woman whose husband was picked up in the raid is terrified to leave her house and worries about how she will care for her three children. She even turned off her air conditioner [and closed her window in the summer heat] because she is afraid [ICE] will come through the window and take her and leave her three kids behind." The woman's husband had been working in local nurseries and garden centers for sixteen years, sometimes laboring for more than eighteen hours a day. "How will I pay [to take care of] my kids?" the woman cried as she spoke by phone during the press conference. "We are not criminals. We are here to work. I will leave this to God because he will help me. We are not criminals," she sobbed. This emotional testimony was one of many shared that evening, including the tearful pleas by children whose parents were detained in the raid. "I don't want my dad to go," one seven-year-old boy pleaded almost inaudibly. "When my brother said my dad was deported, I thought it was a joke." His ten-year-old brother added, "I can't sleep at night because I'm thinking of my dad. He buys us food. I don't want him to go to Mexico. Please let him go."

Once the phone call with caseworkers in the field ended, Victor turned to all of us at the press conference and observed somberly, "These kids are going to need our help. . . . This is not a new problem. Yes, it's getting worse, but it is an ongoing problem. . . . Right now there are children taking care of children in Norwalk [because their parents have been detained]. And just like we did after [Hurricane] María, we [El Centro] will take care of people in need and find ways to help the community."[3] Linking the fates of people displaced by Hurricane María with families ripped apart by immigration detention is a grim reminder of a shared precariousness defining the lives of many Latinas/os in Northeast Ohio. Organizations like El Centro have a long history of working with church leaders, community activists, elected officials, social workers, mental health providers, and faith communities to address the broad range of needs of people whose daily lives are constrained not only by immoral and insane immigration policies, but also by the vulnerabilities produced by what anthropologist Yarimar Bonilla refers to as the "coloniality of disaster."[4] While, as Victor notes, these are not new problems, neither are the resources people draw on as they collectively respond to the challenges they face. Indeed, these long histories of organizing and struggle are precious resources that sustain and animate community responses today.

This chapter focuses on the different ways Latina/o leaders, activists, and service providers respond to experiences of extreme vulnerability produced by the state. Efforts to protect Mexican and Central American families facing immigrant detention and deportation as well as organizing to support increasing numbers of Puerto Ricans relocating to Northeast Ohio in the wake of Hurricane María connect Ohio Latinas/os to broad sets of networks that are deeply local as well as transnational. Just as earlier moments of exclusion and disaster gave rise to powerful moments of coalition building, contemporary efforts reveal new possibilities and the creative strategies that communities employ to support and sustain each other in moments of vulnerability, displacement, state-sanctioned removal, and rebuilding.

For many Latinas/os in Lorain, Hurricane María was a defining moment that captured the layers of vulnerability that connect island and mainland communities as well as the varied responses at the local, regional, national, and transnational levels. As families, organizations, churches, and elected leaders mobilized to meet the needs of people in Puerto Rico as well as those eventually arriving to Lorain and throughout Northeast Ohio, they also put in place networks of support and care that were reactivated nearly a year later as communities scrambled to meet the needs of households devastated by detained and deported family and friends. The swift and organized community response to the June 2018 raids was framed as being of the same fabric of care and support that was woven in the previous months to support a different group of people. As in October 2017, June 2018 saw an influx of people in need of places of refuge, safety, and protection. Indeed, the language of "taking care of people in need" resonated with broader conversations about sanctuary and reflected new ways of being and knowing that suffused many of the conversations, prayer vigils, press conferences, and rallies that brought together so many to affirm that the displaced and detained people were not alone. "*¡No estás solo!*" (You are not alone), the booklet "Bienvenidos a Lorain County" proclaimed to Puerto Ricans relocating to the area following Hurricane María. "There are many organizations, churches, and shops that will make you feel welcomed."[5] This simple yet powerful statement reflected new ontologies and epistemologies grounded in an ethic of care, accompaniment, and sanctuary that guided people's actions during the tumultuous years of the Trump administration.

Refuge, Resilience, and Relocation Post-Hurricane María

In September 2017, Hurricanes Irma and María devastated the Puerto Rican archipelago. Both were Category 5 hurricanes, with Irma having the greatest impact on the eastern municipalities, including Vieques and Culebra, and María "ravaging everything in its path."[6] As one of the most intense and deadliest hurricanes on record, Hurricane María was a catalyst for unprecedented suffering and misery: nearly a year without electricity, more than four thousand dead, and the disruption of basic services from hospitals, funeral homes, and schools to telephone and public services.[7] Like the impact of other (un)natural disasters, the significance of Hurricane María extends far beyond the physical devastation Puerto Ricans endured. As Yarimar Bonilla argues, Hurricane María's importance also lies in what it revealed to the world, "namely, how it laid bare the forms of structural violence and racio-colonial governance that had been operating in Puerto Rico for centuries."[8] According to anthropologist Isa Rodríguez Soto, by the time Hurricane María hit Puerto Rico on September 20, 2017, "the Puerto Rican people were already amid a disaster, an unnatural disaster created by US imperialism. The economy was in shambles; there was a total lack of political will to ensure transparency and accountability; and most people were struggling to survive."[9] One of the most significant consequences of Hurricane María has been a massive exodus that rivals postwar Puerto Rican migration. According to a report by the Center for Puerto Rican Studies on the first anniversary of the hurricane, nearly 160,000 Puerto Ricans had relocated throughout cities in the United States the year following María. "This exodus represents one of the most significant movements of Puerto Ricans to the US mainland in the island's history in terms of both volume and duration [and] is as high as the net migration flow in the previous two years combined."[10] This new migration was preceded by years of significant Puerto Rican out-migration as a result of Puerto Rico's debt crisis, a stagnant economy, and economic policies at the local and federal governments that have devastated the island's economy. As Roberto Vélez-Vélez and Jaqueline Villarrubia-Mendoza noted based on interviews with people following the hurricane, "interviewees consistently reiterate that the humanitarian crisis that people are experiencing preexisted the hurricane. . . . Most organizers point out that the conditions of precarity can be traced to a myriad of factors, such as austerity measures imposed by PROMESA, state mismanagement and/or neglect, a stagnant economy driven by foreign incentives, and a mediocre policy development approach that follows a top-down model."[11] These failed economic policies, as well as the (un)natural disasters that followed, have had two significant consequences: they lay bare what some scholars have referred to as "Puerto Rican cultural trauma" and demonstrate the renewed use of migration as a "form of governance on the island."[12]

Residents in Northeast Ohio quickly witnessed the trauma of displacement and migration in the wake of María. Service organizations, churches, community leaders, and residents organized food drives, collected clothing, and rented trucks to send pallets of food, medicine, and clothes to Puerto Rico to help with immediate relief efforts on the island. As Puerto Rican families began arriving in Lorain and Cleveland, these same organizations, in addition to schools, hospitals, social workers, community colleges, and employers, organized and attended multiple fairs focused on helping those relocating to the area, with a primary focus on securing housing and enrolling children in local schools. According to Victor Leandry, Hurricane María's devastation resulted in new Puerto Rican migration to the region. "When I walk into [El Centro] at nine in the morning, we are already seeing a migration."[13] These sentiments were shared widely throughout Northeast Ohio as cities like Cleveland and Lorain prepared and organized to meet the needs of potentially thousands of new Puerto Ricans, many of whom used family and extended kin networks for temporary housing. As Edwin Meléndez and Jennifer Hinojosa noted, of the ten largest Puerto Rican communities in the United States, Ohio ranked eighth in a list of locations for newcomers and was predicted to be a significant settlement community for people leaving the island in the years to come.[14] Puerto Rican diasporic communities, therefore, were key in mobilizing to respond to the immediate effects of the hurricane on the island, and also drew on what Marisa Alicea and Maura Toro-Morn describe as "existing transnational connections and newly developed networks of aid and support" that connected cities like Chicago, Lorain, and Cleveland to Puerto Rican communities on the island.[15]

As the reality set in that the road to recovery would be long, local leaders focused their efforts on ensuring the long-term needs of newcomers, including providing adequate housing, ESL classes, and clothing for the cold weather, enrolling children in schools, and ensuring they had backpacks, pencils, and other school supplies. In Cleveland a collaboration between Cuyahoga Community College (Tri-C), the Spanish American Committee, the Cleveland Metropolitan School District, and Esperanza Inc. (an organization focused on K-12 education and educational access for Northeast Ohio Latinas/os) resulted in Bienvenidos a Cleveland, an initiative designed to coordinate services and provide information about housing, job opportunities, childcare, and senior care for new Puerto Rican residents. As part of this initiative, Tri-C offered reduced tuition to students from the island, and Cleveland schools "hired nine new staff members to meet the needs of newly-enrolled Puerto Rican students."[16]

Similar efforts quickly developed in Lorain, with El Centro playing a significant role to coordinate efforts with "Lorain Schools, the county commissioners, Mercy Hospital and the Metropolitan Housing Authority."[17] One way El Centro did so was by creating the Spanish-language pamphlet "Bienvenidos a Lorain County: Un guía de nuestra comunidad de Lorain," which listed the range of resources and agencies newcomers could draw on to help in the resettlement process. The ten-page booklet detailed the different ways El Centro could help people—including information on basic necessities such as its monthly food distribution program, SNAP (Supplemental Nutrition Assistance Program), English classes, doctors, and mental health resources; as well as concrete information about the price and size of affordable housing units throughout the city; secondhand stores for clothes, household items, and furniture; public transportation; local schools for children as well as the local community college and vocational schools; the local employment office to connect newcomers to jobs; and contact information for FEMA, with the offer to help people in that process. This information, which anticipated individuals' and families' immediate needs, was complemented by more information about local churches and Puerto Rican and Mexican restaurants and supermarkets, as well as community festivals, banks, local government, and voter registration. By including information about voting and local, state, and national elected leaders, "Bienvenidos a Lorain County" alluded to the possibility of resettlement that would extend beyond the immediate crisis of Hurricane María. It also was intentional in providing historical context for the Latina/o community that was actively working to integrate them by opening the pamphlet with the question, "¿Donde Estoy: Una Historia Breve de Lorain" (Where am I: A brief history of Lorain) that provided brief demographic information about the city—"En esta ciudad, 29% de las personas son hispanas, y la gran mayoría son puertorriqueños, con una minoría de personas de México, países caribeños y centroamericanos" (In this city, 29% of people are Hispanic, and the majority are Puerto Ricans, with a smaller number of people from Mexico, and Caribbean and Central American countries)—as well as information explaining "why there is such a large Latino community in Lorain":

> Many people don't think of Latinos when they think of Ohio, but the Latino community has been here for nearly one hundred years. In the 1920s until the 1950s, factories needed laborers to work in the steel industry in Lorain. The owners of industrial manufacturing participated in a large recruitment campaign to bring workers first from Mexico and many years later from Puerto Rico. For that reason, Lorain has one of the most established Latino communities in Ohio. The Latino community in Lorain has been largely concentrated in South Lorain. *You are not alone!* There are many organizations, churches, and shops that will make you feel welcomed.[18]

While the brochure had the immediate goal of connecting people to resources, it also provided newcomers with a sense of belonging and entering into a community that had the history, capacity, and organizational structure to support and integrate people into a new, welcoming, and culturally familiar community.

As Puerto Ricans increasingly arrived in Lorain, they certainly were welcomed and provided with much-needed support. But it also became increasingly clear that their needs—economic, health, educational, linguistic, and emotional/mental health—posed a particular challenge for a community that already struggles economically with regional unemployment rates higher than the national average and with Puerto Rican households in particular indexing a poverty rate of 29 percent, compared to 22.7 percent nationally.[19] Despite the marginal economic status of large numbers of Puerto Rican families, leaders like councilman Angel Arroyo noted that community members actively supported and provided hospitality for those who needed housing and struggled with getting their children enrolled in public schools. What were desperately needed, however, were greater resources from local, state, and federal officials in the resettlement process for those who had left the island with few resources. "I fear that the next wave of people coming in from Puerto Rico are those that are in even greater need," Councilman Arroyo soberly observed. Thus, while local leaders and community activists noted the critical role local communities play in meeting newcomers' needs, they organized to demand greater federal investment and resources that were in line with relief efforts in places like Houston. According to Councilman Arroyo, "I went to Houston after the hurricane to help and I saw people getting checks for rebuilding in fewer than eight days. In Puerto Rico, they are past 50 days since the hurricane and only 24 percent of the island has power and they are already talking about pulling FEMA out. Yet FEMA stayed in New Orleans and other places for years. Why is Puerto Rico getting the cold shoulder?"[20]

Local churches played an important role in relocation and relief efforts. Immediately following Hurricane María, Sacred Heart Chapel in Lorain became the drop-off site for donations from across the region, with community members coordinating the massive amounts of relief supplies that quickly filled the placita, the large community gathering space adjacent to the church sanctuary. Longtime community member and activist José Mendiola described the ways Sacred Heart Chapel, LOIRA (Lorain Ohio Immigrant Rights Association), and local leaders came together: "When Angel Arroyo helped getting food to the island, LOIRA was involved. . . . A lot of the members of LOIRA were involved. We packed a lot of food. We helped with getting things ready, putting it all in boxes. . . . That whole gym was nothing but a warehouse!"²¹ Sister Cathy McConnell, who has served at Sacred Heart Chapel for more than twenty years, made a similar observation about the community's response: "The gymnasium here looked like Costco! People brought in everything. Seven semi-trucks left from here, and it wasn't just the church doing it. It was the church with the whole great Lorain community bringing things here. And one of the councilmen [Angel Arroyo] was part of that."²² Meeting these immediate needs soon transitioned to continued support to meet long-term needs as well. Celestino Rivera characterized the coordinated efforts of El Centro, community members, and Sacred Heart in the following way:

> The Puerto Rican community really came out to support these families. . . . They had a lot of fundraisers for them. They sent things to Puerto Rico. They did that continuously for about a year. The families that came here, . . . about two hundred families have to come to El Centro for help. That's not counting the ones that came and didn't seek out El Centro because they have family members. . . . [El Centro] is their entrance to schools to make sure they are taken care of there. They helped them with housing. . . . [Everyone] stepped up to the challenge and did what they were supposed to do.²³

This prescient observation, of people doing "what they are supposed to do," speaks to a long history of communal care that brings together churches, civic leaders, and city residents and has defined the community since its beginning. And while Sacred Heart Chapel plays a distinctive and important role for Latinas/os in Lorain, Victor Leandry underscored that meeting the needs of people displaced because of Hurricane María involved a range of faith communities:

> We always have a big collaboration with Sacred Heart. That's the big one. I work with people from different denominations and different churches, but [Sacred Heart] is the largest and it is the most stable, and we have a very good relationship with them. We have a relationship with the smaller churches too. And now we have learned that we need to establish more relationships with more churches. . . . One of the [county] commissioners asked how he could help, and he organized a committee that is still

meeting to deal with the families coming from Puerto Rico. You have the director of Job and Family Services. You have the director of Ohio Jobs. You have me and Father Bill [from Sacred Heart]. House of Praise was there with a representative. . . . It was a good committee that still meets. We are now talking about how to advocate for organizations to develop services for Latinos and to be sure Latinos are served.[24]

While churches and faith communities in Lorain worked closely with El Centro, the crisis and challenge following Hurricane María were not Lorain City problems, but county-wide and statewide problems. "This is a crisis for [Lorain] County," Victor explained. "We have over three hundred families that arrived. For a city, for a county like this, three hundred families is a huge number." As he continued explaining the challenges of meeting the needs of so many families, he offered a trenchant but careful critique of elected officials who were slow to respond:

We know we needed to do something because we knew nobody else [would respond] and we knew it was our people. So we had to do it. But this was not just our issue. It was a county issue, a city issue. So I was a little disappointed. [*Pauses.*] I saw my colleagues from other cities and all the support they received. And here, even though I received support, . . . it wasn't what I was expecting from the government. . . . They didn't step up to the plate. We did receive support from many organizations, but government and a lot of other organizations were missing. Statewide—I don't remember once even seeing the governor of Ohio saying, "We welcome our Latino and Puerto Rican families," you know? . . . That was really hard for me to see.

While state officials were often slow to respond, he noted that local nonprofits like the United Way and national ones like Unidos US offered significant support. He also emphasized that churches from Oberlin played a key role:

I cannot thank all of the churches enough for all of the support we've received, donations and financial donations. Churches in Oberlin were a big one. I underestimated Oberlin's residents [*laughing*]. They are all about responding to crises like this one. . . . The amount of money coming to support a crisis like [Hurricane María], that is good. But on the other hand, it has made me think, like, "Wait a minute. I need employees to run these programs!" When I do fundraisers for [El Centro], people acknowledge we are doing good things. But when we do fundraising, people don't come. The money was coming for the families from Puerto Rico, and we [were happy] and we took that money very seriously. . . . I am glad we didn't use all of it at the beginning because later on, when they were looking for houses, like four or five months later, they didn't have money for a down payment. So that's where we started to use that money. We were very careful . . . so we could use the money for as many people as possible instead of using it for a few.[25]

The critique of the failure of the state on multiple levels—the federal government's hostile and callous response; the failure of the Puerto Rican government; the tepid response by the governor of Ohio and other state-level elected officials—points to the differential inclusion of Puerto Ricans in Ohio and the near-invisibility of the Latina/o population more broadly, even in spite of its long roots in the region and its growing population. But Victor Leandry also offered an additional trenchant critique of the distinctive role nonprofit service organizations like El Centro play in the community, often to the detriment of the staff that provide much-needed services. Moreover, as Victor also noted in his interview with me, the needs in economically struggling regions like Lorain County and Northeast Ohio more broadly are so vast that it is hard to meet all of them and also to compete for the attention of donors who have many options for volunteering time and money. In other words, Victor draws our attention to the limits of neoliberal policies that increasingly rely on the private sector, foundations, and nonprofit service organizations, which not only put a strain on their economic resources, but also take a heavy toll on those who work in these organizations, particularly in moments of crisis. Likewise, churches play an equally pivotal role in meeting the needs of community members, particularly in moments of crisis. This was certainly the case with Sacred Heart Chapel, whose parishioners and pastoral staff have a long history of responding to crises and community needs.

It is not surprising that Sacred Heart Chapel played such a significant role in these efforts. Historian Eugene Rivera has documented the important role the Catholic parish has played in Lorain and how it was founded to meet the needs of the growing Mexican and Puerto Rican communities. He and others have also demonstrated the important nexus between the parish and community organizers since it was founded. José Mendiola, for example, spoke proudly of the way Sacred Heart welcomed César Chávez in 1972 during the grape boycott as he and others supported Chávez's visit and his efforts to cultivate more support in Ohio and throughout the Midwest, particularly given the region's long history as a site of migrant agricultural labor. And as Sister Cathy McConnell observed, one of Sacred Heart's deacons was a founding member of El Centro de Servicios Sociales in 1974. The hurricane relief efforts were just the most recent example of how "we work together on many things," particularly as it was increasingly clear that many Puerto Rican newcomers were likely to remain in Lorain.

> They're not only coming now until things get fixed. They're *staying*. . . . They are staying, and their kids are in school. They have found jobs quickly. . . . I had one couple in here and they were so happy. They had come in because they wanted to get married and their kids to have the sacraments. . . . They were so happy because they each had a job. "Yes! I'm working part-time at Walmart and [my wife's] working part-time at Walmart too!" And I thought to myself, two part-time jobs at Walmart with no benefits because you're part time, was a goldmine to them because they had no work in Puerto Rico. And they came here and they could get hired immediately. At first they lived with relatives, everybody did. But you know, that grows old quickly. As soon as they got jobs and checks, they were able to rent a house, and now they have established themselves and their families here.[26]

One Sunday afternoon in April 2018, Sacred Heart also hosted a fair that brought together a range of agencies, public officials, health professionals, teachers, and social workers to provide information, moral support, and a sense of community. This event was inspired by similar efforts in other cities that sought to bring together in one event the broad array of resources and organizations that could help Puerto Rican newcomers. This was also an opportunity to distribute further the "Bienvenidos a Lorain!" resource guide El Centro had developed. As hundreds of people circulated among tables about local schools, housing, work, and local government and social services, Sister Cathy, Father Bill, and parishioners from Sacred Heart talked with people, listened to their stories, and shared free food—pastelillos, bacalaitos, tostadas, and burritos—that women who, without fail, show up each Sunday to cook to sell to hungry parishioners after each of the day's masses as they socialize together in the same placita hosting that day's fair. Victor Leandry, Centro staff, and other community workers were also in attendance, and this was important not only because it was a way to welcome people and show them that the larger community offered support, but also because it was a way to take pressure off the more individualized attention Centro staff offers through its intake process, which was having an impact on its workers. Victor explained,

> [In other cities] they would put together little fairs once a week. People would show up and they had different tables and services people could be connected to. We [El Centro] were dealing with people individually, family by family, and that was very hard for us because it is time-consuming, especially the first appointment that would usually take three hours. Three hours! For us, it was about confidentiality and welcoming people individually instead of as a big group. We knew we had to do it individually. Other people were doing it in fairs . . . and I would eventually incorporate some of that. But I still wanted to keep the individual essence of family because we wanted to preserve their dignity.

This model, however, was unsustainable. In addition to meeting the needs of newcomers, El Centro continued to meet programming needs—translation services, mental health, housing, the food pantry—that seemed nearly impossible to manage.

> For six, seven months we were dealing with all of this. It was chaos. We continued to provide *all* the other services—we never stopped doing all the other work. And we were doing everything else on top of it. Finally, it was one of those weeks that I started receiving complaints of people saying we weren't smiling, and I knew why. I was defending my staff, but I knew why. I knew coming to work was stressful. After six or seven months doing the same thing, it was like—we didn't have a life. It was work, work, work. Long days. It was so stressful.[27]

This stress and the cost of doing this work caution us not to romanticize the labor of organizations like El Centro or Sacred Heart Chapel. In fact, as Patricia Zavella has documented in her research among reproductive justice activists, burnout is a real and serious problem for people employed in nonprofit organizations and community work. Recognizing this has led women of color organizers to emphasize the importance of self-care and wellness—physical, emotional, mental, and spiritual—for both the people they serve and the activists and organizers themselves.[28] These observations of the toll of community-based work on people is also a reminder of the cost of having smaller, even if well-respected and effective, organizations like El Centro and local churches consistently fill in for the failures of the state. Such insights resonate with narratives celebrating community and individual resiliency that publicly admire and praise people for stepping up and *stepping in* during moments of nearly unimaginable crisis. Resilience is, indeed, a valuable and admirable quality. But it can also be used to undermine efforts and social movements that organize and demand that the very institutions that should, in fact, provide support in moments of crisis—such as the federal, state, and municipal governments—meet their obligations to serve the public. Moreover, this discourse of resilience, as Yarimar Bonilla observes, raises the question, Why are some people always asked to be resilient rather than expect the resources they deserve?[29]

According to Anabel Barrón Sánchez, a local caseworker, immigration rights activist, and co-founder of Lorain Ohio Immigrant Rights Association (LOIRA), mobilizing support for Puerto Rican newcomers is deeply rooted in Lorain's history as the International City and ongoing examples of the Mexican/Puerto Rican solidarity that has been nurtured through years of immigrant rights organizing and advocacy at Sacred Heart Chapel. Embracing solidarity is also deeply personal for Anabel, as a Mexican woman who benefited from community support when she was detained by immigration officials and put into deportation proceedings in 2013. As Anabel recounted in an oral history interview in the spring of 2018, she reached out to fellow parishioners at Sacred Heart Chapel one Sunday morning, sharing her story at each of the English- and Spanish-language masses. "So during the three masses on Sunday—the 8am, 10am, and noon mass—I went to the podium, and I shared my story with the parishioners, and I asked them to support me and I asked them to support my kids." According to Anabel, people were moved to tears, a response that surprised her:

> I didn't think that the church would have that reaction towards me. Be-
> cause after I finished talking there was a line of people, all the way here
> [outside the chapel], just to give me a hug. And the following Sunday I
> came back, and I collected more than a hundred letters to support my stay
> of removal application. These people saw me volunteering and see me
> here, but I never thought they were going to take the time. . . . And they
> were coming to the office and dropping off the letters. I was amazed.[30]

For Anabel, this outpouring of support was significant, not only because Sacred Heart is still largely regarded as a Puerto Rican parish, but also because it enabled profound and generative solidarity between Puerto Ricans and undocumented migrants from Mexico, El Salvador, and Guatemala who increasingly attended mass and events at Sacred Heart, but who didn't feel particularly visible. LOIRA, for example, was established by Anabel and José Mendiola, who are both parishioners of Sacred Heart Chapel, where they hold their meetings; the organization's members include Puerto Ricans, Mexicans, and Central Americans from across Lorain County. "Know Your Rights" workshops, legal clinics, informational meetings with immigration lawyers, and fundraisers have been organized and attended by a range of people, including the Lorain chief of police, Celestino Rivera, who often invoked his family's traumatic experiences migrating from Puerto Rico as being an important point of departure for his role in developing clear policies guiding interactions between his police officers and immigration officials to protect undocumented immigrants.

This is the context in which Anabel observed the importance of offering particular support for Puerto Ricans relocating to Lorain. She also noted that Hurricane María was followed by a devastating earthquake in Mexico City that also preoccupied the thoughts and energies of Latinas/os in Lorain:

> How can I not be compassionate to the Puerto Rican community after
> seeing so many videos that people and clients were showing me. And
> I guess, this is not about niceties, this is about being a human. [*Pause.*]

I know Mexico suffered a lot of losses, especially those kids [lost in the recent earthquake]. [*She exhales and pauses.*] But Puerto Rico was worse. And maybe I'm saying this because I didn't lose anyone in the earthquake, but I know that Puerto Rico—the entire island got wiped out. And Mexico City was just a little, not a little, but a few houses [were lost]. [*Pauses again.*] More failures of [building] structures. So, that's why [I am so focused on the Puerto Rican community]. I would say that the Puerto Rican community supports the fundraiser [for earthquake victims in Mexico] and the Mexican community has supported the hurricane María efforts to welcome this community and these families into our community. So, that's the way that I see it. I don't know if someone else has something else different to say. But now it's like a family, OK. We're all together in this.[31]

Binding oneself up with the struggles of others is what guides the work of people like Anabel Barrón Sánchez. Faith communities work in collaboration with other community organizations to foster these relationships and in doing so, create spaces of refuge for those in need. In the case of Hurricane María, faith communities like Sacred Heart organized locally and operated transnationally to accompany and support those affected by the devastation and to demand resources from the state. Their actions reflect efforts by organizations like the United States Conference of Catholic Bishops (USCCB), which admonished Congress to meet the needs of hurricane victims and be accountable for having produced the very conditions of precarity that characterized the island long before the hurricane. In a statement posted to the Diocese of Cleveland website on November 2, 2017, Bishop Frank Dewane, chairman of the Committee on Domestic Justice and Human Development of the USCCB, declared,

> The people of Puerto Rico have been facing serious problems for many years: economic upheaval and scarcity, persistent joblessness, and other social problems resulting from the financial crisis gripping the Commonwealth's economy. They bear little responsibility for the island's financial situation yet have suffered most of the consequences. Now, the recent devastation has made the circumstances, especially for those in need, unbearable.
>
> As pastors, we share in the suffering borne by our brother bishops and the people they shepherd in Puerto Rico. We stand ready, through

legislative advocacy as well as by means of the emergency funds set up in the aftermath of Hurricane María, to support with compassion our brothers and sisters in such dire need. We urgently beseech all Catholics in the United States to join with all people of good will in supporting these crucial initiatives at this critical point in time for the people of Puerto Rico.[32]

Standing with displaced Puerto Ricans and undocumented immigrants facing immigrant detention through advocacy, accompaniment, and hospitality is the prevailing framework guiding the efforts of activists and faith communities as they collaborate, organize, and develop creative strategies in the face of grim realities.

These networks have long sustained and supported communities that have been adversely impacted by political neglect, racial and gender subordination, economic exploitation, and social marginalization. Indeed, as many scholars have observed, it is precisely these relationships and webs of support that reflect what anthropologist Hilda Lloréns has described as "life-affirming practices" that are passed down through generations and endure across space and time.[33] For Afro-Puerto Rican women living in Puerto Rico's southeast coastal regions, for example, these life-affirming practices "resist long-term oppressive systems, such as the racial capitalism with which Caribbean people have long grappled," as well as "ecological crises and gendered and racialized exploitation."[34] In Lorain, life-affirming practices are also shared across generations and develop and respond to the particular circumstances in Northeast Ohio. Once knitted together, these practices of solidarity and mutual care were key for the community mobilizations following the Corso's raid and for ongoing sanctuary work that endures today. As José Mendiola observed, "It really made a big difference. The community came together. . . . The entire city of Lorain came together."

"I Can't Live without My Mom": Accompaniment, Solidarity, and Immigration Raids

On July 8, 2018, Bishop Nelson Pérez traveled to Lorain to celebrate a special mass for immigrant families at Sacred Heart Chapel. This was not his first visit to Sacred Heart—indeed, while bishop of the Cleveland Diocese, he frequently noted how much he enjoyed celebrating mass in the largely Latina/o parish. But in the frenzied and mournful days and weeks following the Corso's raid, in which members of Sacred Heart parish were detained, the presence of Bishop Pérez and his clear articulation of the church's position regarding immigrants offered much-needed solace to a grieving and fearful community. Following his installation as the first Latino bishop in the Diocese of Cleveland on September 5, 2017, he was consistently vocal in his support of immigrant families and comprehensive immigration reform and offered his first public articulation of his position on September 7, 2017, in response to President Trump's decision to end DACA. Affirming his commitment to stand with DACA youth as well as his call for Congress to develop legislation to protect them, he observed that during his installation mass just two days before, he had called on people to "accompany those in difficult situations."[35] Bishop Pérez returned to this notion of accompaniment in his homily at Sacred Heart Chapel ten months later, proclaiming,

> For the church, there are no borders. The church cannot be detained. And the same church that was present in the lives of our brothers and sisters in their countries of origin—that encountered them and accompanied them—well they come here, and they're embraced by the same church.[36]

Accompaniment is a defining value guiding new initiatives and much of the work in the Diocese of Cleveland under Bishop Pérez. In 2018 the diocese launched its Parish Companion Program, designed to "accompany parishioners who are in the final stages of immigration removal proceedings, or who are at risk of removal."[37] A key element of the program is to provide training to "prepare companions for the different scenarios they may encounter and offer an opportunity to meet people from other church communities who care about similar issues of immigration and the realities facing undocumented sisters and brothers."[38] The training includes a focus on legal issues and practical matters immigrants in deportation proceedings face, and it offers concrete ways to accompany people in this process as well as being clear about the scriptural basis for the Church's position regarding immigrants and immigration.

And while the notion of accompaniment has a long history in Catholic social teaching, with its clearest manifestation in liberation theology and faith-based social justice struggles throughout Latin America beginning in the 1960s, its current manifestation takes on a particular resonance when applied to Latina/o communities in the United States. In workshops, casual conversations, and discussions around issues ranging from immigration reform to family separation, family relocation due to natural disasters, and meeting the needs of the poor, the language of accompaniment is embraced and suffuses faith-based advocacy, programming, and pastoral care. Accompaniment, therefore, is not exclusive to Catholic social teaching. Indeed, it is what informs many faith communities' embrace of hospitality and "welcoming the stranger" in their work with immigrants and immigrant communities in Northeast Ohio and beyond.[39]

In an interview two days following the mass at Sacred Heart Chapel, Bishop Pérez elaborated on the significance of accompaniment as a way of being in the world and a framework for understanding the work of faith-based solidarity:

> For me, Sunday [mass at Sacred Heart] was the coming together, first and foremost, to pray as a people. To pray for this whole [problem around] immigration and not just the things that have fueled it in the last couple of weeks. . . . This has been going on for a long time. [So we gathered] to pray for God's intervention. . . . The other part was to gather in a community together, not only physically there, but symbolically, to gather the community symbolically in prayer, but also in solidarity. So the key words are "prayer" and "solidarity"—that we are in this *together*. And not only does God listen to us, but we listen to each other. We listen to each other and *walk* with each other and *accompany* each other. . . . Accompaniment is rooted—corre por las venas, it runs through the veins of the Judeo-Christian experience of pilgrimage, of journey, that we are on a pilgrimage and peregrinaje. That we are passing through. . . . Accompaniment is the way the Church does business. It accompanies people in their great moments and in their difficult moments. And it's God sharing compassion for his people. It's incarnated now in the life of the Church, through people that do [the work of accompaniment].[40]

Bishop Pérez's emphasis on the importance of accompaniment underscores a number of important issues. First, it affirms the value of

Catholic social teachings that challenge the privileged—in terms of class, citizenship, education, and social status, for example—to stand with the most vulnerable. Second, it is a reminder that faith-based advocacy and activism that embrace pilgrimage, walking with, and solidarity—in other words, accompaniment—are not new and have a long history in Latina/o communities in the United States and Latin America. And finally, this emphasis on accompaniment underscores the creative ways faith-based organizing challenges dangerous legislation and the politically powerful. While moments of state-sanctioned terror and violence are not new to faith-based activists, it is hard to overstate the fear, danger, and vulnerability experienced by immigrants, economically marginalized communities of color, and others during the Trump administration. Increased deportation and immigrant surveillance, race-based violence and rising white nationalist sentiment in mainstream public discourse, anti-immigrant sentiment, and the vulnerability produced by callous and incompetent responses to the aftermath of natural disasters all contributed to increased precarity and the need for those with certain protections and status to offer protection. Accompaniment emerged as one of these strategies and offered a new language for those who engaged in the work that was increasingly criminalized in public discourse and public policies.

In some ways, the language of accompaniment became a way to circumvent the language of sanctuary, which was (and in some circles, continues to be) incredibly polarizing and politicized. As we saw earlier, debates about sanctuary, particularly those focused on sanctuary jurisdictions, were often vitriolic on the national, state, and local levels. Ohio was no exception to these trends. While some elected officials aligned themselves with President Trump's vicious attacks on sanctuary cities and those who advocated for meaningful immigration reform, others worried about how they might resist these efforts effectively. Schools, universities, colleges, city governments, and churches, for example, were some of the places where these conversations took place and were also the object of potential sanctions. In the face of these real consequences, some began to offer strategies to navigate this uncertain and punitive landscape, including a shift in language. This focus on the value of a new language became very real to me one day after mass when José Mendiola and his wife spoke with me and my husband at Sacred Heart Chapel. As we sat together eating tostadas and pastelillos in la placita, José talked about the work he and his wife were doing visiting local prisons and how important it is to have married couples and families involved in this particular kind of pastoral work. Having his wife present to talk with the wives of incarcerated husbands provided invaluable support, he explained. "In the work we are doing here and with immigration, I really think we need to think about this as a kind of hospitality. Maybe we need to talk more about *hospitality* rather than sanctuary," he said. "Sanctuary," he worried, has become such a loaded word, a sentiment shared by a number of people. Indeed, discussions around developing rhetorical strategies that captured the spirit and values guiding activist and community organizing aimed at supporting immigrant and Latina/o communities, as well as implementing concrete programs to offer aid, were recurring themes among many leaders, activists, and community workers. Accompaniment was one of these strategies. Thus, while many embraced and deployed sanctuary practices, arguing for its historical and continued spiritual power, others considered alternate framings and approaches in the face of increased deportation and family separation.

During my interview with Bishop Pérez, for example, he detailed the diocese's approach to supporting immigrant families and explained why offering physical sanctuary was not a viable option for Catholic parishes. This, he admitted, followed many long, emotional, and sometimes contentious discussions in parishes across the diocese, a point that other faith-based activists noted with frustration and disappointment. According to Bishop Pérez, "'sanctuary' is a very complex word and means many different things," and physical sanctuary runs the risk of creating additional problems. He continued,

> First of all, [sanctuary] doesn't solve anything. We're not really set up for it either. . . . In some ways, it creates another prison. . . . The reality is that there is no real sanctuary in the sense people think, that law enforcement can't go into a church and remove a person. Well, actually, they can. There's no law prohibiting somebody to go into a church. Now, there is a document, a memo that talked about sensitive locations. And it listed churches and hospitals and schools. But it's not codified in law. . . . So we talked about how [physical sanctuary] might not be the wisest thing to do.

But that doesn't mean we can't do something. . . . There are families that are going to get deportation orders, and we can't stop that deportation order. However, those families are a family and have needs. And many times they don't even know what to do. So we talked about *accompanying* those families, to help them to get their business in order, to deal with the issues of [caring for] their children. What do they do with their children? So we put together a training program that was put together from different [offices of the diocese], by lawyers, by Catholic Charities, casework management, counselors, to give them a sense of what a family would face if they have a deportation order. What are the things they need to take care of? And then to *walk with them*. And walk not only *during*, but *after* that and with those who *remain*. . . . So that's *accompaniment*. That's *walking* with people, meeting them where they are, . . . to meet people where they're walking and then walk with them, anticipate their needs. *That's accompaniment*. It's what we do with our friends sometimes. Just go for a walk. It may not be directed towards anything. It's just, "Let's walk together." . . .

[Physical sanctuary] is a very powerful tool. That's why I said there are different ways of *walking with* and accompaniment. [Some churches] have made a decision in a very physical way . . . and I applaud and admire that. . . . In some instances, it's a very powerful statement. . . . There has always been in the Judeo-Christian tradition the spirit, the idea of "acoger," which is really the idea behind sanctuary, right? De acoger, you know, to gather, to protect. And there are many different ways that is done.[41]

By definition, the verb "acoger" means to welcome, receive, and take in someone to your home and protection. And it perfectly captures the specific ways the Diocese of Cleveland, as well as much of the Catholic hierarchy nationally, committed themselves to support immigrants through accompaniment, welcoming the stranger, and hospitality, even while they resisted calls both within and outside the church to embrace physical sanctuary, both in word and in practice. While, indeed, "there are many ways" to accompany and support immigrants, physical sanctuary for them was not one of them. Yet Bishop Pérez was unequivocal in mobilizing resources, supporting programming, speaking publicly, and offering a clear pastoral message on the value and centrality of accompaniment. In doing so, he was part of a robust community of faith leaders, activists, and community members who were indefatigable in their efforts to navigate the incredible needs and feelings of vulnerability in a punitive legal and political landscape that required not only creative strategies, but also a new language to frame their efforts. Accompaniment, therefore, also reflected an ecumenical practice that bound up the efforts of diverse groups of people. In short, in both word and practice, accompaniment captured the ways faith-based organizing was stretched and refashioned, and rearticulated a commitment to create, offer, and extend networks of safety, refuge, and sanctuary.

This commitment to accompaniment was enacted most vividly in the days, weeks, and months following the Corso's raid. On June 11, 2018, hundreds of people gathered in the city of Norwalk to pray, speak, listen, and march in response to the raids. This gathering was remarkably diverse, with African American, white, and Latina/o faith leaders, elected officials, and community members speaking out against the raids. When Father Ken Morman, pastor of St. Paul the Apostle Catholic Church in Norwalk, took the microphone at the gazebo, he immediately shared the news that "all the kids are with families," a comment that received sustained applause. In his short speech, he explained that the women were currently being detained in Coldwater, Michigan, while the men were being detained in Youngstown, Ohio. And he also thanked people for their donations and invited others to put money in accounts that would go directly to people being detained. He ended by noting soberly that he and others were doing all they could to meet the immediate needs, but that there were also long-term needs: "We have to change these laws." Father Morman was followed by Reverend Herman Robinson from ACORN—A Christian Organization for Right Now, who began by saying that "we are all precious in God's sight," and offered a familiar trope in American civil religion about how "America is great when we feed the hungry and have compassion for the marginalized. . . . We need to stop tolerating injustices everywhere. You can believe in God and the goodness of America, but we also need to have the courage to do the right thing. If it affects the Hispanics, it affects all of us." Councilman Angel Arroyo from Lorain followed, offering an impassioned speech about the negative effects of ICE in his community and the commitment offered by organizations like El Centro, Sacred Heart Chapel, and others in Lorain to the families and communities affected by the raids. Democratic political candidates also spoke, linking these local events to the broader anti-immigrant policies of the Trump administration. These comments by a white Catholic priest, an African American pastor, and a Puerto Rican councilman reflected the diversity of people who turned out that day to support the families and communities affected by the Corso's raid. This raid had lasting and extensive repercussions that highlighted the feelings of vulnerability and precarity that characterized many Latina/o communities in Ohio and throughout the United States.

One of the most moving comments of the day came from Ruben Castilla Herrera, who arrived from Columbus to offer support and demonstrate his solidarity with a community more than two hours away. In a short, powerful speech, he called for an intersectional approach to organizing that would work "inside, outside, and against" an immigration system that is separating families and causing so much harm and pain. "What direct action are you willing to do?" he asked solemnly to the diverse crowd of white, Black, Latina/o, young, and old assembled. "We *need* each other," he insisted as he recognized the important role of organizations like HOLA immediately following the raid, which included being there for a community that was in crisis and traumatized. But it was the anguished words of fifteen-year-old Juan Pérez, the son of one of the women detained in the raid, that moved the crowd to tears. Juan spoke of his pain and how much he and the other children and families left behind desperately needed the support of people in concrete, immediate, and symbolic ways. Juan began his comments by simply stating, "My mom was taken in the raid." After a pause he continued, "I am so happy to see so many Americans here today. It costs [money I don't have] to talk with my mom [in detention], and so many people have given me money to talk with her." Unfortunately, this was not Juan's first encounter with immigrant detention: his father had been deported two years prior. And as he struggled to recount the stories of friends who were detained despite being US citizens and who had to prove this in order to be released; children left alone because their parents had been detained; and the uncertainty of what would happen to him and his thirteen-year-old brother and five-year-old sister, he observed, "There are lots of kids like me or worse on Jefferson Street where I live." Although Juan and his brother and sister at the time lived with their father, he worried that his father could be taken away again, leaving them with no choice but to enter into the foster care system. "My dad still works at Corso's. And they want ten thousand dollars to get my mom out. We don't have ten thousand dollars. I can't live without my mom," he sobbed as people quickly rushed to his side to console and support him. Immediately the crowd began to chant the familiar UFW slogan "¡Sí se puede!" followed by "¡Los niños de Corso's!"[42]

"¡Los niños de Corso's!" became a rallying cry for the broad range of groups that spent the following months and years organizing support for the families and communities affected by the Corso's raid. By focusing on "los niños de Corso's," the slogan had the intended effect of drawing particular attention to the devastating impact that immigrant detention has on children, most of whom are American citizens. Media coverage of the raids focused on families. This was a point that was emphasized by a gathering of law enforcement and elected officials, faith-based activists, and community members who attended a press conference at El Centro two days after the raid. "Children are taking care of children in Norwalk," Victor Leandry exclaimed when a local news reporter asked what people can do to help. "Reach out to your congresspeople, senators, and governor. Help to register people to vote, the *Latino* community to vote. They need Pampers, baby formula, and money to buy more. LOIRA is helping, and we need money for lawyers. . . . There is an informal network of support developing in Norwalk, Willard, and Fremont [and El Centro will continue to support those networks]." Sister Cathy from Sacred Heart Chapel also noted at least one family from the parish that was directly affected by the raids. And caseworkers like Anabel Barrón Sánchez and Thelma Cruz, who were in Norwalk, called into the press conference to share their grim observations about how traumatized people were and how many children were moving from home to home as they tried to determine what they would do in their parents' absence. "[St. Paul's Church in Norwalk] helped *fifty* kids yesterday," Victor stated grimly. He described the challenge of working in a community so far away from Lorain, but also how Norwalk and the surrounding communities, despite their significant Latina/o population, did not have organizations besides local churches to provide much-needed services: "Sandusky has one of the largest percentages of Latinos in Ohio. But there are no organizations like El Centro to help them. They fall between Toledo and Lorain, so it's hard to help them. We were one of the first organizations who got on the ground immediately to help after the raid. And we are going to feel the effects of these raids for years to come. It's going to be *our* issue in Lorain months from now." As a small town whose Latina/o population has grown over the years, Norwalk is part of surrounding rural communities with Spanish-speaking Pentecostal churches that have developed to serve the needs of largely agricultural workers in the area. Unlike larger urban centers like Lorain, Cleveland, and Toledo, however, the area has no social service agencies that serve the needs of these communities. Organizations like El Centro, LOIRA, and HOLA, therefore, played an indispensable role in providing support, organizing weekly food drives, and offering legal support that attenuated already overextended human resources.

Victor's observations were prescient as staff from El Centro, parishioners from Sacred Heart Chapel, volunteers from First Church in Oberlin, and dozens of others organized donation drives of food, diapers, baby formula, toilet paper, clothes, and cleaning supplies and brought them to a small, Spanish-speaking Pentecostal church in the town of Willard outside Norwalk. St. Paul the Apostle Catholic Church and one of the local Latino evangelical churches in Norwalk also continued to collect and distribute donations. The Latino Pentecostal church in Willard played a particularly significant role, since it offered a place for people to gather to receive goods and donate money and items, and also a place for undocumented parents to complete legal affidavits detailing instructions for their children's care should they be deported. For months following Sunday religious services, lawyers from the Cleveland area donated their time, and volunteers from across faith communities and activists across the region all came together in the church hall brimming with items to distribute. Some volunteers organized the vast number of items to make it easier for people to find what they needed and quickly leave if they chose to do so. Other volunteers would warmly greet wary visitors and ask questions to ensure that they were able to leave with enough food and other necessities to care for family members and friends. Still others were trained to work with parents in completing their affidavits, and the mostly Latina notary publics who were also volunteering as well were able to notarize documents on the spot free of charge. Although everyone did their best to offer a heartfelt welcome to those seeking different kinds of support, it was clear that people's hearts were heavy. Sometimes people would arrive just to talk about what they had experienced the day of the raid. One group of young Puerto Rican men, for example, recounted their horror at being detained and how hard it was to "prove that we were American citizens." "We came here from Puerto Rico after [Hurricane] María to work at Kalahari [water park]," one explained to me and my husband as we waited for someone who needed to complete an affidavit. "Working at Kalahari was terrible, so we went to work at Corso's." As Spanish-dominant language speakers, they described the hours it took to convince immigration enforcement to listen to them long enough to allow them to call a family friend to bring their identification so they could be released. While they could at the time laugh at the irony of the situation now that they were beyond the terror they had once felt, one of their friends quietly asked whether the diapers were for free and whether he could take some for his child at home. When we assured him that he could, he asked about what services we were providing and paid particular attention when we explained that we were helping people make arrangements for their children in the event the parents are detained. He listened intently and said he might return the following Sunday.

This young man's reluctance was shared by many who walked through the church halls on Sundays. This hesitancy was particularly notable for the people who agreed to serve as legal guardians to children. One Puerto Rican couple, who were also pastors at a Spanish-speaking con-gregation in Lorain, arrived one Sunday morning and agreed to be the guardians of several children across multiple households. As they signed the paperwork and learned more about what would be involved should they have to care for children whose parents were detained, the pastor's wife turned to her husband nervously as well as to the parents signing the papers for their children, seemingly to affirm that they were all doing the right thing. These were heavy, weighty moments that people tried to muscle through by saying things like "por si acaso," just in case, knowing that these were precisely the kinds of circumstances that brought all of us there together each Sunday.[43]

Local and national media focused extensively on the impact the raids had on children in the area. The *Washington Post*, for example, provided vivid detail about the experiences of children like twelve-year-old Alex Gálvez and his eighteen-year-old sister, Estefany, who remained in their trailer with "a rotation of older relatives—two more children adjusting to a life without their parents as a result of US immigration policies" after their mother, Nora, was detained during the raid.[44] As residents of a close-knit trailer park in Norwalk, Alex and Estefany were two of the "more than 90 children . . . missing one parent and at least 20 . . . left with no parent at all."[45] As many journalists, scholars, and activists have noted, detained migrants often have deep and long-standing roots in communities like Norwalk, which means that workplace raids resulted in American citizen children left without parents, aunts, uncles, and other extended family and community members who provide precious emotional, financial, social, and cultural sustenance to each other. The terror, trauma, and economic, social, and cultural loss of deportation, however, were not new under the Trump administration. In fact, as journalist Eli Saslow observed, the tears and heartfelt surprise shared by non-Mexican/Latinas/os and their laments that this does not represent America did not resonate with children like Alex and Estefany:

> One of the things that had confused him during the past few weeks was the shock he sometimes saw reflected back at him in strangers' faces—the volunteers who toured the trailer park in utter disbelief, or the TV anchors who broke down in the middle of their live broadcasts from the US border. They said separating a parent from a child was cruel and un-American. They said the United States was in the midst of a singular humanitarian crisis. They said these were the actions of a country they no longer recognized. But, to Alex, the act of family separation seemed quintessentially American. It was the cornerstone of his American experience.[46]

As a son whose father was deported years before in another workplace raid during the Obama administration and who had an aunt, an uncle and other relatives and community members detained, deported or who simply moved away to evade deportation, Alex and his sister share a similar experience with millions of others who are part of mixed-status families that are enmeshed in a deportation regime that devastates families financially and emotionally.[47]

Local news accounts also documented the fear the raids instilled in the community broadly and the impact that it had on the children. According to Pastor Elvin González of Bienvenidos Templo Genesaret in Norwalk, "It's hard for these kids. . . . [They] are left behind with relatives, sometimes with babysitters, so they just had to take them in. The children are just crying, asking for Mom or Dad. They don't know. They don't fully understand what's going on."[48] Pastor Elvin, Father Morman, and others across faith communities opened their churches to receive donations of food, money, diapers, and toiletries, and to bring in lawyers and social workers to meet with family and community members struggling to meet the needs of those left behind. Their efforts were supported by other volunteers from across Northeast Ohio. Along with other faith leaders and secular advocates beyond the region, they were also vocal in their condemnation of the raids and their concern for those suffering in their wake. Columbus-based Imam Horsed Noah of the Somali Islamic Center of Ohio announced, for example, "As an Imam and a parent, I believe rounding up and deporting our neighbors, students, coworkers, friends, and family is a great injustice. Although people can be given labels such as 'alien,' 'undocumented,' and 'illegal,' people of faith know that immigrants—regardless of their legal status—are individuals deeply loved by God and created in God's Divine image. Let's love and not deport."[49] This condemnation was shared by Cantor Jack Chomsky of the Congregation Tifereth Israel, who declared, "I raise my voice along with many clergy of different faiths and denominations to speak out strongly against the recent raids by ICE in Sandusky, Ohio. What a complete violation of our communal and religious values. Our country needs reasonable immigration policy reform, something Congress has failed to do for a generation. Victimizing hard-working people in our communities, no matter their immigration status, tears apart the social fabric of our society and is a terrible waste of public resources."[50] Indeed, African American, Latina/o, and white pastors as well as Catholic nuns, rabbis, and imams from faith communities throughout Ohio were united in their condemnation of both the raids and the family separation that followed. "This is a moral dilemma," Sister Jane Omlor wrote in the nearby city of Tiffin's local paper. "There is a higher law and anyone who professes to be Christian needs to recognize this: Welcome the stranger, love your neighbor, let the little children come to me. . . . How dare we break God's law of compassion and mercy? How dare we take children away from their parents? How dare we cause such suffering? . . . This is not a

Democrat or Republican issue; it's a moral, human issue. We must vote for people who have the courage to lay aside partisanship and work together so all those who seek refuge from violence and poverty can have a chance to find a safe home."[51] As Sister Cathy from Sacred Heart Chapel succinctly noted, "These children do not know where their parents are. That is a trauma."[52]

And while many of these faith leaders mobilized to meet the immediate needs of the affected communities, they also directed our attention to the ways migrant labor is integral to the local political economy and the need for comprehensive immigration reform. Father Morman, for example, explained that undocumented workers in places like Corso's meet employers' needs for workers, but then are criminalized and suffer the consequences from a broken immigration system. Noting the irony of detaining undocumented migrants while local employers "are hurting for workers," he offered a critique of the immigration system more broadly: "It has to be fixed from the Congress side. We have to change the laws. It doesn't help anybody."[53] According to the *Sandusky Register*, Bishop Daniel Thomas of Toledo made a similar critique and visited St. Paul's Catholic Church to meet and pray with family members whose loved ones were detained. "We recognize our current immigration policies are broken and actively contributing to the suffering and separation of vulnerable families. . . . No matter our political persuasion, when families are broken apart, as in this raid, we should all recognize that the common good is not served."[54] Bishop Pérez's statement affirmed this sentiment:

> This latest event in Erie County again makes clear that our current immigration system contributes to the human suffering of migrants and the separation of families. The bishops of the Catholic Church have a duty to point out the moral consequences of a broken system. The Church is advocating for comprehensive and compassionate reform of our immigration system so that persons are able to obtain legal status in our country and enter the United States legally to work and support their families. Since this is a responsibility of our Congress, I would encourage you to speak with your legislators advocating for reform of our present system. We do this remembering the words of Jesus as he calls upon us to "welcome the stranger," for "what you do to the least of my brethren, you do unto me." (Mt: 25–35, 40)[55]

While local media coverage rightfully underscored the trauma and impact of workplace raids on families and communities, the children of deported parents organized to advocate for themselves, their family members, and immigrant communities in Ohio and beyond. Los Niños de Corso's emerged as a hopeful, defiant, and visible force in the aftermath of the Corso's raid. Fifteen-year-old Natalia Alonso from Fremont, Ohio, founded the group following the Corso's raid. As a child whose father had been deported years before, she responded to the Corso's raid by reaching out to the young people affected by their family detentions. She described Los Niños de Corso's as "a Latino youth group. We're here to support any of the kids who were affected. They can reach out to us on our [Facebook] page and tell us what they need and we will gladly help them."[56] Working with churches, immigrant activists, and young people like Juan Pérez who were directly affected by the raid, Los Niños de Corso's played an important role helping to meet the immediate needs of families as well providing a space for young people to come together. Throughout the summer, the group had a particularly visible profile at political rallies, summer festivals, arts fairs, and marches throughout Northeast Ohio. Its local visibility as an organization *by* children of detained and deported parents *for* youth affected by these experiences was buttressed by national attention to the US-Mexico border and the new family separation policy. As the American public was increasingly bombarded with images of children in cages, parents separated from children as a way to deter unauthorized migration, and the news of hundreds of children lost through an inept and callous process of placing them in an underfunded and ill-equipped foster care system, Los Niños de Corso's continued to attend rallies and draw connections between their circumstances and those of migrant children at the border. For the political and religious right that for decades promoted family values as its organizing platform against women's rights, school integration, reproductive justice, and other issues, the hypocrisy of seeing families ripped apart led even Reverend Franklin Graham, the North Carolina-based evangelist and Trump ally, to the surprise of many, to criticize Trump's family separation policy at the border.[57]

This outcry, however, did not prevent further immigrant detention. In August 2019, 680 workers were detained in a Mississippi poultry plant, replacing Corso's as the largest workplace raid under the Trump presidency and in US history. The scenes of children alone with parents in immigration detention and the ripple effects in schools, workplaces, neighborhoods, and communities were resonant with Northeast Ohio communities from the year before. Los Niños de Corso's mobilized quickly in response. They held fundraisers, gave talks, and used social media to seek financial support and food, clothes, diapers, and baby formula once again to provide immediate material and emotional support for the children of detained parents. Using social media, they documented their efforts, including a twelve-hour drive Natalia Alonso and her family made from Northeast Ohio to Morton, Mississippi, to bring the items they had collected to share with the affected communities and families. In a short video produced by AJ+, Natalia described her feelings and how, in particular, seeing children crying because their parents had been detained motivated her to go to Mississippi: "It reminded me of me. . . . I am the child of immigrants. People don't understand the trauma children have. I went through this without my dad for a while, because of his situation, his status. It was a hard time. We had to live with our grandma. We couldn't afford things anymore."[58] Throughout the video, we see Natalia and her family unloading food they have brought to share with families. Her father, Margarito Alonso, assures people in Spanish that they can trust him. "Don't be afraid of us," he says to them as he opens up the back of his SUV. "Come closer. You can trust us. We aren't bad people." The distrust is palpable in the short video— people appear understandably wary of outsiders given the fear that ICE may use the information they gathered during the raid to detain more people. But they also shared their desperate circumstances with Natalia, Margarito, and Monica, Natalia's mother. "His wife was also taken in the raids," Monica explained, referring to her conversation with a man we do not see. "She hasn't been returned. And he has, I think, two or three children." Natalia talks with a woman who reluctantly accepts what Natalia and her family have brought, but also laments that she cannot pay her for anything. While Natalia reassures her that she does not need to pay anything, the woman continues, saying that "God will repay you. He will give you opportunities to study in the future. You are young. Thank you, thank you for being so kind." At the end of the video, Natalia emphasizes, once more, her shared connection to people who live more than a thousand miles away: "Our father, our mother . . . they tell us their stories about their families and about what they had to go through. They received help. I have to repay my dues, you know. In a certain way, I want to help my people out."

While it is clear that young people like Natalia want to "help my people out" and see their efforts as being one way to meet the immediate needs of those whose experiences are similar to their own, what is even more remarkable is her understanding of what her presence can mean to people who feel afraid, uncertain, anxious, and alone. In the days prior to her family's journey to Mississippi, Los Niños de Corso's worked closely with organizations like El Centro in Lorain as well as faith-based communities in Oberlin, Lorain, and beyond, as well as local restaurants and businesses to collect food, money, and other necessities to share with the families in Mississippi. As Anabel Barrón Sánchez pulled into a school parking lot in Oberlin one afternoon to fill up one of El Centro's vans with donations from across the city, she grimly remarked that just a year prior, we had been doing this for members of our own communities not far away. And here we were, once again, collecting donations from Oberlin and throughout Lorain County for the families of detained migrants. Members of First Church, Peace Community Church, the Quakers, and Sacred Heart Catholic Church in Oberlin, for example, collected money and items for Los Niños de Corso's, as did groups like Indivisible Lorain County, students, faculty, and staff connected to Oberlin College, and local activists active in various social justice and immigrant organizing in the town. These efforts were familiar gestures of solidarity. But they were also an attempt to support the efforts of groups like Los Niños de Corso's and others as well as to remind people that in some of their darkest and most painful moments, they are not alone.

Conclusion

In her remarkable ethnography *Making Livable Worlds: Afro-Puerto Rican Women Building Environmental Justice*, anthropologist Hilda Lloréns writes evocatively about the ways Afro-Puerto Rican women have responded to long histories of crisis, turbulence, and dislocation that colonial conquest has produced in Puerto Rico. "In the face of calamity, Afro-Puerto Rican women on the archipelago and in the diaspora did what they had done for generations: they continued to make livable worlds."[59] Making livable worlds, according to Lloréns, includes the daily and often overlooked instances of "solidarity, reciprocity and an ethics of care that are the center of the lives and communities" they are a part of.[60] Latinas/os in Northeast Ohio have also been engaged in making livable worlds and have both participated in and collaborated with faith-based workers, organizers, social service providers, and local community activists in order to do so. As Lloréns and others have amply documented, these efforts of creating spaces of care, refuge, and sanctuary—in short, spaces to sustain livable worlds—are not at all new. Yet the specific historical and political contexts in which they are forged do, indeed, respond to the distinctive challenges that each moment presents. As faith communities, activists, and service providers seek to create and sustain spaces where newcomers and long-term residents can survive and thrive, they draw on the language of accompaniment, solidarity, and sanctuary to frame their work and guide their actions as they move forward. Doing so entails not only meeting the immediate needs of people, but also critiquing the state for producing these crises in the first place. These efforts affirm that those who live in state-produced precarity are not alone. These actions also proclaim to a broader public a commitment to walk with and accompany those who are most vulnerable and disposable in the contemporary American political economy. Efforts to sustain and demonstrate solidarity with Latinas/os take on a number of guises—accompaniment, direct action, physical sanctuary. But ultimately what faith communities and local activists demonstrate is a commitment not only to make livable worlds, but also to center safety, refuge, and connectedness within these spaces.

4

Becoming Sanctuary People

Faith, Solidarity, and Social Justice Organizing

In her important book *God's Heart Has No Borders: How Religious Activists Are Working for Immigrant Rights*, sociologist Pierrette Hondagneu-Sotelo documents the distinctive role faith-based activists have played in immigrant rights struggles and how, in the course of conducting her research, she was profoundly transformed:

> Interviewing religious-based activists for this book . . . opened my agnostic eyes to the progressive potential of organized religion. In fact, I developed deep respect and admiration for these people, who, acting out of religious faith, work to make the social world a better place. Religion can act as a progressive force, lessening human social conflicts, exclusions, and inequalities. This occurs through interfaith dialogues, social services, the infusion of moral values into civic engagement, and, I think, even through prayer and the singing of songs.[1]

Like Hondagneu-Sotelo and so many ethnographers, I, too, have been indelibly transformed through the time I have spent with faith-based activists, religious leaders, community organizers, service providers, and people doing the hard and often thankless work in nonprofit organizations supporting immigrants, Latinas/os, and those most impacted by political, economic, and social policies. And I also have observed the ways that people have committed themselves to work across significant differences of class, race, language, citizenship status, and educational background to make the world a safer and better place, particularly for those who are most vulnerable. As Hondagneu-Sotelo and others poignantly document, this happens in myriad ways, including through the power of prayer and song, such as the weekly prayer vigil a group of interfaith activists and leaders organized in front of the ICE office and detention center in Brooklyn Heights, just south of downtown Cleveland. In the snow, rain, heat, and rare midwestern idyllic spring afternoons, anywhere from a handful to dozens of people gathered to read Bible passages, sing songs, and chant in support of detained migrants and to protest immigrant detention. I first heard of these prayer vigils through a group of faith-based activists in the city of Oberlin with whom I have worked throughout my years of living in the city and teaching at the college. These vigils were largely led by and comprised of white, educated, faith-based workers and organizers who ranged in age, but mostly older and middle-aged, some with young children in tow. They were solemn affairs whose consistent presence served as a powerful reminder of the distinctive role faith and religious beliefs play in social justice struggles, as well as the challenges and opportunities of faith-based organizing in these efforts. In short, these prayer vigils, as well as myriad efforts supporting Latina/o and immigrant communities, are examples of the labor of sanctuary people.

In this chapter, I use Ruben Castilla Herrera's notion of sanctuary people to capture and elevate the work of solidarity across difference. Becoming sanctuary people and doing the work of solidarity is largely unglamorous, tedious, and hard. It is the work of communities of color who are directly affected by policies and practices that have an immediate, direct, and unrelenting impact on them. And it is also the labor of white allies who play a distinctive role and who are deeply committed to working across difference. This chapter, therefore, documents the coalitions people forged across race, class, citizenship, and faith boundaries with an explicit goal of supporting Latina/o communities in a time of danger and contextualizes their efforts within longer histories of faith-based activism. Many activists, members of faith communities, and religious leaders frame the work they do as a political response to displacement as a result of unjust immigration policies, economic crises, and (un)natural disasters, but they also regard their engagement and solidarity work as a form of radical hospitality that sometimes puts them at odds with state power. For some faith communities, solidarity through sanctuary practices is not new; for others, a different understanding of "welcoming the stranger" has compelled them to respond in ways that lead to powerful instances of solidarity. In doing so, we see the various ways Latina/o residents, activists, and leaders respond and organize as they work to create spaces of refuge, hospitality, and safety for all.

What follows is not a new story. Instead, it is one that has been told by many others—activists, scholars, faith leaders, elected officials—but it has a particular urgency today because it offers a road map forward during a moment of deepening division, suspicion, cynicism, and erosion of trust. It is not a seamless narrative that fails to acknowledge mistakes, challenges, and limitations. In fact, drawing on oral history interviews with people actively involved in this work demonstrates a profound humility that undergirds the ways people come together in moments of adversity, pain, frustration, and fear to create spaces of safety, refuge, and sanctuary and how past actions and activism have nurtured these efforts. While there are diverse and often circuitous pathways sanctuary people take, what binds them together is a profound sense that their faith compels them to act and refuse to be silent witnesses to people's suffering. As Celestino Rivera soberly observed in his interview with me as he described how he hoped to focus his efforts after nearly five decades in law enforcement, "I feel the need to make a difference. . . . I want to do it on a visceral level. . . . In the past couple of years I've had this passion for not only the undocumented, but about our communities and the whole environment [the Trump administration] has created. . . . I feel the need to speak out more about it. . . . Everything that's going on disappoints me. But the silence disappoints me even more."

The Work of Solidarity

Ruben Castilla Herrera often invoked the notion of sanctuary people. At press conferences, workshops, public lectures, prayer vigils, and public protests, Ruben reminded people of the importance of the work they were doing and invited people to consider what it means to be sanctuary people. At its core, sanctuary people reflected a commitment to understanding social justice struggles as inherently intersectional. At a lecture at Oberlin College in October 2018, for example, he began by acknowledging that we were living in difficult times. And in this difficult time, he explained, all of us need to reflect on the ways we can work within, outside, and against the system to realize how collectively we can achieve liberation. Sanctuary people are those who actively work to create places of safety, protection, and justice for others and who are, in turn, transformed by these experiences. All of us are called to be sanctuary people, Ruben proclaimed, and the obligation for sanctuary people is to grow the movement. He firmly believed that growing the movement required us to have an intersectional analysis to understand the distinctive yet overlapping struggles of immigrants, victims of police brutality, and other forms of state-sanctioned violence. For many involved in sanctuary work, this was only one facet of what it means to be sanctuary people. Indeed, as Ruben and many activists in Ohio and nationally demonstrated, sanctuary people would embrace what Naomi Paik refers to as abolitionist sanctuary—a commitment to challenging all forms of oppression and political, racial, social, and economic marginalization.[2]

This notion of sanctuary people resonates with what historian Barbara Ransby describes as the liberation and freedom struggles of the BLM/M4BL that are queer, feminist-led, and largely advanced by Black queer youth. Barbara Tomlinson and George Lipsitz have referred to these movements as emerging from "insubordinate spaces" of possibility for a more just and egalitarian world. Understanding sanctuary people in this way—as part of larger collective struggles for freedom and a more just world emerging from spaces of shared exclusion—invites us to consider the relationship between sanctuary people and solidarity. In other words, is the decision to become sanctuary people an expression of and commitment to familiar and new forms of solidarity, or is it something different? While Ruben often reminded people of the importance of being in solidarity with others, his reference to what it means to be sanctuary people suggested something a little more radical. It was also a deliberate and conscious choice to develop new vocabularies for the kind of organizing he envisioned. As the historian David Roediger has argued, solidarity frequently evokes deeply emotional responses of a romanticized past, of what is possible today, and how we can imagine our futures. These imaginings can be generative and inspiring, but they can also obscure the difficulties in solidarity and raise questions about "what and whom solidarity leaves out and how it is premised on those leavings out."[3] Grappling with the complicated history and present of solidarity struggles, or what Roediger refers to as the process of "making solidarity uneasy," is important for understanding "an erratic pattern of the ways in which solidarity actually comes and fails to come into the world."[4] This interrogation of solidarity is not meant to diminish its value. Rather, it is crucial for understanding the successes and failures of various collective struggles. More importantly, it has the potential to direct our attention to powerful catalysts for meaningful social transformation that we might overlook otherwise. Such insights are advanced by activists and scholars alike, including Robin D. G. Kelley's powerful claim in his book *Freedom Dreams*, "I have come to realize that once we strip radical social movements down to their bare essence and understand the collective desires of people in motion, freedom and love lay at the very heart of the matter."[5]

When I first heard Ruben use the term "sanctuary people" in January 2018 at the sanctuary workshop in the Columbus Mennonite Church where Edith Espinal lived, I was intrigued, but was so consumed with listening to the experiences of people in public sanctuary who convened in person and virtually that day that I didn't pay particular attention to it. At a workshop in June 2018, I took note of the ways Ruben called those in attendance to become "sanctuary people." He reiterated this call during Miriam Vargas's press conference on July 2, 2018. But it wasn't until Ruben spoke at Oberlin College in October 2018 that the phrase truly resonated with me. As one of several guest lecturers for a set of courses in American and Africana studies focused on sanctuary, refuge, and resilience, Ruben spoke passionately about the work he and others in the Columbus Sanctuary Collective were engaged in.[6] This included organizing against police violence and anti-Black racism and supporting queer and racial justice organizing that also advocated for no-cash bail. Hearing Ruben repeatedly challenge/invite people to become sanctuary people and locating them as a central feature of sanctuary, social justice, and faith-based organizing inspired me to think critically about what it means to be sanctuary people and to include in my analysis the actual people who do this work, how they come to it, and what it means for them. Through casual conversations with people over the years of conducting this research, I was often struck by how many people located their current commitments within longer histories of activism, volunteer work, and social justice organizing and how they made connections between current and past work. The work of the past grounded their actions in the present, and they were mindful of the lessons learned from previous efforts and how those lessons guided them in the present. This was particularly the case for white, middle-class activists. And perhaps most importantly, it was clear that while faith-based organizing certainly grounded contemporary sanctuary efforts with some congregations and parishes playing a particularly visible role, not everyone belonged to religious communities. Indeed, many held deep admiration for faith-based organizing even if they didn't profess religious affiliation.

In what follows, I sketch out some of the circuitous routes sanctuary people traveled prior to their work in the Trump years. For some, personal experiences of migration, displacement, and race- and class-based marginalization were the foundation for their current commitments. For others, international peace and solidarity struggles provided fertile ground. And finally, local histories and context play an important role in making certain practices and positions possible. Ultimately, what binds sanctuary people together is not only Celestino Rivera's observation of the importance of speaking up and refusing silence, but also a commitment to seeing interlocking struggles as one's own.

Personal Histories of Displacement and Migration

Anabel Barrón Sánchez often remarks in public lectures and private conversations that she never imagined she would be an immigrant rights activist.

> I didn't choose to be part of this immigration activism or whatever you want to call it. I was *pulled* into it. . . . I was *one* immigrant, undocumented for so many years. So you know how they say immigrants live in the shadows? I was one of them. And I still feel like one of them, but with a little bit more freedom. I never thought in a million years that I was going to be doing whatever I'm doing right now.[7]

As a caseworker at El Centro de Servicios Sociales, Anabel has played a pivotal role in helping to solidify El Centro's role as a trusted institution that is responsive to the needs of immigrants, particularly undocumented migrants seeking much-needed services such as ESL and citizenship preparation classes. And as a parishioner of Sacred Heart Chapel, she is a visible and beloved community member who is deeply respected for her leadership in immigrant rights organizing as well as a caseworker helping a range of people receive the services, resources, and support they need. Her journey as an immigrant rights advocate and activist, however, is the result of her own painful experiences as an undocumented resident and newcomer to Lorain many years ago:

> I started doing the work because of my own defense, because as other immigrants, we don't know our rights. . . . It's not that we don't want to get educated, but you want to keep a low profile so no federal agency knows that you're here. But once I got caught, they put me in deportation proceedings and I didn't understand a single word that they were telling me. I didn't understand what [they meant when they said] "We want to put you in deportation proceedings." What is that? "And we want to remove you." Those terms that they used for me—it was unfamiliar. So I said I need to learn. I need to learn. *I need to know my rights.* I need to educate myself. So that's how I became the person who I am right now, by going to trainings. Going to different conferences. Talking to lawyers. And I started working [at El Centro] because I became very public. People know me in this community, especially here in Lorain.[8]

While her role as a caseworker at El Centro has allowed her to provide support to so many in Lorain County, she describes the distinctive role Sacred Heart Chapel and her faith have played in her commitment as an immigrant rights activist:

> When I was first living [in Lorain], for so many years, the only place that I used to go was Sacred Heart Chapel. That was my house. That was my second house. So if I wasn't in my home, I was in Sacred Heart volunteering in the kitchen. So I used to do that because I couldn't work. . . . My kids were going to school and I was going to church to help out every day. . . . The people in Sacred Heart Chapel . . . for me, they were family. They felt like they were family. And when my detention happened, they showed me a lot of support. So for me knowing—as an immigrant, an undocumented immigrant, you feel like you're alone. Your family is away from you. And I have no siblings. My mom and dad have already passed away. So for me, it was like, OK, this is on you, Anabel. But I was wrong. It *wasn't* on me. A lot of people stood by my side. And every time that I needed someone to lift me up—because there are times when you want to

give up. You are human beings like everyone else. And that's what made me think that if I find someone that cares for *me*, I want to be someone to lift up the others.[9]

Her desire "to lift up others" emerged from a sense of belonging and community she felt at Sacred Heart:

When I first came, I didn't have friends. And I have been going to a Catholic church since I was little. . . . My mom used to take me. So I went to Sacred Heart . . . and it was my, my little piece of my tierra. My little land. Knowing if I was going there, I can speak Spanish freely. I don't have to speak English there. And people were welcoming. And I got to know other Mexicans there. They were there in the same situation that I was in. So that was the reason that I was going. Plus my faith. I find peace in my faith. When [I had] the most trouble in my life, I got very close to God. . . . And I really feel like he's always taking care of me, but at the moment of my [greatest] struggle, he showed me that he was there by putting all of these people together.[10]

Anabel frequently returns to both her faith and her personal experiences facing deportation as the foundation for the work she does. She also is clear about how her relationship with Celestino Rivera, the Lorain chief of police for twenty-five years, transformed her life forever. She became quite emotional as she described the meeting she and Father Bill Thaden arranged at Sacred Heart Chapel that would help set in motion a new set of relationships between the Lorain police department and residents of the city.

[Celestino Rivera] was called into a meeting by LOIRA—at that time we were HOLA—and he was called to a meeting at Sacred Heart Chapel. . . . So, as you know, Celestino is a member of Sacred Heart Chapel and has a good relationship with Father Bill, and Father Bill was the one inviting him into this meeting. So when [Celestino arrived], all of us were hiding. There [were people] sitting where he was and tables and chairs. . . . But all the men, all the ladies and the kids, we were hiding. And we all were wearing white. And [while Celestino] was sitting and saying hi and this and that [to people sitting at the meeting] and just saying hello and thanking people for inviting him, we started coming [into the placita]. We led all of our kids, holding hands, with white T-shirts saying "Stop deportations." And all of our kids were holding hands—there were close to, I would say sixty kids in that meeting. And [Celestino] couldn't hold back his tears. He was crying. . . . I remember that we were telling him, "You are separating families because of the traffic stops. If we get stopped without our driver's license or [police] meet an undocumented immigrant, the police officers from Lorain were calling ICE or Border Patrol." He didn't know that. He didn't know that that was a practice here with his officers. So in that meeting—I was the one interpreting in that meeting. After it was done, he came up to me and said, "Thank you, thank you for opening my eyes." And since then, he would call me. "How are you doing, Anabel?" He learned my story that day as well. That I was stopped by a police officer, not in Lorain, but in Sheffield Lake. It was a different [police] department, but he felt like I was one of the people that got in all of this mess because of [what they were doing in Lorain and] because they didn't understand the law.

And that's why I feel like it is not knowing that we have rights [that can be a problem]. That we can [change things if we know our rights]. What do [police officers] do if [they] stop a US citizen with no driver's license? And that's the question that we asked him [in the meeting] and he said, "Well . . . we give them a citation and they can go home." "So why don't you do that with us? Why do you have to call the Border Patrol?"

So that night [Celestino later said] he couldn't rest, he couldn't go to sleep. So he changed the policy. And since the new policy has been there, deportations for traffic stops have stopped in Lorain. That's how [Celestino and I] started our relationship. It happened at an event at Sacred Heart.[11]

When I ask about the significance of this meeting taking place at Sacred Heart with Father Bill, she immediately explained the unique role the church played:

As an immigrant, an undocumented immigrant, you feel safe in a church. You feel safe that the people you trust are not going to hurt you. We knew that Father Bill wasn't going to hurt us. But we were afraid. To be honest, we were afraid of the Lorain chief of police coming to a meeting and talking to us. It was very intimidating. We were like, "What are we going to do?" But thank God, everything went so smooth and easy. I mean, I think what opened up the conversation was bringing our kids [to the meeting]. There were two little boys . . . whose parents were picked up by Border Patrol here in Lorain. And they had the picture [of their parents] on a T-shirt. So we told the story about them. And [Celestino] was like, wow. . . . It was one of the ladies' ideas. She said, "Let's bring our kids because in the end, they're the ones who are suffering." And that's true. When [I was] in the process of deportation, being a mother, I remember all I could think of was, "What's going to happen to my kids?" You really don't care about yourself anymore while you're there. *You* know what's going to happen. But you just pray it never happens. But when it happens, it's your kids, your family [you're thinking about]. So for [one of the ladies to say] we should bring more kids, we should do it because in the end, like I told you, they're the ones asking, "Where's my mom? Where's my dad?" [it was to send a message]. And we felt Sacred Heart Chapel was a safe place for all of us to get together and talk to him. We couldn't have done it in any other place.[12]

It is not surprising that Sacred Heart Chapel would play this role in Anabel's journey in faith-based organizing and activism. As Eugene Rivera has documented, the chapel itself emerged from years of community organizing to create a church that reflected the cultural, linguistic, and religious practices of a diverse Latina/o Catholic community beginning in the 1950s. And it has been a place that has nurtured other faith-based activists whose efforts to support migrant farmworkers, the civil rights movement, and Central American solidarity struggles in the 1980s were sustained by priests, nuns, and fellow parishioners over the years.

José Mendiola, for example, draws a clear line connecting his work with LOIRA to his involvement with the United Farm Workers in the 1960s and 1970s and the role his faith and involvement at Sacred Heart Chapel have played in these efforts. As the child of migrant agricultural workers, José was born in Texas and was part of a burgeoning Mexican and Mexican American community who began settling in Lorain beginning in 1921.[13] When I asked José how he came to his most recent work with immigrant communities in Lorain, he explained, "When I was a kid, there were a lot of organizations like the church and St. Vincent de

Paul, organizations like that that helped out our family. And as I grew older, I decided I was going to give back to the community. And in the process, I got caught up in the Chicano movement."[14] His involvement included working with groups in Cleveland, Lorain, and Toledo to support the United Farm Workers and the grape boycott, and organizing a visit by César Chávez to speak at Sacred Heart Chapel in the 1970s.

> Cleveland was an organizing office for the grape boycott . . . and they had an organizer that came to Lorain. . . . I and a few other people from the community decided to listen about what was going on in California and with the help of that organizer from Cleveland, we started a boycott committee. The boycott committee ended up raising a bit of money for the United Farm Workers. As a matter of fact, I know there was a letter that was signed by César Chávez thanking us for all the work we did. . . . César Chávez came out to this area, and we were on the picket lines against stores that were selling grapes and wine. And we were successful because of our efforts . . . and the efforts throughout the country to help César Chávez.[15]

While José speaks proudly of his work during this time, he acknowledges that he prioritized work and raising a family and was quite distant from faith-based activism and service until recently. Once again, being a member of Sacred Heart Chapel created a space for him to become involved, this time in immigration issues. He first became involved by participating in "Know Your Rights" workshops and fundraising for bond money for parishioners in immigrant detention. He has also worked with HOLA, a nonprofit organization based in Painesville, just east of Cleveland, that is focused on "providing programs and services to Hispanic workers, families and children."[16] And when it was clear that the needs in Lorain included not only immigrant advocacy but also social service provision, he worked closely with Victor Leandry from El Centro and Father Bill from Sacred Heart to establish LOIRA, the Lorain Ohio Immigrant Rights Association. He explains, "We started having meetings twice a month. And we would bring in [groups] like the Free Clinic. . . . And we were also able to work with the Lorain County Health Department to do vaccinations. . . . And one of the most important things we did [was make sure immigrants received] the series of shots they needed to apply for a visa or citizenship. . . . That was saving them around $450. People also came to update their health records. . . . LOIRA did all those things and also took immigrants whenever they had to go in for biometric [screenings] in Cleveland." José Mendiola consistently identifies both the Chicano movement, César Chávez, and the UFW in shaping his activism, as well as the role his faith has played in deepening his understanding of the obligations he feels to work for others. More specifically, he identifies the Cursillo movement—an influential movement among Latina/o Catholic laity that includes weekend workshops and retreats to foster spiritual growth and development—as playing a pivotal role in grounding his immigrant rights activism after years of feeling distant from the church. He explains, "When I went back and did my cursillo, I did a lot of workshops . . . and in the process I found out that [what] I was doing—looking out for the immigrant community—that it was based in Catholic social teaching. These are Christian values that everybody is supposed to be doing."[17]

That the Cursillo movement played a significant role in José's commitment to immigrant rights as a part of Catholic social teaching is not surprising. Indeed, scholars like Adrian Bautista have documented the powerful role cursillos play in the spiritual life of Latinas/os, and specifically its singular role in Latino men's lives throughout Ohio.[18] This renewed sense of obligation to Catholic social teaching also led José to be involved at the diocesan level with programs like Welcoming the Stranger and the Compañeros Program, and also to participate in a delegation to the US-Mexico border. These experiences also cultivated a space to critique the Cleveland Diocese's decision not to be involved in public sanctuary efforts. This was something that was deeply disappointing to many who wanted a different response from the Catholic Church during the Trump years. And while José acknowledged and praised the diocese for its diverse efforts to support undocumented immigrants—Welcoming the Stranger, raising funds to pay for bonds for immigrant detention, and offering extensive legal advocacy through Catholic Charities—he expressed a sentiment shared by many: a deep admiration for other faith communities who embraced public sanctuary.

Like José and Anabel, Celestino Rivera also spoke about the ways his faith grounded his work. As someone who dedicated nearly his entire life to public service, first through the military during the Vietnam War and then as a police officer in the Lorain police department for forty-nine years, Celestino consistently shared—in formal interviews, casual conversations, and public events—his desire to be remembered as an activist who made a positive impact on the world. This desire, he explained, was grounded in both his own experiences growing up in a Catholic orphanage and his faith:

> I became a Catholic by accident. My father didn't have any religion. But when they took us away from him [when] I was five, they put us in a Catholic orphanage, Parmdale. So I lived with nuns every day for almost seven years. . . . And of course, faith is a big part of being in a Catholic orphanage. You went to mass often. You learn to serve mass. You celebrate May with the rosary. You actually celebrated feast days—they're still in my head! [*He laughs.*] So it was a big part of my growing up.[19]

After seven years at Parmdale Orphanage in Parma, Ohio, Celestino returned to live with his father in Lorain, but was soon put into a foster home when it was clear that his father was unable to care for him and his siblings. As he grew up with his foster family—he was separated from his brother and sisters as they all went to different homes—Celestino describes feeling angry and searching for meaning and a sense of belonging that he ultimately found at Sacred Heart Chapel:

> Somehow during that time, I became really close to the priests at Sacred Heart. . . . They had a real sense of social justice. And even in their sermons, they spoke about African American issues and how you have to deal with social justice. So I think that is where I really developed a sense of those issues. . . . When I was thirteen and fourteen, I lived in a predominantly Black neighborhood [in Lorain] and I became so interested in the civil rights movement. And some of it also came from a little magazine called *Jet* magazine [*laughs*]. . . . It was the news you didn't find in the regular media or magazines.[20]

Celestino's interest in the civil rights movement and the incredible admiration he felt for Black leaders at both the local and national levels continued to grow and were sharpened while he served in the army in Vietnam and the conversations he had with fellow soldiers.

Even the soldiers I talked to in Vietnam, the Black soldiers, they always had this feeling, "Why am I here? Why are we here dying? We don't get any respect back home. When I go back home, it's going to be the same old thing. I want more." A lot of them were from big cities, but more from the South. And so I think just listening to them [made an impact on me].[21]

Celestino's experiences were transformational and significant: they remind us of the ways the shared experiences of racial exclusion and economic marginalization in cities like Lorain and institutions like the US military created affinities and understandings that led to solidarities and coalitions across race, ethnicity, immigration status, and class. They also led people like Celestino to read and learn more about the Black Power movement, the Chicano movement, and the Young Lords movement, and to get involved with the farmworkers' movement and other struggles for meaningful social change. "I was just looking—I always think I have had a leaning towards [social justice and activism]. And for me, faith [*pauses*] I've said that I look at [my work] in the police department more from a *service* perspective than an enforcement [perspective]. That is how I always felt about my faith. It came more from a social justice perspective as opposed to a traditional approach."[22]

This social justice perspective is a defining feature of Celestino's life, and his experiences highlight important continuities among faith-based activists. Not only do their personal experiences of migration, labor, and displacement inform their embrace of sanctuary practices, but their experiences with social movements—Black Power, civil rights, as well as the Young Lords, Chicano, and farmworkers' movements—grounded and guided their understandings, responses, and activism during the Trump years. These activist histories grounded in racial and immigration justice are largely US-based, although many scholars have amply documented their international dimensions as well.[23] It is precisely this international, global solidarity that serves as a connecting thread that binds up the work of Latina/o faith-based activists with their white counterparts whose routes are distinct, but somewhat parallel connecting the work of faith-based activism across differences of race, ethnicity, class, education, language, and citizenship.

International Solidarity Struggles

In *Meatpacking America: How Migration, Work, and Faith Unite and Divide the Heartland*, Kristy Nabhan-Warren offers much-needed analytic attention to the ways "the Midwest is a place where many are working to make their communities inclusive and more welcoming."[24] Such insights build on pathbreaking work of scholars like Sujey Vega, Theresa Delgadillo, and Sergio González with their focus on Latina/o communities in the Midwest that also centers the ways faith and religious practices play a critical role in community building. While Ohio's labor and political-economic landscape shares some similarities with those in Iowa and other midwestern regions, it is also distinct in its migration histories, Latina/o settlement patterns, and economic landscape that is characterized by the impacts of deindustrialization, robust agribusiness, and burgeoning service sector jobs. In this context, migration from Mexico, the Caribbean, and Central America as well as domestic agricultural migrant circuits have always been part of Ohio's labor and economic history. As religious scholar Felipe Hinojosa has amply documented, the circulation of religious practices, faith-based social movements, and faith communities that bring people together across race, ethnicity, language, class, and citizenship have similarly been part of these regional histories. Recognizing these religious circuits connecting people across differences should not be romanticized, nor should it obscure the ways religion sometimes hardens lines dividing different groups of people, particularly around issues of race. Instead, these studies, as well as my own research findings, draw our attention to the ways faith and migration can unite communities as well as the challenges that continue to emerge.

Throughout my conversations with people at workshops, peace vigils, rallies, protests, planning meetings, and fundraisers, it was clear that many white faith-based activists have long histories working for social justice causes that they drew on throughout their sanctuary work beginning in 2016. While there were a range of activities and organizations different people belonged to, there were a number of historical moments and specific social movements that capture the variety of faith-based activism that defined them and that were different from the activism of Latinas/os. In what follows, I focus on two specific eras—the anti-war movement of the 1960s and 1970s and Central American solidarity work of the 1980s—and how these experiences provided fertile ground for people's faith-based activism during the Trump years.

The Realm of God

Without exception, older white faith-based activists I interviewed and worked with over the years identify the Vietnam War and the anti-war movement as being some of the earliest and most transformative moments in their lives. These were also experiences that, for many, coincided with their growing awareness of racial justice and the civil rights movement as they moved from largely white, conservative, rural communities to multicultural, racially diverse urban settings. For John Gates, who grew up in rural West Virginia, studying and working at Kent State University in Ohio played a pivotal role in his political consciousness and activism. "It was the Vietnam War," he explained to me when I asked him to share what led him to his faith-based activism. "Until that time, [my wife, Linda] and I were not really political at all. I think the fact that we came from West Virginia and the economic status of our families sort of lent itself to [this way of thinking]." At Kent State, he took classes that, as he describes, "opened my eyes" not only to anti-Black racism, but also to the contradictions in American democracy:

> I can remember when Carl Stokes became mayor of Cleveland. I thought, "Wow! This is a great country. Only in the United States could this man pull himself up by his bootstraps and become mayor." But . . . after that I thought, "Yeah, he did that and that's great. But there's no reason why he should be just the first mayor, you know? There should have been others before and there should have been governors and presidents." And then, of course, Kent State became the center of controversy with the invasion of Cambodia and the Nixon administration and the National Guard that shot four students. . . . I had graduated mid-year and I was working at the post office. Linda was still teaching at Kent State when this happened. And we saw the National Guard come in. The city was cordoned off, and when you entered or left, you had to go through checkpoints . . . and there was maybe one tank at a central checkpoint. . . . We became more politicized [because of our experiences at Kent State].[25]

While John is clear about the way his experiences at Kent State politicized him, he explained that his faith was something distinct from his burgeoning political consciousness. While he and Linda explored different churches, he described how he grew up in a more conservative and traditional faith community:

> I grew up in . . . a Southern Baptist church. And it was really about the Bible and, you know, "Jesus died for your sins." We had meetings where . . . after a long, impassioned sermon by the minister, maybe he would cry and he'd get really emotional and invite people from the congregation to confess. You didn't actually have to say anything, but you could come to the altar and he would bless you. It was all very emotional. But as far as taking any political actions, no, I don't remember that at all.[26]

Like John, Reverend Steve Hammond, who was co-pastor at Peace Community Church in Oberlin for more than three decades, also describes how the anti-war movement shaped his political development and how this differed from the more conservative environment in Green Castle, Indiana, where he was raised:

> When I was in high school, I was very much into political and anti-war stuff and all that. . . . I had the long hair . . . and always in the principal's office—you know, "You've got to cut your hair. You've got to stop wearing armbands," and all that kind of stuff, you know. I said, "No. I'm not going to do that. . . . You can't make me." When I got to college [at Indiana State University], [my wife] Mary and I got involved with a Christian group that was conservative. And there wasn't a lot of emphasis on social justice. . . . I thought, well, maybe that's not part of this, but it was a great community of people that was really caring and loving and good folks to be around. So that's where I developed a sense of community. And the social justice part was dormant until I went into seminary, really. Then it all just blossomed.[27]

As a student at Northern Baptist Theological Seminary, Steve was increasingly exposed to a range of faith traditions and ideas; he was also influenced by Mennonite professors at his seminary and took classes at Bethany Theological Seminary. All of this, he explained, had a significant influence on him. When I asked him how it impacted him, he explained, "The kind of peace and justice people were talking about and how they understood the gospel in terms of peace and justice. And . . . what the realm of God is about, what that means, and Anabaptist thought. It just . . . made sense to me."[28] Steve's anti-war work and commitment to social justice, therefore, were nurtured in what he and others describe as a dynamic intellectual, spiritual, and political space where faith-based activists created ecumenical communities as students attending and connected to the many theological seminaries in Chicago and the surrounding area.

Nancy Finke, for example, described how the anti-war activism she and her husband, David Finke, were involved in was grounded in faith-based understandings of social justice that adhered to the belief that "everyone is a child of God." Before enrolling at Chicago Theological Seminary, David already had a long history of attending Quaker programs that included anti-war and antinuclear arms protests. Once they moved to Chicago after graduating from Oberlin College, Nancy and David were part of an interdenominational/ecumenical community of faith-based activists protesting the war and supporting the civil rights movement. "David and I were married in 1964. And that summer was the Gulf of Tonkin. . . . For both of us, [our activism] grows out of the New Testament." Nancy continued to describe how their work with the anti-war movement was also her introduction to the idea of sanctuary:

> My first experience with [sanctuary] was during the Vietnam War when we were housing AWOLS [absent without leave]. They were all white Americans . . . and this was part of our work with AFSC [American Friends Service Committee] in Chicago. There were so many men who either—well, there were lots and lots who just refused induction. . . . David was in charge of monitoring the federal courts. It was a huge number. More than half of the people coming through the federal courts in Chicago were draft refusals during those few years. So we were meeting with draft refusers. But at the same time, these guys were turning up who had just left after they had been inducted or they'd been in the army. . . . And for the AWOL people, there was a network set up called the Midwest Committee for Military Counseling. They had lawyers and there was one chaplain at the Great Lakes Naval Base who was willing to work with

these guys to help them get discharged. . . . And there was also a couple who were in charge of the AWOLs, so I knew whenever [they] called us, it meant they had someone who needed a place. . . . David and I put them up for a while and found places with Quakers for others. And there were people willing to drive folks to Canada. We didn't ever drive anyone to Canada, but I know at least one other Quaker who did. So that was a sanctuary project.[29]

When I ask Nancy whether at the time they regarded what they did as sanctuary work, she explained,

> No, I don't think so. But now looking back, we've talked and thought about it a lot. . . . I see it connected [to sanctuary work today] in that we were protecting people from evil law enforcement and protecting people from the military. The military would be after them, and there was one guy who actually took sanctuary in a Quaker meeting house, and the people in the meeting resisted. When the MPs came for him . . . I remember the Quakers—we stood around the military car and I think he went with them finally. But people stood and resisted and . . . some people were telling the police, "Guys, don't start driving because those people won't move!" [*Nancy chuckles, remembering this moment.*] Well, all of them were a little crazy, but yeah. I'm not sure we used the word "sanctuary," but we definitely viewed it that way. We were giving them safe haven.[30]

Nancy recalls that these efforts were interfaith, although as she and others have noted, much of the activist work they did also involved people who were not part of faith communities. But it was this notion of "the realm of God" that grounded the anti-war efforts of people like Nancy, Steve, David, John, and Mary and that many of them referred to specifically. David described the realm of God as the belief that "the eternal life happens here and now. We recognize God's realm or kingdom that is already breaking out in the world. We engage in that and we get into that flow and become part of that. And I think that as people of faith, that's what we are called to do. To recognize that realm of God that is all around us and help other people to see it and to be in step with it."[31]

It is this belief that guided faith-based activists to protest the war, engage in antinuclear weapons activism, and support the civil rights movement, and to do so while reaching out across faith traditions. Nancy recalled, for example, walking with nuns, laypeople, and civil rights activists and leaders in Chicago when Reverend Dr. Martin Luther King led open housing marches in the city in the summer of 1966:

> What I remember about the nuns is [how angry people were with them for marching]. . . . We were marching through neighborhoods where Black people were refused housing. You know, the real estate was redlined and real estate agencies refused [to offer Black people housing]. And we were walking through the neighborhoods and the people on the streets were just livid. They were just furious. They threw rocks and firecrackers and bottles. And Dr. King got hit with a brick. And it was the nuns who got the most horrible abuse from people along the street. And I thought it was because people must have felt betrayed [seeing the nuns marching]. "How can this Catholic nun—" I mean, that's another question about how this squares with people's faith. . . . But it was scary. But you know, it was like, we just have no choice. We *have* to be there. We have no *choice*. I remember having an argument with one of the guys in the Quaker meeting in Chicago who had grown up in a working-class neighborhood. And he just thought we were being really intrusive, pushing these people around, you know, pushing these white people around. And that we had no business going into their neighborhoods. Which astounded me at the time.[32]

While this notion of the realm of God compelled some to engage in this kind of faith-based activism, there were powerful dissenting voices and perspectives as well. This was evident during the tumultuous years of the 1960s and 1970s, and persisted in the 1980s as faith-based activists described their involvement in Central American solidarity work and the ways these movements, as well as the powerful influence of feminist and liberation theology, served as a basis for their sanctuary work three decades later.

Accompaniment as Unflinching Commitment

As we saw earlier, the Central American sanctuary movement of the 1980s has played a significant role in informing the New Sanctuary Movement. This is not at all surprising, given that many faith-based activists today were profoundly transformed by their solidarity work with Central America in the 1980s. Moreover, while the notion of accompaniment is certainly bound up with the teachings and practices of liberation theology, some—particularly younger activists—come to this understanding of accompaniment through their work with secular organizations in both Latin America and the United States. Groups like NISGUA (Network in Solidarity with the People of Guatemala) have worked for decades to "build and strengthen ties between the people of the United States and Guatemala in the global struggle for justice, human dignity, and respect for the Earth. NISGUA accomplishes this through an integrated strategy of international human rights accompaniment, digital organizing, strategic campaigns, political education, and horizontal exchange."[33] As an organization that began in 1981 to "coordinate US activism to fight state support for Guatemala's brutal military regime" and that shifted its focus to accompaniment of Mayan refugees, genocide survivors, land defenders, and water protectors, NISGUA reflects the trajectories of many faith-based activists whose efforts were first nurtured in Central and Latin American solidarity movements, that have ranged from secular to faith-based organizing and that have also shifted to meet the changing needs of vulnerable immigrant communities.[34]

After graduating from Oberlin College in 2012, for example, Sarah Johnson spent a year with NISGUA as a human rights observer, something that she describes she came to through her involvement with Ecumenical Christians of Oberlin, a student group connected with Peace Community Church. Through this organization, Sarah not only developed a deeper sense of the relationship between faith and social justice, but also learned more about Central America and liberation theology specifically. Sarah's experiences also draw our attention to the enduring, albeit often overlooked, ways these struggles have always been intersectional, with an understanding of the ways sexuality and LGBTQ organizing have often been bound up with anti-imperialist liberation struggles in Central America. Sarah explains that she was drawn to an approach to Christianity that insisted that "we need to take a stance for justice and love and care about others." This involved supporting organizations that provided services to those in need in the United States, as well as progressive social policies. These commitments also led Sarah to the work of the Santa Elena Project of Accompaniment (SEPA), an Oberlin City-based project that works with rural communities in Guatemala and also raises money and provides other kinds of support.

> SEPA isn't a religious organization, but just going through the list of the people on the board, I'm pretty sure most of the people who have been involved for a long time are deeply involved in their religious communities. I think part of what was so compelling about Guatemala for me was that it felt like this is the place where the privilege I have is partially the result of harm done in this community by groups that I'm a part of, and it can be put to meaningful use. The whole model of human rights accompaniment is that human rights violators are less likely to commit crimes when they know that the world is watching. And so the visibility of a person's privilege is a powerful tool.[35]

For Sarah, this decision for people from such different social locations, places, and positions of privilege to help others was incredibly inspiring. She admired not only people she met through SEPA and NISGUA, but also "folks from different parts of the world, faith leaders who acted in solidarity [with the people in Guatemala] and who sometimes lost their lives. I drew a lot of comfort and inspiration from knowing there are other folks who have done similar work—well, not even necessarily similar work but who have been animated by a similar spirit" in their accompaniment work. She shared the story of one priest who worked with Indigenous groups near Lago Atitlán in the 1980s and who was assassinated: "And the part of the story that I think was the most meaningful to me was that the community he worked with asked his family if they would give permission for the community to bury his heart under the cathedral in town. And they said yes. The rest of his remains were transported back to the US. . . . That really inspired me, that kind of unflinching commitment. There is an element of being an outsider from the community who nonetheless sacrificed tremendously and were accepted and integrated into those communities. There is something beautiful in the mutuality of it."

Sarah's collaboration with SEPA was made possible because of the decades-long efforts of people like John Gates, who co-founded the organization in 1997 as part of international efforts to accompany returning communities in Guatemala. According to its 2020–2021 annual report, SEPA "has remained steadfast in its mission to support education in the returned refugee communities Santa Elena 20 de Octubre and Copal AA La Esperanza in Northern Guatemala, in addition to providing support to accompaniers to protect human rights defenders through NISGUA."[36] As John Gates reflected on his work supporting sanctuary struggles during the Trump years, he identified a clear connection to the work of SEPA and the Overground Railroad in the 1980s.[37] In 1985, he explained, First Church in Oberlin went through a discernment process similar to the one in 2018 that led to the church's decision to declare itself a sanctuary church:

> We had a fairly long discernment process, and we brought refugees from El Salvador to First Church to speak about why they left and why they came to the United States and the problems they had in being accepted here and what they were having to go through with Immigration and Naturalization. And we listened to people. . . . We went to Cleveland to talk with immigration officials about what they were doing. . . . There was one person named Cindy . . . who was a former nun . . . and her mother worked at [the Oberlin College library]. And one of Cindy's good friends was one of the four nuns murdered in El Salvador in 1980. . . . She [helped] organize the Interreligious Task Force in Central America and came [to Oberlin] and talked with us about what she was doing and how she was doing it. . . . It was probably around six weeks or so that [our congregation] studied this, and then we brought it to the congregation and said, "Let's discuss this and take a vote on whether or not we should become a sanctuary church." It was really contentious. And actually we never did take a vote because [Pastor] John Elder did not want to have a vote of 50 to 49. That would have split the church. So it was tabled. And then John discovered this organization in Evanston, Illinois—the Overground Railroad that was created by Mennonites.[38]

According to John Gates, First Church, Peace Community Church, and Sacred Heart Church in Oberlin all worked together to sponsor the "landed immigrant" families and individuals whose cases were being processed and who were allowed to stay in sponsoring communities during this process. Approximately five families as well as a number of single men came to live in Oberlin at that time, and the ecumenical group helped find housing, covered the cost of rent, and located temporary jobs as they waited for their immigration papers for Canada to be processed. While migrants often stayed from six to eight months, their impact significantly exceeded their stay. Indeed, as John shared, one of his daughters was so transformed by this experience that she became an accompanier after she graduated from college and was one of the motivators for Oberlin residents to establish SEPA in 1997.

Like John, Reverend David T. Hill (pastor of First Church in Oberlin) and Reverend Steve Hammond (co-pastor at Peace Community Church in Oberlin) also trace much of their contemporary faith-based activism back to their solidarity work with Central America. They identified the important role these efforts played in deepening their understanding of US foreign policy in Latin America and how this transformed their perception of politics and social movements. David, for example, described how he first learned about US foreign policy in Central America in his peace and justice classes in college. He later incorporated this information into materials that he used when he taught Sunday school in Florida and in his work when he moved to Cleveland Heights in 1985. Although he was beginning to learn about the Overground Railroad during that time, he didn't have direct involvement in the movement, but it made an impression on him when, years later, he moved to Oberlin to be the pastor at First Church. For Steve Hammond, learning and being involved with the Overground Railroad affirmed what he refers to as "Jesus's critique of empire." Reverend Mary Hammond, co-pastor of Peace Community Church in Oberlin, was also influenced by the events in Central America in the 1980s, but she also had a remarkably distinctive path that included the ways feminist theologians and specifically feminist liberation theology transformed her spiritually and politically. As a seminary student in the 1980s, she learned about liberation theology when it was first translated into English and attended an International Ministries conference in Wisconsin on liberation theology that dramatically changed how she continued her seminary education. After the three-day seminar on liberation theology in 1985, she explained, "I couldn't *not* start writing papers in a more grounded way. I committed myself to doing all my biblical studies in a grounded way."[39]

For Mary, writing and thinking about her seminary studies in a grounded way involved reading scholarship by feminist theologians like

Mary Daly, which, in turn, sharpened her analytic focus when learning more about liberation theology. "Women are present in a silent way,
even if they aren't foregrounded," she explained to me. As she began
to imagine and reimagine women's lives and her own life in different
ways, she also did so with attention to Central America. Thus, while
Mary identified the groundbreaking book *Unexpected News: Reading the
Bible through Third World Eyes* as having a significant impact on her, it
was the Nicaraguan priest and poet Ernesto Cardenal and his reflections
with the poor, peasants, and artists in the community of Solentiname in
Nicaragua that moved her deeply.[40] Indeed, *The Gospel in Solentiname*
was a pivotal and globally significant publication in liberation theology
that centered the experiences of poor, marginalized, and persecuted as
a direct challenge to the repressive regime of Anastasio Somoza. Books,
conferences, workshops, international solidarity brigades, and work in
the United States nurtured these international ties and collaborations,
such as Mary's work with a woman working in El Salvador during the
civil war in the 1980s. "I was writing letters to a missionary in El Salvador. I had written a study about Jesus and women here [in the United
States, titled *Jesus, Women and Me*]. We met at a conference for just a
week, and we clicked so much that she took that study, recontextualized
it for women during the civil war in El Salvador, and then led that study
all over the place, even in Costa Rica, for the next two or three years."
The inspiration from feminist liberation theologians and the transnational collaborations their writings and experiences engendered were
transformative for Mary. She explained, "It's powerful to hear scripture
from the underside—not from empire or white privilege. Many people
don't see that we live in the belly of empire and to understand Jesus's
death as a result of not going with empire and not some transactional
analysis or individualistic analysis that makes you OK and everyone else
not OK."[41] This feminist and Third World liberation theology lens also
led Mary to become deeply involved in supporting women from developing countries in selling their art and crafts in the United States: "Jubilee Crafts was part of a progressive Christian magazine called the *Other
Side*. It was really fair trade stuff before people talked in the language
of fair trade. But it was selling crafts from what were then called 'Third
World' countries. . . . And they did education; they gave you resources
to do educational programs as you sold them and to know the stories of

every craft and craft maker. . . . I eventually wound up on the board of Jubilee Crafts . . . and that learning really gave me a chance for myself, as opposed to just osmosis from Steve's seminary education, to get a bigger worldview."[42]

Women's labor—as Third World women crafters, as the wives of pastors during and after seminary school, as theorists in feminist and liberation theology, and as pastors and faith leaders themselves—is the irrefutable center for this work. As Mary and other feminist theologians have observed of women in the Bible, women's faith-based activism was always present in a silent way and indelibly shaped the lives of other faith-based activists. The people I worked with, for example, often referred to the nuns and other women leaders who played pivotal, if sometimes hidden, roles in the civil rights and sanctuary movements, a crucial point scholars documented amply. And women also played an important role as mothers and grandmothers whose largely unpaid labor volunteering with the poor, immigrants, single mothers, and those in need served as the foundation for faith-based activism. Nancy Finke, for example, described how growing up in her mother and grandmother's faith tradition of the Disciples of Christ Christian Church in Missouri laid the foundation for her pacifism, her decision to become a Quaker, and her religious and political values. Her grandmother was a pacifist and her mother was deeply interested in international solidarity work. They were the first to instill in her the values and beliefs that led to her faith-based activism as a Quaker. When describing the basis of her activism, she explains,

> I would say it was the New Testament. I'm not sure that's how I thought of it in the beginning. It has to do with equality and believing there is value in everyone and the idea that it's not right to kill other people. My family—my grandmother and my mother—had a lot to do with that. My grandmother put it in religious terms. She would say, "You know, Jesus doesn't want us to kill." She was against the death penalty. And [she believed] everyone should be welcome. . . . My mom was just voracious about international relationships. She was constantly seeking out people from other countries [who lived in Missouri]. . . . She and my aunt and my grandmother, all of them had been schoolteachers. My mom set up sponsorship for a woman, a teacher from Cuba, to come and spend a year

teaching at Webster Groves High School. And that family eventually left Cuba and came back to Missouri through an AAUW scholarship. She met people from China, Taiwan, Finland, and Germany. . . . I remember all these people in our house, from Colombia—just coming through. . . . She was also active in the National Council of Christians and Jews in St. Louis. She had her faith . . . and that has had a big impact on me.[43]

Scholars of American religion have long noted the role gender plays in religious practices and faith formation. These roles are not always visible, nor are they uniform. For some, like Mary, feminist awakenings informed their religious and political activism that was quite different from the conservative religious upbringing of their families. For others, like Nancy, women like her grandmother and mother laid the foundation for her pacifism and faith-based activism in later years.

While these narratives demonstrate the ways that historical moments can serve as shared moments of faith-based activism, their stories also highlight the importance of place in cultivating their identities and practices as people of faith committed to the work of sanctuary. Thus, while Nancy hails from a progressive Protestant faith community that emphasized actively welcoming strangers and helping others, others like John Gates and Mary and Steve Hammond shared how they grew up in more conservative religious faith communities. Still others, such as Sarah Johnson and David Hill, were raised in moderate and tolerant religious congregations where activism and social justice were supported, even while there were limitations with regard to cultural and social issues. What unites them all, however, is the way that living, working, and building community in Oberlin transformed them. These insights highlight the importance of place in locating, grounding, and nurturing the specific sanctuary practices of sanctuary people.

The Power of Place and Religious Practices

The Jesuit Retreat Center is a quiet, bucolic space in the bustling city of Parma just south of Cleveland. In addition to its more than fifty acres of meadow, woodlands, and walking trails, the retreat center is also home to four beautiful chapels, including the small Martyr's Chapel dedicated to nuns, priests, and laypeople who were murdered during the civil war in El Salvador. Inside the sparsely decorated chapel are two comfortable chairs and a simple wooden altar. Natural light filters in from the south-facing window that looks out onto a garden courtyard. Along the walls are framed lithographs, drawings, and watercolor portraits that together tell a story about martyred men and women serving God through their dedication to the poor. The watercolor painting features the faces of the six Jesuit priests, the caretaker, and her daughter who were brutally assassinated in their residence at the Universidad Centroamericana on November 16, 1989. Words like "truth" and "history" appear around some of the faces, as well as carefully handwritten reflections about service, community, and social justice. Along another wall are two draw-ings of four women—Ita Ford, Maura Clarke, Dorothy Kazel, and Jean Donovan. One of the drawings features the faceless profile of each of the women done in soft dark charcoal with the title "Martyrs for Justice" appearing below. The other pencil drawing features their smiling faces, a drawing quite familiar to those who mourned their vicious murder on December 2, 1980, nine months after the assassination of Archbishop Óscar Romero on March 24, 1980. On a small wooden table, there is a typed narrative protected in plastic that provides a brief description about these women's lives in El Salvador as well as excerpts from letters and journal entries they wrote during their time working with the poor and war-displaced. Below the heading "Martyrs for Justice" is the fol-lowing text:

> These four North American churchwomen, Ita, Dorothy, Maura and Jean responded to God's call to be one with the poor of El Salvador. Aware that the depth of their compassion and commitment could cost them their lives, they freely chose not only to live with them and for the people of El Salvador but also to die with them.
>
> On December 2, 1980, they were brutally tortured and murdered by members of El Salvador's National Guard. Through the memory and wit-ness of the life and death of Ita, Dorothy, Maura and Jean, may we too respond to God's continuing call to solidarity with the poor.[44]

Sister Dorothy Kazel, OSU, was one of many nuns, priests, and laypeople from the Cleveland Diocese who had served in El Salvador beginning in the mid-1960s and had been part of the Cleveland Diocesan Latin

BECOMING SANCTUARY PEOPLE | 141

American Mission Team in El Salvador since 1974. Jean Donovan joined the Cleveland mission in 1979 and worked with Dorothy, as well as Sister Ita, MM, and Sister Maura, MM, who had arrived in El Salvador earlier that year after years of working in Chile and Nicaragua, respectively.[45]

Like thousands of others who were inspired by liberation theology's call to serve and embrace a life dedicated to a preferential option for the poor, Dorothy, Jean, Ita, and Maura remained in El Salvador, even when it became clear that their work was increasingly dangerous and as priests, nuns, laypeople, and thousands of Salvadorans were detained, tortured, and killed during the brutal civil war. Dorothy explained her decision to remain in a letter to fellow Ursuline Sister Martha Owen:

> We talked quite a bit today about what happens *if* something begins. And most of us feel like we would want to stay here . . . if there is a way we can help, like run a refugee center or something. We wouldn't want to just run out on the people. . . . I thought I should say this to you because I don't want to say it to anyone else because I don't think they would understand. Anyway, my beloved friend, just know how I feel and "treasure it in your heart." If a day comes when others will have to understand, please explain it for me.[46]

This fierce commitment to remain in El Salvador was echoed by Maura Clarke, who wrote,

> I am beginning to see death in a new way. We have been meditating a lot on death and the accepting of it, as in the Good Shepherd reading. There are so many deaths everywhere that it is incredible. It is an atmosphere of death. The work is really what Archbishop Romero calls "acompaña-miento," accompanying the people, as well as searching for ways to help. This seems what the Lord is asking of me, I think, at this moment. We are on the road continually, bringing women and children to refugee centers. Keep us in your heart and prayers, especially the poor forsaken people.

Ita Ford also wrote about her commitment to accompaniment, explaining, "I have no solutions to this situation, but I will walk with you, search with you, be with you." Jean Donovan reflected on how this process had forever transformed her, leaving her with little choice but to remain in El Salvador: "I love life and I love living. . . . Several times I decided to leave. I almost could, except for the children—the poor, bruised victims of this adult lunacy. Who would care for them? Whose heart could be so staunch as to favor the reasonable thing in a sea of their tears and loneliness? Not mine, dear friend, not mine."

In an article commemorating the fortieth anniversary of Dorothy, Ita, Jean, and Maura's death, Margaret Swedish explicitly connects the violence, trauma, and unrest of the 1980s in El Salvador with the injustice, violence, and unrest in the United States in 2020:

> In any historical moment, we are called to enter the reality in which we live and together to read the signs of the times. The violence and injustice experienced by the people of El Salvador was the foundation from which the four US churchwomen discerned what it would mean to accompany the poor and to follow Jesus in their time.
>
> So what of our time? How do we understand this moment in the human journey as we come to the end of this traumatic year? The list of the year's sufferings is long: the pandemic, the collapsing economy and increase in poverty and hunger, the police killings of Black men and women that sparked angry protests around the nation, the resurgence of white nationalism, the raging wildfires in the West and a record Atlantic hurricane season fueled by our warming planet.
>
> We have seen the collapse of good governance and furious political polarization that threatens our democracy. Fear of change, fear of things getting out of control, extreme individualism—these are all signs of a society in crisis, fragmenting as our problems appear increasingly insurmountable.
>
> We must ask ourselves: Where will we take our stand in the midst of such uncertainty?[47]

Swedish continues by reflecting on the importance of discernment—a process that should be done in community rather than in isolation— and that she describes as a "lost skill in a culture where we never seem able to take the time to just stop and think about what we are doing and why. But it requires some radical shifts in our vantage points, not least of which is stepping into the reality of the suffering ones of our world and seeing the world through their eyes." A crucial feature of this discernment process is understanding history and hearing stories like these so we understand the "historical thread that runs through our history to this day." These sentiments echo those of the sanctuary people whose work is grounded in their understanding of the relationship between faith and social justice activism, and also the importance of the history of particular places and how those histories and the "historical thread" connects their actions in the present with those of the past.[48]

The Cleveland Diocese's decades of work in El Salvador is an example of how history, place, and faith ground contemporary faith-based activism. Every person involved in sanctuary work in Lorain and connected to Sacred Heart Chapel, for instance, made reference to this history, even if they had varying degrees of understanding of the details of the relationship to El Salvador. Sister Cathy from Sacred Heart Chapel, for example, described the many ways the parish was unique and distinct as a specifically Hispanic/Latina/o parish that emerged as a result of community organizing in the 1960s and whose mission has always been guided by a commitment to working in Latin America. "This is a unique parish," she explained. "And I think the parishes that have the missionaries from El Salvador from the diocese are the parishes that are the most socially conscious and who have a heart for the immigrant." While Sister Cathy's religious community, Sisters of the Humility of Mary, sent community members to Chile, she reflected on the impact of the Cleveland Diocese's enduring relationship with El Salvador:

> The Cleveland Diocese responded by opening up a mission in El Salvador and offering priests and sisters and laity of the diocese to parishes. This enabled other communities to send sisters there instead of opening their own missions. . . . The Sisters of St. Joseph were a part of it. . . . Akron Dominican sisters were a part of it. And the Ursulines . . . made a commitment to always send sisters. . . . There were about ten years where the missionaries would watch the temperature increase in El Salvador before the war. Then there was the war and then there was the postwar. We never left. Other dioceses opened up missions, then when there was a revolution, they took their missionaries back. Cleveland never did. And even when Dorothy and Jean were killed, the team met with the bishop and said, "They can't leave." And the bishop let them stay.[49]

This history not only inspired and instructed, it also shaped the priorities and set the expectations of people responding to the rising anti-immigrant sentiment and policies that had a devastating impact on the communities in Lorain. José Mendiola, for example, explained his involvement in programs like Welcoming the Stranger and Compañeros (the Parish Companion Program) that were designed to "accompany parishioners who are in the final stage of immigration removal proceedings, or who are at risk of removal."[50] He also participated in a delegation sponsored by the Cleveland Diocese to the US-Mexico border in 2019, worked with Sister Rita Mary Harwood from the diocesan office to collect items for the families affected by the Corso's raid in June 2018, worked with immigrant families at Sacred Heart Chapel, and participated in the parish's prison visitation program. All of this work, according to José, is grounded in his understanding that Catholics should welcome immigrants, welcome the stranger, and was a guiding feature of his faith-based activism. It is probably for this reason that he expressed disappointment when the Cleveland Diocese stated its decision not to be involved in offering physical sanctuary to immigrants seeking to avoid deportation. José described attending meetings throughout the diocese beginning in 2017 where this question was repeatedly raised, debated, and ultimately rejected by the Catholic Church hierarchy in Cleveland. In one meeting with Bishop Pérez, it became very clear that the diocese's position would be to continue to support its important work with valuable programs like Welcome the Stranger, develop new ones like Compañeros, and continue to train and offer legal resources to those who needed them. But sanctuary was not an option. José explained, "The Diocese of Cleveland said, no, we will not do sanctuary. . . . I was very disappointed. There were a lot of other people that were disappointed." And although he praised the diocese for its other interventions and support, he also expressed admiration for Protestant churches that, despite the legal concerns that were raised about offering physical sanctuary, chose to do so anyway:

> I really have to hand it to the other denominations. They didn't care [about repercussions]. They went ahead and did what they thought was right. Not that we did the wrong thing. We just went about it in a different way. I truly believe that what we're doing at the diocese level with the Welcome the Stranger Committee has had a real impact on our community. They go to different churches and talk to people who are not informed about immigration. I'm talking about Anglo people who don't

know anything about immigration. I talk to them and tell them, "These are the facts. Now you decide what you want to do and believe."[51]

José was, of course, not the only one disappointed with the diocese's response. Celestino Rivera, for example, described tense meetings where he was told not to pursue this issue. This was particularly painful since Celestino knew that there were priests who believed that the Church was being called to offer sanctuary as a way to challenge an unjust legal system and state power as well as to be a fearless witness. He explained,

> We were having a meeting about sanctuary about the same time [people in Oberlin] were having meetings. And they were talking about the reality of churches being sanctuary and whether that's a good move. . . . If I had to judge the mood, I would say that most of them felt like it's not the right thing to do because at some point they have to leave sanctuary. Where do they go from there? And that's the kind of pragmatic conversations we were having.
>
> When Bishop Pérez came, he cut the conversation off almost immediately and said, "We're not doing it. Period." . . . Well, [one Franciscan priest] said to the bishop, "Bishop, I have to differ with you. How can we teach the Word on Sunday and then not live it Monday through Saturday? . . . Respectfully, I want to tell you that in my parish, they understand what you do unto others—they understand. They understand welcoming the stranger. They want to do something to live that. And if somebody comes to our church and asks for our help, I believe they're going to offer that help." And the bishop says, "I'm telling you, we're not doing it." And so I say, "I'm sorry for this, Bishop, but you know what? If you've ever dealt with these people, and I am sure you have, they are so humble. They are so full of faith. If their church doesn't speak up for them, then what chance do they have?" That's all I said to him. Now he turned his anger to me and said, "You should know better, because it's the law." And I said, "Bishop, *you* know and *I* know and *everybody* knows that sometimes they make bad laws. And it's people of faith, it's people of goodwill who make those sacrifices to get those laws changed. There was a time when . . . people had to ride in the back of the bus. There was a time when [African Americans] couldn't drink out of the same fountains [as whites]. . . . But good people came forward and sacrificed and it changed."[52]

Celestino's frustration during this meeting was exacerbated by what he knew about the history of the diocese and a visit to El Salvador he had taken years before with one of the priests whom he deeply admired. He recognized the courage of people who, in the past, challenged the status quo in order to remain faithful to their beliefs, even at great cost to themselves. This is what animated people like Celestino, José, Anabel, Sister Cathy, and Father Bill. And it is an important point of reference for the work they continue to do, even when there might be disagreement about the strategies, tactics, and decisions they make. But what guides them is this history of resistance, offering refuge, and bravely challenging state and even clerical power when necessary. As Anabel observed when she reflected on her own experiences,

> I never thought that the Lorain chief of police would be on my side, that he would be taking the day off to go with me to my check-ins. For me, that was awesome. Undocumented immigrants are afraid of police officers. Having now the chief of police coming with me and standing by my side saying, "She's not a criminal." That was just God's grace.[53]

Anabel's comfort in having Celestino, the chief of police, on her side also points to another example of the importance of place. Lorain, for example, never declared itself a sanctuary city. This was a deliberate decision that reflected a keen understanding of the local political culture of Lorain, a city with a long and proud history as the International City, but one that, like other formerly progressive spaces in Ohio, became increasingly conservative politically in ways that shaped conversations and approaches around immigration. As we saw earlier, Celestino Rivera navigated these dynamics carefully by putting in place clear policies governing when the Lorain police department would or would not collaborate with federal immigration officials, policies that ultimately protected undocumented residents. In doing so, he demonstrated admirable courage, but was also acutely aware of the ways local political, economic, and cultural forces shape what is possible and what is not.

Oberlin, however, has a completely different history. And this history not only enabled it to be public in its sanctuary city declaration in 2018, but also facilitated religious congregations and local activists to take bold actions following the 2016 presidential election. In fact, many of the faith-based activists I interviewed and talked with over the years explained that it was living in Oberlin and being inspired by the city and college's history that, in many ways, facilitated, supported, and even compelled them to take public and decisive action. As historians Gary Kornblith and Carol Lasser have meticulously documented in their book *Elusive Utopia: The Struggle for Racial Equality in Oberlin, Ohio*, both the city and college were founded as "an experiment dedicated to radical racial egalitarianism" where the residents believed "that they followed the teachings of Christianity in their embrace of racial equality and that, by ridding the world of the sins of slavery and color prejudice, they would bring about the redemption of humankind." While Kornblith and Lasser also note that this utopian vision was both short-lived and elusive, Oberlin's history of standing "at the vanguard of the abolition and black freedom movements" is frequently invoked as activists justify and persuade others of the need to support contemporary social justice movements.[54] Indeed, it is one of the reasons many offer for choosing to live in Oberlin and an explanation of how either they first came to faith-based activism or how it was further cultivated.

As Steve Hammond shared his experiences in seminary and his search for a church that he could be a part of once he was done with his studies, he described the challenge of finding a place that shared his "vision of the church":

> I realized when I left seminary that I was not going to be able to go to your typical Baptist church. . . . My vision of the church was more social justice-oriented, more community building, trying to give people—the big phrase that came to me in seminary that I should have heard long *before* seminary was "the Kingdom of the Realm of God." And I was trying to piece that together, because that's what Jesus talks about so much—the realm of God, this world being the realm of God. So I talked about that [in my interviews with executive ministers in seminary helping graduating students find a job]. And one not only shooed me out of his office, but he wrote a letter to me afterwards, despairing about the state of the church that they were turning out graduates like me [*laughs*]. That the church was going to have absolutely no future. . . . But one of those meetings was with a guy named John Sundquist, who was the executive min-

ister in Ohio. And our fifteen minutes turned into an hour and a half, and we had a great conversation. He understood, and we understood each other. And then he said, "I'd love to have you in Ohio, but there's no place for you in Ohio." So I got up to leave and was on my way out the door when he said, "Wait a minute, wait a minute." And he got his briefcase and said, "Have you ever heard of a place called Oberlin? . . . There's a church there. . . . I think you ought to give it a try."[55]

Steve and his wife did, indeed, give Oberlin a try, even though the job had an uncertain future. There had been talks about closing the church, but they decided to hire Steve for two years to see whether the church would grow, which it did, providing a spiritual home and community that shared Steve and Mary's vision of social justice. Later in my interview with Steve, he returned to this prescient conversation with John Sundquist that led him to take a job with an uncertain future in Oberlin. "That professor said, 'Oberlin's where you want to be.' He knew the history of Oberlin. He knew me and he knew that this is where I should go. He said, 'Go there. Whatever it takes to go there, because that's the place for you.' That heritage sure inspired me. . . . You walk through Tappan Square and you think about all the people who have walked through there. It's pretty crazy to think about."[56]

Oberlin's heritage includes a powerful abolitionist movement, challenging the Fugitive Slave Act of 1850, welcoming Japanese American students in the wake of the passage of Executive Order 9066 in 1942, and welcoming students and faculty following the Kent State tragedy in May 1970.[57] Steve and others invoked this history when explaining why they supported sanctuary and grounded this commitment in their religious beliefs as well:

I think Jesus would offer people sanctuary. If Jesus is head of the church, shouldn't the church be a place of safety? Not just the building itself, but our church communities. Shouldn't they be sanctuary? And again, if you live in the empire, you're going to have to choose now and then. The empire may not like it if you're harboring people. But you know, that is what this town's about. From the slavery abolitionist days, the government didn't like what they were doing [in Oberlin]. But they did it anyway. And they understood it as what it meant to be Christians . . . That's the heritage of the church in this town. And we need to keep it going.[58]

Part of how they kept this work going is through the peace vigil that a small, committed group of protestors participate in every Saturday morning on the corner of Main and College Street, which began following the September 11 attacks in 2001. They have also kept this work going by participating in activism that does not emerge only from faith-based organizing, but that benefits from ecumenical collaborations, like Sane Freeze in the 1980s and, more recently, Black Lives Matter organizing.

John Gates also described how living in Oberlin and its history played a pivotal role in nurturing his social justice activism and inspiring him to be involved in faith-based work. He described how when he and Linda first arrived in Oberlin in the early 1970s, they didn't have a church community, but that soon changed when he learned about First Church:

> Oberlin's history played a role in it too. . . . The first college to admit women and people of color. I really think it played an important role for me, you know, this is the kind of society I wanted to be a part of. So I tried to emulate the people that were here and that I thought were speaking out for justice. . . . Oberlin played a very important role in my wanting to become more involved in political action that would bring justice to the United States. . . . What First Church was trying to do and what the history of Oberlin [shows us] is to do what is right. That's what we all should be working for. For a common understanding of brotherhood, sisterhood and [against] the unequal distribution of wealth.[59]

Being inspired by a history of social justice led John and Linda to decades of faith-based activism, including housing and working with Central American migrants fleeing US-fueled wars in the 1980s, solidarity with returning communities in Guatemala beginning in the 1990s, and the New Sanctuary Movement beginning in the mid-2000s. These efforts, John explains, are part of the way he both honors the history of Oberlin and contributes to a vision of community he seeks to help create. "A lot of it has to do with the community that I want to live in. I think the community in Oberlin is really rich in that regard. . . . I owe it to the community to do better and to give back. To strengthen areas of compassion and justice and love wherever I can."

Like John, David Hill also shared how Oberlin's history shapes the work he and others do around sanctuary and how the kind of activism that seemed exceptional and life-changing when he was younger is a regular part of people's lives in Oberlin. When he worked as a pastor in Jefferson, Ohio, the county seat of Ashtabula County, he described attending vigils to protest the US invasion of Iraq and how it would be

> me, the Lutheran pastor, and two United Methodists. And that was the whole crowd. . . . I discovered [something] through that. I started going to protests because I wanted to change things and discovered pretty quickly that it didn't matter how many thousands of people showed up in Washington, it wasn't going to change policy. But I kept going because it changed me. It had an effect on me. . . . It gave me a chance to hang out with other people and listen to how they expressed their concerns, how they connected it with their faith life. And that was instructive to me so I could better lift that out of people. And then I came to Oberlin where we have protests and vigils all the time.[60]

These protests and vigils, of course, included anti-war demonstrations and the regular Saturday noon protest for peace on Main Street, and they also included immigration issues. On July 23, 2008, ICE agents raided the restaurant Casa Fiesta in Oberlin and detained five employees. This was one of eight workplace ICE raids that summer that included seven other Casa Fiesta restaurants in Northeast Ohio and resulted in a total of fifty-eight immigrants being arrested and some ultimately deported.[61] Activists and community members in Oberlin mobilized protests and offered support. For some, including David Hill, this was their first experience feeling the outrage of losing valued community members and confronting the consequences of immigration enforcement and the deportation regime that ripped apart families and communities. David described the challenge of wanting to be a pastor who could speak to people as they struggled to make sense of the impact immigration detention had on their community, particularly on the family members of detained migrants who resided in Oberlin and were devastated by the raid. As a faith leader, he also had conversations with the Oberlin police chief and attended community meetings and sessions of Oberlin City Council where it was clear that there was a divide between what the police chief believed was his job to enforce laws and broader community outrage at immigration enforcement policies that were ripping families and the community apart. David observed, "My sense was that [the Oberlin police chief] had a good sense of what Oberlin was all about and was trying to walk this very challenging line between Oberlin's values and what the law calls him to do and the values of his colleagues in the broader Lorain County that were different than Oberlin's."[62]

David's observation about the ways Oberlin's progressive values come into conflict with more conservative ones—and in this case, anti-immigrant sentiment—was on display in Oberlin City Council meetings where largely non-Oberlin residents angrily decried attempts to pass a sanctuary city ordinance. David recalls, "It was really, really ugly. A lot of shouting and . . . repetitive [bashing immigrants]. I remember at one point the chair of City Council—I think it was Ronnie Rimbert at the time, saying, 'No. We've heard that argument. . . . We're not going to have any more repetitive [immigrant bashing].'" Indeed, African American elected leaders like Ronnie Rimbert and African American faith leaders and community activists played an important role in challenging anti-immigrant sentiment and enacting the city's 2009 public declaration to support immigrants. This statement was an important foundation for the passage of Oberlin's sanctuary city statement in 2017. These actions demonstrate how immigration issues in Oberlin are "a natural flow in Oberlin's history." Yet the resistance also confirms Kornblith and Lasser's prescient observations about the elusive quality of Oberlin's quest for racial equality. The utopian vision that defined Oberlin's founding was similarly challenged by racist resistance. But perhaps more importantly, it was undermined by "well-meaning actions that can have unintended consequences." They write, "Amid today's continuing struggle for the conscience and soul of America, we need the courage to envision a future of racial justice, an inclusive and productive multicultural politics, an economy of abundance widely shared, and a society of mutual respect, generosity, and dignity. Dreams are dangerous, imperfect, and powerful. They are also elusive, as are the utopias we imagine."[63]

The elusive power of dreaming into being egalitarian and inclusive places of safety clearly animates the work of sanctuary people. It requires constant vigilance and the labor of dedicated people who are willing to reach out across difference, to see ways to connect people who are often structurally and socially distant, and to illuminate the ways one's well-being is intimately bound up with that of others. This is not easy work. Sarah Johnson, for example, spoke quite poignantly about how challenging it was to bridge often vast divides and how emotionally difficult it felt "being the only link in the chain" that connected people who clearly needed, depended on, and relied on one another. These chains form bridges that span linguistic, cultural, educational, race, class, and religious communities and are rooted in the unglamorous work of sanctuary people. Victor Leandry, for example, often reflects on the important work of bringing different communities together. And although his role as the director of a social service agency like El Centro seems to fall beyond the realm of faith-based organizing, he is also a vital bridge between different communities—secular and religious; white, upper-middle-class and Latina/o working-class; long-term African American and Latina/o residents of Lorain; community foundations, philanthropists, and service providers and those receiving services. These differences map on to geographies of opportunity and disinvestment that have a profound impact on how people respond in moments of crisis. But they are also spaces of opportunity to bring people together in surprising and mutually beneficial ways.

Conclusion: Overcoming Evil with Valor y Dignidad

Nancy Finke described how after years of living in Chicago and then back in Missouri where she grew up, she and her husband, David, wanted to return to live in Oberlin, something they had been "thinking about" and "planning for a long time." Although she and David had been involved in faith-based work as students in Oberlin, she said they originally planned to not get involved in anything once they returned to Oberlin in 2016 "for a year, although we knew that was kind of impossible." They didn't intend to join anything, rather "just kind of live here and get to know everybody and get to know people at Kendal and at the Quaker meeting and the college. I expected we would be doing more with the college . . . because we were here [as students]. But then two months [after we arrived], Trump was elected. And we just got sucked up into the political work. So we have been pretty active with Lorain County Rising and Community Peace Builders and the Quaker Community." While working with immigrants and sanctuary work were new experiences for Nancy, she sees a connection between that work and the range of activism she has done in Oberlin, Chicago, Missouri, and now in Oberlin once more. As she reflected on the sanctuary work she has been involved in, she elaborated on how her own personal history also influenced her:

> Just wanting to live, wanting to help. To help fill a need. . . . I think maybe for me—my dad was killed when I was two, and so I think about how my mom and I were separated from him and I think that's part of the strong feeling [I have] about this. The notion that children would be deliberately taken away from their parents and . . . that parents put their children on a train and say, "Leave." I just can't imagine that. . . . And somehow to alleviate that would be a good thing. [*Long pause.*] I guess one thing that gives sanctuary its power is that we're defying evil. Quakers don't talk about evil very much. They [*chuckles*]—we laugh sometimes because in the Quaker hymnal, some of the hymns have been revised to take out works like "sin." We see God in everyone, which is a good thing. But still, there is evil. There are enemies. One of our Quaker friends gave a lecture and said, "Jesus said, 'Love your enemy.' But he never said there is no enemy" [*nods approvingly at that statement*]. That's good. I'll write that one down.[64]

Acknowledging that there is evil in the world was not something that people like Nancy did very often. In fact, it is rather remarkable how little faith-based organizers talked about evil. Injustice, racism, xenophobia, white supremacy, homophobia, fascism, and anti-immigrant sentiment were the terms they used to describe the problems they sought to ameliorate in their modest ways.

Doing so, however, was no easy feat and required sustained efforts across time and space. And it also required organizations, institutions, churches, faith communities, and, above all, personal commitment. Celestino Rivera poignantly referred to this as valor y dignidad—courage and dignity, the name that he hoped to give his own nonprofit one day. As he spoke about his disappointment with the Catholic Church hierarchy's position on public sanctuary, his disillusionment with what he perceived to be a lack of broader outrage about the political climate, and his plans after his retirement, Celestino reflected on the trajectory of his career in law enforcement and how to build something different, meaningful, and enduring through his dream organization, Valor y Dignidad:

CR: I guess the way I look at it is, I've got limited time. And I want to make an impact while I can. Do you know what my biggest goal is? [*Pauses and smiles.*]

GP: What?

CR: I already know what my obituary is going to say. [*Pauses again.*] "Former police chief dies." [*Laughs.*] If I could somehow change that to "Community activists dies," I'd be a happy person. I don't want that to be my [only] legacy anymore. I know that doesn't sound right.

GP: No, no. It doesn't sound bad.

CR: I'm trying to figure that out. How can I best impact the world? I thought maybe writing would do it. But I don't know how to do that. And I don't know anything about a blog. And I don't know anything about starting one. I just thought maybe if I [started] an organization like Courage and Dignity, then maybe I would just do that work under that organization. And then reach out to certain people who I know. . . . I love working with people who actually do things. Who just really care. You can tell right here [*points to his heart*].[65]

Celestino was absolutely right when he predicted what his obituary would say. Sadly, on June 22, 2022, Celestino Rivera died unexpectedly of heart failure. His obituary did, indeed, pay homage to his many years as Lorain's police chief. But it also detailed the extensive contributions Celestino made to Lorain, his family, Ohio, and beyond. And it also included the dozens of organizations he belonged to and helped create, and the surprising number of awards and recognitions he received. Celestino humbly served so many in so many ways. And his reflections on the importance of valor y dignidad—courage and dignity—capture what was at the core of his vision of what it means to be a sanctuary people. For José, Anabel, Sister Cathy, John, Sarah, David, Nancy, and thousands of others in Ohio and beyond, being sanctuary people is about a fierce commitment to community, to justice, and to accompanying others along journeys that are not easy, but are made lighter when done in communion. It is also about having courage in the face of state power to fight and preserve the dignity of others. Valor y dignidad—courage and dignity—are at the heart of being sanctuary people.

Conclusion

The Spiritual Power and Political Uses of Sanctuary

On September 14, 2022, nearly fifty Venezuelan migrants arrived by plane on Martha's Vineyard, a small island and elite vacation destination in Massachusetts. Arriving without warning or coordination with local officials, migrants like Luis appeared confused about where they had landed after surviving what has become an increasingly familiar, long, and dangerous journey by land by tens of thousands of Venezuelans to the US-Mexico border. After being processed by immigration officials in Texas, Luis, his family members, and dozens of others boarded planes in San Antonio headed to Martha's Vineyard. Many of the migrants arriving on Martha's Vineyard shared a similar story with reporters, volunteers, and local officials of being approached by a woman named Perla who offered them McDonald's gift cards and a free flight to Massachusetts, where, according to one migrant, they were told there would be "people waiting for you with food, shelter, and ready to help you with whatever you need."[1] In reality, migrants arrived at a place with no family, no immigration infrastructure, and limited local resources to meet the needs of people whose journeys had unexpectedly led them to a small island in the Atlantic Ocean after months of travel through harrowing conditions and multiple countries. Although migrants like Ardenis Nazareth were surprised that they ended up "on this little island," they also conveyed a desire to find work quickly to support families back home, as well as profound gratitude for the reception they received: "We're getting food, clothing, all our needs met. I love Massachusetts!"[2]

As immigration lawyers rushed to take ferries to Martha's Vineyard and residents mobilized at St. Andrew's Episcopal Church to meet the needs of migrants like Ardenis, Luis, and others, it was clear that the polarizing debates around sanctuary cities and immigration continued to have salience and evoke political drama beyond the years of the Trump administration at the expense of vulnerable migrants who have the most to lose in these political battles. Indeed, reporters quickly revealed that although the migrants arriving in Martha's Vineyard were from Texas, it was *Florida* governor Ron DeSantis who authorized and used his state's funds to fly the Venezuelan migrants to Massachusetts. Following the lead of Texas governor Gregg Abbott and Arizona governor Doug Ducey, who beginning in the spring of 2022 used state funds to send thousands of migrants by bus to places like New York City, Washington, DC, and Chicago, DeSantis boasted, "All those people in DC and New York were beating their chest when Trump was president, saying they were so proud to be sanctuary jurisdictions. The minute even a small fraction of what those border towns deal with every day are brought to their front door, they all go berserk."[3] The political theater at migrants' expense included Abbott busing hundreds of migrants to vice president Kamala Harris's home in Washington, DC, where mayor Muriel Bowser, according to the *New York Times*, "declared a public emergency . . . in response to the arrivals."[4] Similarly, New York City mayor Eric Adams publicly worried about the strain of months of busloads of migrants arriving in the city, with approximately eleven thousand migrants entering into the city shelter system from May to September 2022, was putting on an already overextended system that was "nearing its breaking point."[5]

By October 2022, just a few short weeks following the arrival of migrants on Martha's Vineyard and with unabated new arrivals, Adams also declared a state of emergency and sought "state and federal funding to help pay for housing and services, and urged the federal government to allow newly arrived asylum seekers to work legally and to slow the northward flow of migrants from the border."[6] And while the rising number of asylum seekers certainly contributed to the strain on the system, housing and immigrant rights advocates were unequivocal that migrants were not to blame for the crisis. Rather, increasing rents, the paucity of affordable housing, the rising number of evictions, and understaffing in government offices tasked with overseeing the city's housing voucher system were problems that predated the arrival or migrants and were critical factors contributing to the growth of homelessness in the city.[7] This did not prevent Adams from criticizing Abbott yet again for failing to coordinate migrant arrivals with officials in New York City and asking El Paso mayor Oscar Leeser to refrain from sending more migrants to the city.[8] In a speech where Adams announced that New York City was "doing our part, and now others must step up and join us," he also observed, "New Yorkers are angry. . . . I am angry too. We have not asked for this."[9]

Mayor Eric Adams's assertion that people must "step up" and that he and fellow New Yorkers "have not asked for this" could not be more prescient and painfully true about the ongoing global migration crisis. As countless studies, news reports, memoirs, and personal stories can attest, migrants fleeing economic crises, political violence, and the devastating impacts of climate change and (un)natural disasters in their countries to build new lives in the United States, Europe, and elsewhere certainly have not asked to live in conditions that necessitate such drastic changes in their lives. And the myriad numbers of volunteers, service providers, community members, activists, and faith-based workers and religious leaders have likewise demonstrated the dramatic ways people have stepped up to meet the needs of people whose circumstances are seemingly beyond the assistance of local, national, and global entities charged with protecting the rights of migrants. In short, the increasing reliance on civil society to address state-produced population movements is a global phenomenon with particular local and national implications.

Predictably, volunteers at St. Andrew's Church on Martha's Vineyard did what so many have done before and what they will continue to do, namely, responding to a crisis and creating welcoming spaces of refuge, hospitality, and care. They provided food, clothing, and COVID-19 testing for migrants and helped to find places for them to sleep. According to the *New York Times*, "The Rev. Chip Seadale said St. Andrew's had decided to take in the migrants for the night after learning that they had nowhere to go. A parishioner had reached out to him, knowing that the church helps house homeless people in the winter." Given that the island's only homeless shelter could accommodate only ten people, the lack of affordable housing in an area where "the medium home price is about $1 million," and the limited number of jobs available in a community where tourist and service sector jobs are largely seasonal, migrants were arriving in a place that would not be able to support them in a sustained and meaningful way. According to Barbara Rush, the warden at St. Andrew's, "There are literally no jobs in the winter, and there is no affordable housing on Martha's Vineyard. . . . The bulk of people that work a lower- to middle-income job live off island and commute." Nevertheless, restaurants, community members, and churches—all part of what Rush described as "a strong and capable community"—mobilized to meet the needs of migrants and made them feel welcome and safe.[10]

Migrants on Martha's Vineyard shared their feelings of profound gratitude for the generosity people extended to them, particularly after experiences of feeling vulnerable and being taken advantage of during the long trek to the United States. These sentiments were echoed by migrants who continued to arrive throughout the fall of 2022 and who were met at bus stations, homeless shelters, churches, food pantries, and employment agencies by people who volunteered their time, money, and efforts to bring them clothes and food and offer translation services, medical attention, housing, legal advice, gestures of solidarity, and companionship. On October 17, 2022, the *New York Times* detailed the experiences of recently arrived migrants in New York City, including Renee Chicaiza, and reported, "Ms. Chicaiza broke down in tears as she recalled how moved she was by the warm reception they received when they arrived at the Port Authority Bus Terminal. The last stretch of the trip through Mexico had been particularly difficult, with corrupt police demanding money and people refusing them any help. The bus ride itself had seemed like a blessing, and the sight of friendly faces filled her with a profound sense of relief. 'They hugged us, they told us welcome to the country, they gave us clothes,' Ms. Chicaiza said, wiping away tears. 'It was beautiful.'"[11]

This book has documented the efforts of people across different social locations of class, race, ethnicity, religious affiliation, education, language, and citizenship status to create spaces of support and care for Latina/o communities during a time of particularly visible hostility, danger, uncertainty, and precarity. It has used the notion of sanctuary people—a frame that the late community activist Ruben Castilla Herrera often used and that captured the prevailing ethic of care grounded in faith-based organizing during the Trump years—to draw attention to Latinas/os' coalitional, community-building practices and the particular role faith-based organizing plays in building and sustaining networks of support, defying unjust laws and callous state policies of neglect, and working to change punitive policies and practices through mass mobilization, electoral politics, and grassroots organizing. Sanctuary people reliably respond to the immediate needs of others in moments of crisis, yet they do so understanding the interconnectedness of people's struggles and seek to build enduring relationships of protection, support, and empowerment. Indeed, drawing on the language of sanctuary and protection to encompass a diverse set of experiences of precarity underscores the power of a word, an approach, and a practice that people at the mercy of state power have accessed in different, historically and culturally contingent ways for millennia.

Throughout my research, I consistently asked people to explain what they believed gave sanctuary its power. They often hesitated when answering this question and then tended to describe how faith, religious mandates, and the power of sacred spaces infused sanctuary practices with a divine quality and power that compelled them and others to act, even in the face of opposition from elected officials, religious leaders, activists, and powerful community members. And while this book documents the ways that contemporary sanctuary practices have a long and varied history in the United States, sanctuary's reemergence in political discourse, organizing strategies, and modes of resistance has been taken up not only by the political left, but also by the political right in surprising ways. Throughout my research, I was often surprised by the vitriolic responses sanctuary evoked—such as governors DeSantis, Abbott, and Ducey scornfully busing and flying migrants to sanctuary jurisdictions—and tried to understand the source of these passionate responses and how the word—and the practices that it characterized—became so vilified in American political discourse.[12] For this reason, I was completely surprised and more than intrigued when I began to notice the embrace of sanctuary rhetoric by the political right near the end of Trump's presidency and well into the Biden administration to talk about everything from ending abortion access to expanding gun rights.

In the fall of 2021, for example, the state of Texas passed one of the most restrictive abortion laws in the country. While this reflected well-funded and carefully organized strategies to overturn *Roe v. Wade*, a strategy that relied on the mobilization of conservative evangelical Christians and the political right on the local, state, and national levels, this particular victory was also a story that involves town-by-town organizing by people like Mark Lee Dickson, who has been at the forefront of what he calls the building and proliferation of "sanctuary cities for the unborn." In May 2021, voters in the city of Lubbock, Texas, overwhelmingly passed a city ordinance to declare itself a sanctuary city for the unborn, which would prohibit abortions within city limits.[13] Although more than twenty municipalities in Texas had passed similar ordinances between 2019 and 2021, Lubbock was notable because with a population of over 250,000, it was the largest city to do so through a voter-approved ordinance, rather than having it be enacted by local elected officials. And while the majority of towns in Texas and beyond that passed sanctuary cities for the unborn ordinances were small rural communities, cities like Lebanon, Ohio, with a population of more than twenty thousand, passed a similar resolution in May 2021, the first city in Ohio to do so.[14] Dickson's strategy of organizing "one small town at a time" was credited for helping to pave the way for the statewide abortion ban in Texas in September 2021, and was unapologetic in adopting the language of sanctuary city policies designed to protect immigrants. As Emily Wax-Thibodeaux of the *Washington Post* reported on Dickson's comments as he preached at College Heights Baptist Church in Plainville, Texas, in September 2021, "'An abortion clinic in Waskom, Texas, is not an Austin problem or a Washington, DC, problem. It's a town problem,' he said, urging the audience not to wait for state or national leaders and instead to pass their own local ban."[15]

The overturning of *Roe v. Wade* in June 2022 accelerated the circulation of sanctuary rhetoric on both the political right and left beyond Texas. San Clemente, California, for example, witnessed one of the most visible clashes when in August 2022 the city council was preparing to consider a resolution to declare the city a "sanctuary for life where the dignity of every human being will be defended and promoted from life inside the womb through all stages of development in life up and until a natural death." And while the three-to-one vote removed the resolution from the San Clemente City Council agenda that month, the heated debates and the publicity they received underscored the ways activists deploy sanctuary rhetoric in contradictory ways. In his efforts to support making San Clemente a sanctuary for the unborn, Mark Lee Dickson observed, "Gov. Newsom has been very clear that he wants California to be a sanctuary for abortion access."[16] Indeed, as dozens of states set in motion plans to restrict abortion access, governor Gavin Newsom and California state legislators quickly put into place abortion protections following the Supreme Court's rule on *Roe v. Wade*, and in September 2022, Newsom signed a dozen bills "establishing some of the strongest abortion protections in the nation" and affirming its leading role as "an abortion sanctuary."[17]

The proliferation of Second Amendment sanctuary jurisdictions has followed a similar path as the sanctuary cities for the unborn, a path that also leads back to Texas. On June 16, 2021, governor Gregg Abbott signed seven bills to strengthen the state's gun protections, including HB 2622, which specifically "makes Texas a Second Amendment Sanctuary State by protecting Texans from new federal gun control regulations."[18] According to the Southern Poverty Law Center, Second Amendment jurisdictions to protect gun rights are not new. In fact, "in 2013, municipalities in 38 states passed bills to 'protect' against any federal gun legislation proposed by the Obama administration in the aftermath of the mass shooting at Sandy Hook Elementary." What is relatively new, however, is the use of the term "sanctuary" to characterize these strategies, which emerged first in May 2018 in Monroe County, Illinois, and is now a designation for hundreds of jurisdictions across the country. Increased suspicion and anger over mask mandates, public health measures, and alleged government overreach during the global COVID-19 pandemic fostered what the Southern Poverty Law Center characterizes as new trends "away from 2A sanctuaries and toward broader 'constitutional sanctuaries' that refuse laws perceived as infringing on any constitutional rights, not just Second Amendment rights."[19] In a surprising twist and co-optation of progressives' use of sanctuary to protect immigrants' rights, conservative advocates of sanctuary policies that seek to enshrine the protection of guns and restrict abortion access selectively embrace a strategy they once viciously excoriated. This is mendacious propaganda and a cynical ploy.

This book has argued for a broader understanding of sanctuary, one that has "expanded in practice and the demographics of its seekers."[20] I have detailed the ways contemporary sanctuary practices in Ohio respond to the precarious circumstances that defined the lives of many Latinas/os in Ohio as they confronted the Janus-faced power of the state, characterized by intense and relentless immigration surveillance, enforcement, and detention as well as a callous disregard, neglect, and willful disinvestment. As displaced Puerto Ricans in the wake of Hurricane María drew on long-standing diasporic connections to relocate to Lorain and Northeast Ohio, migrant laborers from Mexico and Central America were detained in workplace ICE raids, and undocumented community members and families sought physical sanctuary in houses of worship for months and years to evade deportation and family separation, they bound themselves up with a diverse set of faith-based activists, service providers, volunteers, and community members who themselves drew on long histories of resistance, political organizing, and solidarity work that helped to create spaces of safety and refuge. These sanctuary practices were generative and reflected the ways that the most inspiring and successful social justice struggles are ones that reveal the interlocking systems of political, economic, and social stratification and illuminate pathways forward grounded in an ethic of accompaniment and solidarity. Such insights affirm the power of slogans like "sanctuary everywhere" and contemporary racial justice movements that, as historian Barbara Ransby argues, invite us to reimagine freedom in the twenty-first century.[21]

But what are the consequences of this broadening of sanctuary? What do we gain and what do we lose when sanctuary circulates in more capacious ways that unmoor it from its religious and spiritual foundations? Is there danger in secularizing sanctuary? Anthropologist Aimee Villarreal first posed this final query to me and Oberlin College students in the fall of 2018 when giving a talk about Native and Indigenous sanctuaryscapes in the American Southwest. It's a question that has stayed with me and helped guide this research. What gives sanctuary its power? And why have people from a range of political, religious, epistemological, and spiritual traditions embraced, deployed, and refashioned it in ways to frame their struggles and ground their actions in moments of significant danger and uncertainty?

From its inception, sanctuary's appeals to divine power and the authority of God have been a powerful way to challenge the secular and punitive power of the state. Both then and now, these appeals were grounded in the recognition of the sacredness of particular places—churches, synagogues, mosques, temples, and shrines—that were imbued with divine authority and offered protection, shelter, and safety to those evading punishment and retribution, albeit in temporally circumscribed ways, which underscores the liminal quality of sanctuary practices. The continued salience of the sacredness of place is visible in campaigns led by Indigenous communities and activists to protect water and mountains, as well as mounds, stones, and rock formations, from pipelines, border walls, and extractive mining. Efforts to extend this recognition of the sacredness of place inform strategies to proclaim cities, streets, states, and college campuses sanctuary spaces, places where those who inhabit them should be assured of their safety and protection from harm. It is this epistemological position that also helps explain why church takeovers by the Young Lords and other Latina/o freedom movement activists in Chicago and New York captured the public imagination in the 1960s: it demands not only that we recognize the authority of God, but also that we acknowledge the inherent dignity and sacredness of people themselves. Sanctuary, therefore, rests fundamentally on our understanding of a divine mandate on how to treat others and what we are both willing and required to do to protect one another.[22]

These concerns, of course, extend far beyond contemporary sanctuary practices. Indeed, the global pandemic revealed profound divisions as we all tried to make sense of what was for many of us a new reality defined by lockdowns, social distancing, mask mandates, and the reckoning with racialized state violence and senseless loss of life that marked the summer of 2020. While these tragedies seem far removed from the struggles over sanctuary in the preceding years, Edith Espinal eloquently captured what binds them together. In an interview with a local newspaper during the early months of the pandemic in 2020, she soberly acknowledged the weight and pain caused by pandemic lockdowns and social distancing. But she also observed how these experiences were ones that she and others living in public sanctuary had endured as they lived sequestered from family, with limited interactions with a small number of people, and with an omnipresent element of fear. "Last week, two people sent me messages saying they were starting to see how difficult it is to be stuck inside. I hope now more people can support the sanctuary movement because they also are understanding now."[23] What moral obligations do we have to protect each other, and how much are we willing to sacrifice of ourselves in order to take care of one another?

When I shared my colleague's concern about the secularization of sanctuary with Reverend John Fife, he responded by saying that she made a good point and that it's a real concern. And although he articulated the need for faith communities to work with secular and global entities like UNHCR (United Nations High Commissioner for Refugees) to protect the most vulnerable populations globally—"because faith communities' status within secular society is diminishing globally. It's true of Muslim, Jewish and Christian traditions"—he was also ambivalent about the secularization of sanctuary. "Our experience in the 1980s was that all of our secular institutions were declaring sanctuary in support of the faith communities. Now they've kind of co-opted the idea of sanctuary as a secular term. I think that makes them much more vulnerable to attack by the government and therefore tends to diminish the aura of a spiritual world of *faith communities* as sanctuary."[24] Reverend Fife's comments were not meant to criticize secular groups' use of the language of sanctuary in their organizing efforts. Instead, he wanted to make the case for the particular role of spirituality and faith in sustaining movements and imbuing them with the spiritual sustenance they need to persevere. Sanctuary's power provided meaning and sustenance to Edith Espinal to remain in a Mennonite church for over three years. It animates Lorain's Latina/o community and others to aid, respond quickly, and build infrastructure to aid people who lost everything in Hurricane María and still struggle with the long-lasting trauma to build a new life in Northeast Ohio far from the home, people, and communities where they want to be. Sanctuary also became the resonant framework to guide the work of the same community in Lorain and beyond as they met the material, emotional, and spiritual needs of families ripped apart following the workplace raid in Corso's garden center that instilled fear and turned a formerly bustling, vibrant community into a ghost town as people retreated from each other in mistrust and fear. And sanctuary affirms and sustains the efforts of faith-based activists whose long histories of work with the United Farm Workers, the civil rights movement, anti-war organizing, Central American solidarity groups, and feminist liberation theology movements of the twentieth century were the foundations nurturing their responses to the pitched battles in the twenty-first century.

As I noted earlier, just before his untimely death on June 22, 2022, Celestino Rivera remarked that when he died, he hoped that he would be remembered as a community activist. At his prayer service at the Spitzer Center at Lorain County Community College, hundreds of people joined together to mourn his passing and celebrate his life. The grief was nearly unbearable as people spoke of their love and admiration for a public servant and man dedicated to his family who was a self-described orphan, veteran, police officer, and former police chief and who dedicated his final years in that latter role to put into place policies to protect, support, and assure undocumented residents that they were valued members of the communities he served. This often put him at odds with powerful people in city government, law enforcement, community leaders, and even the Catholic church communities he worked with in a variety of capacities. But like so many other sanctuary people, Celestino Rivera engaged in the work of building safer, inclusive, and welcoming places with valor y dignidad, the courage and dignity he had hoped to name the nonprofit he dreamed of establishing one day. The work of sanctuary people is not glamorous. It entails great sacrifice from sanctuary leaders like Leonor, Miriam, and Edith who endured separation in order to remain connected to their families. And it is fortified by tireless community leaders and activists like Anabel, Victor, José, John, Nancy, Steve, Mary, John, David, and Sarah who are guided by a call to work collectively and in solidarity to make sanctuary everywhere.

ACKNOWLEDGMENTS

I want to offer a special thanks to my students and colleagues at Oberlin College who inspired me from the early moments of the sanctuary campus organizing in November 2016 to develop teach-ins, campus lectures, film screenings, public presentations, and new courses, and ultimately to write this book. I especially want to thank Jesus Martínez, Zurisaday Gutiérrez-Avila, Julio Reyes, Marcelo Vinces, Adrian Bautista, RaShelle Peck, Art Phung, Shelley Lee, Steven Volk, Meredith Gadsby, Baron Pineda, Wendy Kozol, Pam Brooks, Meredith Raimondo, Naomi Campa, Ellen Wurtzel, Elizabeth Wueste, Kirk Ormand, Drew Wilburn, Benjamin Lee, Chris Trinacty, Irene Garza, Tim Elgren, Sandhya Subramanian, Marvin Krislov, Ferd Protzman, Eder Aguilar, Dulce Cedillo, Belkis Moreno, Kaytlen Cruz, Marissa Ramirez, Brendan Aleman, Paola Quevedo, Abby Parker, Wren Fiocco, Casey Troost, Mikala Jones, Colby Fortin, Callie Howard, Rachel Marcus, and Levy Reyes. I am particularly grateful to the leaders and members of student organizations like Obies for Undocumented Inclusion and staff of the Multicultural Resource Center, including Rut Mérida, Dulce Rincón, Adriana Vergara, Della Kurzer-Zlotnick, Ellie Lindberg, Ana Robelo, and Joelle Lingat, as well as other students whose scholarly and activist work and example beyond the classroom were instructive to me—Brian Cabral, Zia Kandler, Ashley Suárez, Sophie Newman, Caela Brodigan, Emily Belle, Mia Rosenberg, Becca Cohen, Clara Lincoln, Katie Wilson, Miriam Entin-Bell, Sophia García, and Soluna Amen. During this time, I was also fortunate to be part of the Oberlin Sanctuary Project, which brought college and community members together to document and reflect on the history of Oberlin City and College as a safe haven. My thanks to Ken Grossi, Alexia Hudson-Ward, and Meredith Gadsby for including me in this meaningful collaboration.

Activists, community leaders, scholars, and organizers in Ohio and beyond were generous with their time and taught me a great deal about the meaning and experiences of sanctuary. I want to offer my deepest and abiding gratitude and respeto to Edith Espinal and Leonor García, who shared their experiences with me while they were living in public sanctuary, and to Miriam Vargas as well, who entered into sanctuary shortly after Edith and Leonor. John Durst first invited me to meet with Edith in the fall of 2017 when he and I were part of an immigration workshop at the College of Wooster. I want to thank him, Libni López, Ruben Castilla Herrera, and Pastor Joel Miller, who were all part of that first memorable conversation with Edith. I also want to recognize the efforts and work of others who have worked tirelessly alongside sanctuary leaders and other activists and community organizers and service providers, including Deborah Lee, Jeff Johnson, Pablo Morataya, John Fife, Celestino Rivera, Elba Armstrong-Rivera, José Mendiola, Felisitas Mendiola, Anabel Barrón Sánchez, Sharon Shumaker, members of the Forest Hills Presbyterian Church sanctuary committee, Sister Cathy McConnell, Bill Thaden, Rita Mary Harwood, Nelson Pérez, Victor Leandry, David T. Hill, Nancy Finke, David Finke, John Gates, Linda Gates, Ann Elder, Ann Francis, Carmen McFarlin, Carla Van Dale, Sarah Johnson, Mary Hammond, Steve Hammond, A. G. Miller, Brenda Grier-Miller, and all of the members of the Oberlin Community in Support of Immigrants as well as Jessie Ferriols and Sacred Heart Church's Peace and Justice Committee. These kinds of ecumenical movements are truly inspiring and important.

There are so many people whose work as sanctuary people is not included in this book, but whose labors prior to this research and years following it and into the present inspire, guide, and sustain efforts to create spaces of safety. I want to thank especially Libni López, a true model of selflessness who is deeply committed to building and sustaining community in an actively loving way and whose joy, entrega, and fierce dedication defending immigrants is an incredible source of inspiration. Steve and Dinah Volk have been part of countless meetings, protests, vigils, and gatherings, and have offered incredible intellectual insight and ethical grounding over the years. Both John and Linda Gates have modeled for me what it means to live a life of love, integrity, joy, and hope. And thanks to María, Manolo, Alexa, and Emilia for the joy you have brought to my family and our community in Oberlin.

I have been fortunate to be part of an intellectual community at Oberlin that offers pretty miraculous support, love, and care. I am particularly grateful to Wendy Kozol, Shelley Lee, Meredith Gadsby, KJ Cerankowski, Joan Kaatz, Carmen Merport Quiñones, Jess Arnett, Leila Ben-Nasr, and Angie LaGrotteria. I want to offer a special thanks to Wendy and Shelley for taking the time to read and offer edits and comments to make this book better. I am particularly grateful to have had time to bring this book to completion with the support of Research Status from Oberlin College in 2021–2022. I also want to thank colleagues and administrators at Oberlin who have offered support over the years, including David Kamitsuka, Tim Elgren, Pablo Mitchell, Yveline Alexis, Renee Romano, Danielle Terrazas-Williams, Tamika Nunley, Tania Boster, Trecia Pottinger, Megan Mitchell, Candice Raynor, Greggor Mattson, Danielle Skeehan, Harrod Suarez, Daphne John, Rick Baldoz, Charles Peterson, Laura Baudot, Jay Fiskio, Karl Offen, Chie Sakakibara, and Gillian Johns. I am incredibly blessed to have the love and friendship of incredible women along the way: Michelle Boyd, Deborah Parédez, Regina Deil-Amen, Heather McClure, Tita Reed, Melanie Lee, Meredith Gadsby, and Shelley Lee have inspired me to be thoughtful, find time for fun and celebration as well as silence and meditation, and find beauty around me. I want to offer a special thank you to so many people who brought joy, laughter, love, silliness, and competitive tennis fun in the final phases writing this book, especially Griselda Soto Bravo, Lolo Gómez Nuñez, José Gómez Soto, Rania Ziar, Amanda Phillips, Libni López, Ted Samuel, Roni Gilbert, Sue Parkin, Mike Parkin, Chris Romer, Denny Romer, Deborah Roose, David Snyder, Lynn Swanson, Danielle Terrazas-Williams, Andree Underwood, Eric Ishida, Constantine Ananiadis, and Christina Nielson.

I offer a special thanks to my Oberlin students who over the years have reminded me of the power of fierce hope to create a better future and whose engagement in the classroom is matched by their commitment and efforts beyond. A special thanks to Stephanie Shugert, Tzetza Rosas-Pérez, Becky Trigo, Ariana Leandry, and Minerva Macarrulla for reading and offering edits of the near-final version of my book manuscript. And also a special thanks to students enrolled in my sanctuary course, my race, religion and citizenship seminar, and my community-based research course on Latina/o oral history. I'm grateful to the students who

transcribed interviews and offered research support over the years—
Nalin Beckman, Stephanie Shugert, Tzetza Rosas-Pérez, Belkis Moreno,
Karen Cepeda, and Jaimie Yu. My Posse arrived in Oberlin College just
as I was beginning this research in earnest, and I offer my thanks to them
for keeping all of this in perspective—Brendan Aleman, Diana Guzman,
Jacob Thomas, Manny Jones, DeJuan Moore, Danny Montes, Kopano
Muhammad, Mirian Soria, Leilani Vellón, and Rania Ziar.

I am grateful to my colleagues beyond Oberlin, particularly those from
the Association of Latina/o@ Anthropologists and my co-collaborators
on the anthology *Ethnographic Refusals, Unruly Latinidades*—Alex
Chávez, Ana Aparicio, Andrea Bolivar, Sherina Feliciano Santos, Santiago Guerra, Jonathan Rosa, Gilberto Rosas, Aimee Villarreal, and Pat
Zavella. I am incredibly grateful to the School of Advanced Research
for inviting the *Ethnographic Refusals* crew to spend a week in Santa
Fe as part of one of its advanced seminars in April 2019, where I was
able to share my work, sharpen my analysis, and spend meaningful time
together with pretty amazing colleagues and friends. I have learned
so much from the generosity of scholars and friends whose work in
Latina/o studies, religion, faith-based organizing, and social movements
have taught me a great deal over the years—Sujey Vega, Felipe Hinojosa,
Sergio González, Lloyd Barba, Jorge Juan Rodriguez V, Amalia Pallares,
Nilda Flores-González, Yarimar Bonilla, Isar Godreau, Frank Guridy,
Jonathan Rosa, Julio Cammarota, Lourdes Gutiérrez-Nájera, Marisol LeBrón, Arlene Dávila, Carlos Vargas Ramos, Leo Chavez, Almita
Miranda, Dario Valles, Miguel Díaz Barriga, Margaret Dorsey, Carlos
Vélez-Ibañez, and Mariluz Cruz Torres. My thinking about sanctuary
practices was also enhanced through my participation in the Borders
and Migration Workshop sponsored by the Great Lakes College Association in Athens, Greece, in June 2018 and conversations with impressive
scholars like Irene López, Nancy Powers, Rumi Shammin, Brian Miller,
Isis Nusair, Geoff Boyce, Mari Galup, and Chryssa Zachaou.

I cannot imagine seeing this book to completion without the vision,
support, and incisive questions my editor Jennifer Hammer offered.
Working with you, Veronica Knutson, Alexia Traganas, Rosalie Morales
Kearns at New York University Press, and with Luis Plascencia have
made the challenges of writing this book much easier. I am also grateful for the incisive and useful comments of the anonymous reviewers

of my book. A special thank you to Rebecca Gómez and her husband, Manuel, who were gracious hosts in Rincón, Puerto Rico, where I was able to write, read, reflect, and rest during short writing retreats during my research leave. Deep gratitude to my mother, Toni Jo Rideout, for making me café con leche and breakfast for my daughter, Lucia, as I wrote in the early mornings in Rincón and for asking good questions and offering insights about translation, the varied experiences of a diasporic life, and politics. I also benefited from time and reflection at the Jesuit Retreat Center in Parma, Ohio, where the staff offer a quiet and welcoming space for reflection.

I entered graduate school in 1993 planning to study the relationship between politics and religion following two years of living and working as a Holy Cross Associate with remarkably dedicated Holy Cross priests, brothers, sisters, and fellow associates in rural Chile in the years following the end of the Pinochet regime. My deepest gratitude to the people who transformed my life during these years, including Liesl Haas, David Carey, David Morales, Jean Lammers, Bob Dailey, and the people of Pocuro, who were my first teachers about the meaning of accompaniment. I also want to thank Micaela di Leonardo for her mentorship throughout graduate school and for providing me with the analytical tools and training that have allowed me to return to the initial questions that first led me to graduate school more than three decades ago.

From an early age, my parents, Felix and Leeann Pérez, instilled in me and my siblings, Eric, Peter, Lorna, and Teresa, the value of learning, but also of sharing our gifts and talents to give something back to others. It is that ethic of love and care that guides this work. There is not a day that goes by that I fail to give thanks for my children, Lucia, Pablo, and Antonio, for always asking tough questions, offering comic relief, and inspiring me to think deeply and carefully about religion, politics, social change, and how to make the world a better place. And of course none of this would be possible without Baron—for your love, enduring hours of listening to me talk, worry, and process all of this, for encouraging me to get away to write, supporting me as I conducted this research, and for all the years of vigorous debate that I believe has made me smarter and more honest.

While I hope this this book conveys my deep gratitude and admiration for people who work to create spaces of safety and refuge, I am one of many who mourned the passing of people whose lives inspired this work: Amber Evans and Ruben Castilla Herrera both passed away while I was finishing the research for this book. Hearing about their work in Columbus and in particular Ruben's recurring challenge to all of us to reflect on and become sanctuary people was truly inspirational. Celestino Rivera's tragic and untimely death in June 2022 was devastating for so many people. The outpouring of love and grief following his passing is a testament to the incredible impact he made on so many people's lives, including my own. This book is dedicated to him, Ruben, and all the other sanctuary people who have transformed our lives for the better.

NOTES

INTRODUCTION

1 September 5 was also the day that attorney general Jeff Sessions announced the repeal of DACA (Deferred Action for Childhood Arrivals). Edith Espinal announced that the church welcomed her into sanctuary on September 5, left temporarily with the hope of a stay of deportation, and returned on October 2, 2017; she remained in sanctuary until February 13, 2021. Throughout this book, I use the actual names of people rather than pseudonyms, a decision that reflects the wishes of those whose efforts I share in these pages.

2 According to the Migration Policy Institute, "regularizing" one's immigration status refers to the ways millions of unauthorized migrants are given legal status "through programs and mechanisms variously referred to as legalization or regularization." "Legalization/Regularization," n.d., Migration Policy Institute, www.migrationpolicy.org.

3 Kevin Parks, "Sanctuary for Local Immigrant: 'Call to Action' Unites Church," *Columbus Dispatch*, September 11, 2017, www.dispatch.com.

4 Ben Garbarek, "Undocumented Woman Takes Refuge in Clintonville Church," ABC News 6, September 5, 2017, https://abc6onyourside.com.

5 Parks, "Sanctuary for Local Immigrant."

6 Rabben 2016, 6–7.

7 Throughout the book I use "Latina/o" since that is the most common term used by the people I worked with to refer to themselves when using pan-ethnic labels. While there continues to be a range of labels/terms that seek to disrupt the gendered nature of language and capture the diversity of Latinidad—including gender, sexual, racial, linguistic, and ethnic diversity—such as "Latinx," "Latin@," LatinU," and "Latine," I employ "Latina/o" throughout as well as the labels people themselves used.

8 Press conference following Corso's raid, El Centro de Servicios Sociales, June 7, 2018.

9 LeBrón 2019, 330.

10 Buff 2019, 17. Paik, Ruiz, and Schreiber write, "Sanctuary offers a capacious concept with roots in religious and ethical genealogies that it carries with it, even in secular contexts" (2019, 3).

11 Rabben 2016, 31.

12 Rabben 2016, 48.

13 Villarreal 2019, 44. Linda Rabben also notes the ways that "Native American groups that had tense relationships with one another still offered and received sanctuary" (2016, 35). Villarreal in particular characterizes the 1680 Pueblo Revolt and its aftermath as a moment "flooded with migrants and refugees," and describes "the diverse sanctuaryscapes that Pueblo and Athapaskan peoples had forged before and after the revolt" (2019, 55, 57).

14 Paik, Ruiz, and Schreiber 2019, 4–5. Many scholars have noted that the rise of sovereign nation-states signaled a significant shift in sanctuary practices, although they never entirely disappeared. What remains constant is the way sanctuary operates as a way to challenge state power and authority.

15 See, for example, Pallares and Flores-González 2010; Pallares 2015; Rabben 2016; Lippert and Rehaag 2013; Cunningham 1995; Coutin 1993; Paik 2017, 2020; Paik, Ruiz, and Schreiber 2019; González 2022; Barba and Castillo-Ramos 2019, 2021; and Buff 2019.

16 Buff 2019, 17.

17 See Barba and Castillo-Ramos 2021 for a much-needed foregrounding of gender and the role of Latinas specifically in the sanctuary movement. Reverend John Fife is a Presbyterian minister and was pastor of Southside Presbyterian Church in Tucson, Arizona, in the 1980s. Reverend Fife and Jim Corbett played an important role in the 1980s sanctuary movement, something I detail further in chapter 1. Their role gained renewed attention following the 2016 presidential election as stories circulated in popular media connecting contemporary sanctuary movements with previous ones. In February and March 2017, for example, the podcast *99% Invisible* featured two episodes on the sanctuary movement and was one way this history gained renewed visibility among mainstream audiences following the 2016 presidential election. See "Church (Sanctuary, Part I)" and "State (Sanctuary, Part II)," *99% Invisible*, February 28, 2017 and March 7, 2017, https://99percentinvisible.org. Despite the attention sanctuary movements received following the 2016 presidential election, the New Sanctuary Movement dates back to 2007 as immigrant rights activists sought to challenge rising rates of deportations and family separation under President Obama. See Pallares 2015.

18 García 2006.

19 Paik, Ruiz, and Schreiber 2019, 2.

20 Villarreal, forthcoming, 9.

21 Pallares 2015.

22 Barba and Castillo-Ramos 2019, 13.

23 Paik 2020, 103.

24 Ransby 2018, 162. Part of this history and theory necessarily includes careful attention to the experiences of women of color, queer, and feminist organizing, such as the Combahee River Collective, whose "expansive and inclusive radical statement . . . begins by locating its authors in the hierarchy of the society and world we live in and grounds them in a set of lived experiences that create the basis for

(but are not *determinative* of) their radical critique of the status quo—capitalism, empire, white supremacy, and hetero-patriarchy" (Ransby 2018, 162).

25 Rabben 2016, 218.

26 González 2022, 214, 215.

27 See Hobson 2016 for a history of LGBT and radical queer organizing that included a trenchant critique of US imperialism, war, and racism. Erica R. Edwards's important work documents the role of Black feminist artists, intellectuals, and writers in contesting postwar US imperialism, including the poet June Jordan's writings based on her visits to Nicaragua during the US-fueled Contra war that, according to Edwards, "deepened an intrahemispheric analysis of police violence and counterinsurgency" (Edwards 2021, 215).

28 Pallares 2015, x, 23.

29 Paik, Ruiz, and Schreiber 2019, 3.

30 Hinojosa, Elmore, and González 2022; Vargas-Ramos and Stevens-Arroyo 2012; Espinosa, Elizondo, and Miranda 2005.

31 See Cadava's reflections on the elision of sustained and careful analysis of religion and faith in his own scholarship (2022, 301).

32 Hinojosa, Elmore, and González 2022, 3.

33 Hinojosa, Elmore, and González 2022, 1, 5. Referring to the humanitarian work of Sister Norma Pimentel along the US-Mexico border, Hinojosa, Elmore, and González argue that her efforts draw upon "a half-century-long tradition within Latino communities that has fused religion and politics. . . . Latino communities have drawn from their faith and spirituality to build networks of mutual aid, demand self-determination within institutions and social agencies tasked with serving them, organize movements for freedom, and . . . provide sanctuary for those seeking refuge."

34 Hinojosa 2014, 3.

35 Barba 2022, 139.

36 Barba 2022, 127.

37 Rodríguez V 2022, 146.

38 Barba 2022, 160.

39 Rodríguez V 2022, 161.

40 Vega 2022, 95. See also Sujey Vega's work on Latina/o communities in Indiana and the role of faith and religion in laying claim to belonging, Vega 2015.

41 See Hansen 2018; and Orozco Flores 2018.

42 See Zavella 2020, 2022; Bolivar 2022; Villarreal 2022; and A. Martínez 2022.

43 A. Martínez 2022, 255.

44 My understanding of precarity has been enhanced by the work of scholars and writers who have wrestled with similar questions, particularly during the global pandemic beginning in early 2020. I am especially indebted to the insights of my Oberlin College students, including Miriam Entin-Bell, whose honors thesis explored how residents in a multi-abled community navigated community care, collective support, and precarity in the early months of the pandemic. See Miriam

Entin-Bell, "Multi-Abled Community in a Precarious World: Living, Funding, and Caring in Camphill Village," honors thesis for Comparative American Studies, Oberlin College, April 10, 2023.

45 Hinojosa, Elmore, and González 2022, 4.

46 Tomlinson and Lipsitz 2013, 1.

47 Tomlinson and Lipsitz 2013, 1.

48 Tomlinson and Lipsitz 2013, 9, emphasis in the original.

49 Tomlinson and Lipsitz 2013, 9.

50 González 2022, 218. Many writers have demonstrated the cultural and social consequences of neoliberal political-economic ordering, including the rise in punitive governance, racialized policing, and what some have referred to as the "neoliberalization of consciousness" that increasingly characterizes contemporary US society. See, for example, Collins, di Leonardo, and Williams 2008.

51 Elaborating on the Latin American roots of liberation theology, the contributors to the anthology *Ethnographic Refusals, Unruly Latinidades* write in their collectively authored introduction, "Activists and scholars concerned with liberation struggles in the Americas have long been inspired by theologians like Father Gustavo Gutiérrez, with his emphasis on the centrality of 'liberating praxis' as the basis for the kind of solidarity and fellowship that should define interpersonal relationships and struggles to remedy inequality, or Archbishop Óscar Romero, who flouted church practices on behalf of the poor in El Salvador, or educator Paulo Freire, who argued for and lived by the principle of making the road by walking with ordinary people as they take control over their lives in Brazil" (Aparicio et al. 2022, xxiv).

52 Farmer 2013, 127.

53 In Groody 2013, 167.

54 See Orozco Flores 2018. The essays from *Ethnographic Refusals, Unruly Latinidades* (2022) provide detailed discussions of accompaniment as well as examples of how it informs the work of Latina/o ethnographers. My discussion of accompaniment here draws from the anthology's introduction. For examples of organizations using accompaniment as a framework guiding their engagement, see Freedom for Immigrants, www.freedomforimmigrants.org; NISGUA (Network in Solidarity with the People of Guatemala) and its Guatemala Accompaniment Project, https://nisgua.org; the Interfaith Movement for Human Integrity, Post-Release Accompaniment Project, www.im4humanintegrity.org; and the work of organizations like Taller de San José, which "offers accompaniment in a Mexican neighborhood in Chicago, helping service participants navigate health, judicial, and social service systems" (Villarreal Sosa, Díaz, and Hernández 2019, 21). See also Wilkinson and D'Angelo 2019.

55 González 2022, 213.

56 All of these data are from the 2021 American Community Survey by the US Census Bureau and summarized in the report "Ohio Hispanic Americans: Snapshot from the 2021 American Community Survey," https://devresearch.ohio.gov.

57 Rivera 2005.

58 José Mendiola, oral history interview by Emily Belle, Latina/o Oral Histories of
    Northeast Ohio Project, March 12, 2016, Amherst, OH.

59 For more about the negative impact of urban renewal policies on the Latina/o
    community in Lorain and the importance of the vibrant ethnic enclave along Vine
    Avenue, see oral histories and archival materials from the Latino Lorain History
    Project, a collaboration among the Lorain Historical Society, El Centro de Servi-
    cios Sociales, and Oberlin College. See Lorain Historical Society, www.latinolorain.
    org; and Oberlin College, https://latinolorain.oberlincollegelibrary.org.

60 See Pallares 2015; Paik 2017; Paik, Ruiz, and Schreiber 2019; Ellis 2019; Buff 2019;
    Diaz-Edelman 2017; Fuist, Braunstein, and Williams, 2017; J. Martínez 2017; Vega
    2015; and Hinojosa 2014, 2017.

CHAPTER 1. SANCTUARY CITIES, STREETS, AND CAMPUSES

 1 "Sanctuary" definition," Google.com, accessed April 1, 2023, www.google.com.

 2 Orozco and Anderson 2018, 5. The numbers of people living in public sanctu-
    ary shifted between 2016 and 2020 as some were able to leave and others entered
    for various legal reasons. Noel Anderson from the Church World Service noted
    that by 2019 the organization was aware of forty-four people living in sanctuary
    throughout at least fifteen states.

 3 Orozco and Anderson 2018, 6.

 4 Orozco and Anderson 2018.

 5 Paik, Ruiz, and Schreiber 2019, 2–3.

 6 Barba and Castillo-Ramos 2019, 17. Gerardo Cadava (2016) and María Cristina
    García (2006) document these binational, transnational, and regional networks
    that were foundational for the sanctuary movement in the 1980s. Aimee Villarreal
    argues, however, for a longer history of US sanctuary practices in the American
    Southwest that include Native American practices and interrogates the ways that
    the origin story of the US sanctuary movements "and scholarship about them, has
    a notable Protestant overtone that curiously overlooks Native American practices
    of hospitality as well as the robust Catholic tradition of church asylum that flour-
    ished in Spanish colonial America" (2019, 49).

 7 Stoltz Chinchilla, Hamilton, and Loucky 2009, 102.

 8 Stoltz Chinchilla, Hamilton, and Loucky 2009, 106. See also Barba and Castillo-
    Ramos 2019; García 2006; and Paik 2020.

 9 Barba and Castillo-Ramos 2019, 18.

10 García 2006, 98–99.

11 Stoltz Chinchilla, Hamilton, and Loucky 2009, 106.

12 Paik 2020, 107.

13 Gonzales 2013, 5.

14 Barba and Castillo-Ramos 2019, 21. See Díaz-Barriga and Dorsey 2020 for an
    incisive discussion about the contestations around the building of the border
    wall.

15 SB 1070 also made it a misdemeanor crime to be without legal documents. While some provisions of the law were struck down by the Supreme Court, one of the most notorious features, the ability of police to "demand 'papers' and investigate immigration status if they suspect a person is undocumented," was upheld in June 2012. See ACLU website, www.aclu.org.

16 See Chavez 2008.

17 Orozco and Anderson 2018, 4.

18 Pallares 2015, x, 23.

19 This strategy resonates with other feminist movements and organizing strategies such as las Madres de la Plaza de Mayo that used motherhood as the basis for political organizing and, more specifically, to challenge state violence.

20 Barba and Castillo-Ramos 2019, 23.

21 For a thorough discussion of the history and ascendency of family values rhetoric, gender, and gender complementarianism in conservative evangelical churches and political organizing, see Dowland 2015.

22 Reverend John Fife, interview by author, January 24, 2018, Tucson, AZ.

23 Escudero 2020, 3.

24 Beltrán 2014, 246–47.

25 Beltrán 2014, 247.

26 Angelo Mathay and Margie McHugh, "DACA at the Three Year Mark: High Pace of Renewals, but Processing Difficulties Evident," Migration Policy Institute, August 2015, www.migrationpolicy.org. From its inception and continuing into the present, DACA has faced consistent legal challenges both in the courts and in political discourse.

27 Muzaffar Chishti and Faye Hipsman, "All Eyes on US Federal Courts as Deferred Action Programs Halted," Migration Policy Institute, March 13, 2015, www.migra-tionpolicy.org.

28 Reverend Deborah Lee, interview by author, June 21, 2018, Oakland, CA.

29 Paik 2020, 113.

30 Reverend Alison Harrington, interview by author, January 23, 2018, Tucson, AZ.

31 Reverend Jeff Johnson, interview by author, June 15, 2018, San Pablo, CA.

32 Lee, interview by author, June 21, 2018.

33 Harrington, interview by author, January 23, 2018.

34 Reverend Pablo Morataya, interview by author, June 21, 2018, Oakland, CA.

35 Morataya, interview by author, June 21, 2018.

36 Lee, interview by author, June 21, 2018.

37 Harrington, interview by author, January 23, 2018.

38 Rios 2011.

39 Cacho 2012.

40 Jeff Johnson, interview by author, June 15, 2018.

41 Jeff Johnson, interview by author, June 15, 2018.

42 Executive Order 13758, "Enhancing Public Safety in the Interior of the United States," January 25, 2017, www.federalregister.gov.

43 Lee, interview by author, June 21, 2018.

44 Collingwood and Gonzalez O'Brien 2019, 6, 3. There is broad consensus about the difficulty of defining sanctuary cities; Melvin Delgado notes that identifying them is "an art rather than a science" because of the broad, dynamic, and often intentionally capacious ways they and other sanctuary spaces can be labeled and defined. Delgado 2018, 126.

45 Collingwood and Gonzalez O'Brien 2019, 4. See also González 2022. Some have also pointed to earlier examples of sanctuary cities and policies, such as Berkeley declaring itself a sanctuary city in 1971 to provide refuge to US soldiers unwilling to fight in the Vietnam War and the Los Angeles police department's Special Order 40 in 1979, which prevented its officers from making inquiries into someone's immigration status. See Delgado 2018, 105; Collingwood and Gonzalez O'Brien 2019, 6; and Ridgley 2012.

46 Collingwood and Gonzalez O'Brien 2019, 16.

47 Collingwood and Gonzalez O'Brien 2019, 4.

48 This post-9/11 anti-immigrant landscape included the establishment of the Department of Homeland Security, which was home to the new office of Immigration and Customs Enforcement; the Sensenbrenner Bill of 2005 proposing harsh criminal measures against undocumented immigrants and those who sought to help them; policies facilitating local law enforcement participation with federal immigration authorities to share information about deportable immigrants in custody, including the 287(g) and Secure Communities Programs, and sharing with ICE fingerprints of those in custody; and legislative efforts at the state level targeting immigrants, such as Arizona's SB 1070 in 2010, which, among other things, required people to provide documentation of legal residence if stopped by law enforcement, earning the name the "show me your papers" bill.

49 Collingwood and Gonzalez O'Brien 2019, 5.

50 Collingwood and Gonzalez O'Brien 2019, 5, 40. See also Delgado 2018 for an extensive discussion about the ways sanctuary resolutions are key in providing support not only to immigrant communities, but also to social workers and others who provide essential services.

51 Delgado 2018, 111.

52 Cleveland 19 News identified eight sanctuary locations: Columbus, Dayton, Lima, Lorain, Oberlin, and Painesville, as well as Lake and Lucas Counties. On January 30, 2017, Cincinnati formally declared itself a sanctuary city, with other cities like Cleveland Heights passing welcoming city resolutions. See Amanda Horncz, "Ohio's 8 Sanctuary Locations and What It Means for Immigration Matters," Cleveland 19 News, November 16, 2016, www.cleveland19.com; Jason Williams and Dan Horn, "Cincinnati a 'Sanctuary City.' What's That Mean?," Cincinnati Enquirer, January 30, 2017, www.cincinnati.com; Thomas Jewell, "Cleveland Heights Opts for 'Welcoming City,' as Opposed to Sanctuary Status on Immigration," Cleveland Plain Dealer, February 7, 2017, www.cleveland.com.

53 Oberlin City memo from Jon D. Clark, law director, to Ronnie Rimbert and Oberlin City Council members, February 17, 2017. For the city of Oberlin's sanctuary resolution, see www.cityofoberlin.com.

54 Celestino Rivera, interview by author, August 1, 2019, Oberlin, OH.

55 Rivera, interview by author, August 1, 2019.

56 See, for example, Georgetown Law's Institute for Constitutional Advocacy brief filed in Los Angeles, which included an amicus brief filed by elected prosecutors and law enforcement, including Celestino Rivera. "Prosecutors and Police Warn: DOJ's Sanctuary Cities Stance Endangers Public Safety," Georgetown Law, January 30, 2018, www.law.georgetown.edu.

57 Jackie Borchardt, "Ohio Treasurer Josh Mandel Backs Bill Banning 'Sanctuary Cities' in Ohio," *Cleveland Plain Dealer*, February 6, 2017, www.cleveland.com. See also Gina Pérez, "In Defense of Ohio's Sanctuary Cities," *Cleveland Plain Dealer*, February 24, 2017, www.cleveland.com.

58 Jeremy P. Kelly, "State Reps Want to Ban 'Sanctuary' Schools and Cities for Immigration," *Dayton Daily News*, March 26, 2019, www.daytondailynews.com.

59 "What's a Sanctuary Policy? FAQ on Federal, State and Local Action on Immigration Enforcement," National Conference of State Legislators, June 20, 2019, www.ncsl.org.

60 Collingwood and Gonzalez O'Brien 2019, 23–24.

61 Delgado 2018, 135–36.

62 Movimiento Cosecha, press release, March 3, 2017, www.lahuelga.com.

63 "Protect Undocumented Students at Berkeley," open letter to Chancellor Nicholas Dirks and Interim Executive Vice Chancellor Carol Christ, n.d., https://docs.google.com/forms/d/1Kfnc2CfrQFqp5pBkmImJN5zQsicVUTtzqErnotOA5kA/viewform?edit_requested=true. The idea of a "Fourth Amendment campus" or "constitutional campus" emerged as one possibility to ensure the kinds of protection people demanded without offering the "false sense of security" that sanctuary allegedly offered.

64 See Young 2019, 171. See also the Oberlin Sanctuary Project for more about the history of the college and town in sanctuary movements, https://libraries.oberlin.edu.

65 The letter in its entirety is as follows:

Dear President Krislov,
Given the outcome of the Presidential election, we call on Oberlin College to stand with other colleges and universities and investigate how to make Oberlin a sanctuary campus that will protect our community members from intimidation, unfair investigation, and deportation. The City of Oberlin has been a sanctuary city since 2009, and along with the city of Lorain is one of two sanctuary cities in Lorain County. Making Oberlin College a sanctuary campus supports these local efforts and demonstrates our commitment to support some of the most vulnerable members in our community.

The student group Obies for Undocumented Inclusion and the Undocumented Student Initiatives of the Multicultural Resource Center recently issued a call to action to raise awareness of and support undocumented students at Oberlin College. They also reminded us of the early efforts by concerned students who in fall 2013 issued a letter to the Board of Trustees in which they urged:

"We must remember that immigration and access to education are not new issues and that they weave into a history of inequality in this country . . . We need to contribute to this movement and remember that it is not just an action against global and national systems of oppression, but an action to support human dignity and respect in our communities."

This action will honor Oberlin's stated commitment to social justice, diversity, and inclusion, while extending its history of providing refuge for those seeking freedom. We urge you to immediately investigate how to make Oberlin College a sanctuary campus. Doing so will demonstrate our commitment to ensuring that Oberlin remains an institution of higher learning that actively protects the safety of all members of our community.

Sincerely,
Shelley Lee, Comparative American Studies and History
Gina Pérez, Comparative American Studies
Julio Reyes, Multicultural Resource Center
RaShelle Peck, Africana Studies
Pam Brooks, Africana Studies
Wendy Kozol, Comparative American Studies
Marcelo Vinces, Center for Learning, Education and Research in the Sciences

66 Young 2019, 171.
67 Marvin Krislov, "Statement in Support of Undocumented Students," December 1, 2016, www.oberlin.edu.
68 Elizabeth Redden, "Can a Campus Be a Sanctuary?," *Inside Higher Ed*, November 15, 2016, www.insidehighered.com.
69 Collingwood and Gonzalez O'Brien argue, "The sanctuary debate is thus not only about policy but also about the respective roles of local, state and federal officials in immigration enforcement" (2019, 8) and detail the ways both practical and ideological goals shape sanctuary debates. See also Young's analysis of how the sanctuary campus debates highlighted "whether schools or local governments should be required to cooperate with federal immigration enforcement" (2019, 172).
70 Villarreal, forthcoming, 10–11.

CHAPTER 2. "HAY UNA VIDA FUERA DE SANTUARIO—THERE IS LIFE OUTSIDE OF SANCTUARY"

1 Danae King, "Woman Says She Is in Sanctuary at Columbus Church for Her Family," *Columbus Dispatch*, October 4, 2017, www.dispatch.com. See also Jennifer Smola, "Mexican Woman Again Seeks Sanctuary in Columbus Church," *Columbus Dispatch*, October 3, 2017, www.dispatch.com. Edith Espinal remained in sanctuary at the Columbus Mennonite Church for forty months until receiving an order of supervision from Immigration and Customs Enforcement on February 18, 2021. She was one of many who left public sanctuary shortly after President Biden assumed office in January 2021.

2 Edith Espinal, interview by author, October 23, 2019, Columbus, OH.

3 Alexis Moberger, "Julian Castro Meets with Edith Espinal ahead of Democratic Debate," ABC News 6, October 15, 2019, https://abc6onyourside.com; Geneva Sands, "ICE Rescinds Half-Million Dollar Fine against Undocumented Immigrant Living in Ohio Church," CNN, October 22, 2019, www.cnn.com; Gabe Ortiz, "Undocumented Immigrant Formerly in Sanctuary Calls on Biden to Rescind Outrageous ICE Fines," *Daily Kos*, March 30, 2021, www.dailykos.com.

4 Espinal, interview by author, October 23, 2019.

5 Chavez 2008 describes diminished citizenship as the qualified citizenship that US-born children in mixed-status families experience as a result of the trauma and stigma of illegality and the pervasive Latino threat narrative.

6 Hilda Ramírez and her son entered into sanctuary in St. Andrew's Presbyterian Church, in Austin, Texas, where they remained until April 2021. See "Hilda and Alirio Walk out of Sanctuary and into Freedom for One Year," press release, Austin Sanctuary Network, April 14, 2021, https://austinsanctuarynetwork.org.

7 Samuel Oliver Bruno entered into sanctuary in CityWell Church, a multicultural Methodist church in Durham, North Carolina, in December 2017 and remained there until he was detained by ICE agents while visiting a government office and was deported to Mexico in December 2018. At a prayer service in front of the Wake County Detention Center, where Samuel was being detained, the civil rights leader Reverend William Barber II joined hundreds of others and explicitly connected state policies enabling immigrant detention and family separation of Latin American immigrants to those that ripped apart African American families as well, announcing, "This snatching of families has a deep and long and evil history and we will call it out for what it is . . . It's evil." Yonat Shimron, "Sanctuary Church, Supporters Resist Arrest and Deportation of Congregant," *Christian Century*, December 19, 2018, www.christiancentury.org. Sadly, Samuel died in Mexico in 2021 following a car crash in 2020. See "Immigrant Who Lived at Durham Sanctuary before Deportation Dies in Mexico after Car Crash," WRAL News, July 6, 2021, www.wral.com.

8 Eliseo Jiménez entered into sanctuary at the Umstead Park United Church of Christ in Raleigh, North Carolina, on October 10, 2017, and remained there for more than

three years until he left in March 2021. According to one report from the United Church of Christ, Eliseo was one of "three men, fathers with young children, [who] were welcomed into sanctuary by United Church of Christ congregations in October 2017." See Connie Larkman, "Eliseo Jimenez Soon Plans to Leave Sanctuary of North Carolina Church," United Church of Christ, March 25, 2021, www.ucc.org.

9 Carmela Hernández and her four children—Fidel, Keyri, Yoselin, and Edwin—entered into sanctuary at Church of the Advocate in North Philadelphia on December 13, 2017, and remained there for more than three years. In a sermon the church's pastor, Reverend Dr. Renee McKenzie, emphatically proclaimed the church's support for Carmela and her family as a radical act of love that is part of the church's DNA: "The Church of the Advocate is a place for radicals. No, I am not saying that the Advocate is a place for extremists. This is a place that believes and knows and lives the simple truth that God calls us to love radically, serve radically and welcome radically." See Jason Jensen, "Carmela Libre: Grant Asylum to Mother and Children in Sanctuary at Church of the Advocate," New Sanctuary Movement of Philadelphia, n.d., www.sanctuaryphiladelphia.org. Like Edith, Carmela and her family left sanctuary in the early days of the Biden administration in March 2021.

10 The use of ankle monitors is a common method of surveillance for migrants as well as people awaiting trial or on probation or parole. According to the ACLU, "Jurisdictions use this tracking technology to limit how long a person can stay outside and where they can go," and has been steadily on the rise. Ayomikun Idowu, Allison Frankel, and Yazmine Nichols, "Three People Share How Ankle Monitoring Devices Fail, Harm, and Stigmatize," ACLU, September 29, 2022, www.aclu.org.

11 Espinal, interview by author, October 23, 2019.

12 Reverend Joel Miller, interview by author, October 23, 2019, Columbus, OH.

13 According to the US Senate website, "A private bill provides benefits to specified individuals (including corporate bodies). Individuals sometimes request relief through private legislation when administrative or legal remedies are exhausted. Many private bills deal with immigration—granting citizenship or permanent residency. Private bills may also be introduced for individuals who have claims against the government, veterans' benefits claims, claims for military decorations, or taxation problems. The title of a private bill usually begins with the phrase, 'For the relief of. . . .' If a private bill is passed in identical form by both houses of Congress and is signed by the president, it becomes a private law," www.senate. gov. See also "Joyce Beatty Introduces Bill to Help Woman in Sanctuary Fight Deportation," press release, September 6, 2019, https://beatty.house.gov.

14 HR 4224, "For the Relief of Edith Espinal Moreno," www.congress.gov.

15 See Orozco Flores 2018 for extensive discussion of the pastoral and insurgent approaches to faith-based organizing.

16 According to its website, "HOLA is an award-winning, 501c3 charitable non-profit organization based in Painesville, Ohio, providing programs and services

to Hispanic workers, families and children. HOLA was founded in 1999 to serve the growing Hispanic community in Lake and Ashtabula counties, and has since expanded its reach to most of northern Ohio and beyond." www.holaohio.org.

17 Orozco Flores 2018, 169.

18 Pallares 2015, x.

19 Pallares 2015, 23.

20 King, "Woman Says She Is in Sanctuary."

21 Espinal, interview by author, October 23, 2019.

22 Stephanie Russell-Kraft, "Edith Espinal Has Spent 18 Months Hiding from ICE in a Church. How Much Longer Will the Authorities Let Her Stay?," *New Republic*, January 17, 2019, https://newrepublic.com.

23 Abrego 2014, 196.

24 Ashton Mara, "Two Days before Deportation, Akron Woman Claims Sanctuary," WOSU, September 13, 2017, https://news.wosu.org.

25 Michael Sangiacomo, "Akron Woman in Sanctuary in Cleveland Heights Church Wishes Ordeal Would End," *Cleveland Plain Dealer*, November 5, 2017, www.cleveland.com.

26 Espinal, interview by author, October 23, 2019.

27 In his powerful essay "Witnessing in Brown: On Making Dead to Let Live," Rosas also vividly conveys the pain, violence, and trauma of what it means to "make dead to let live." Refugees and asylees, he writes, "cannot represent themselves; they must be represented. Their lives and homelands must be represented as full of despair, pain, and hopelessness; mired in relations of precarity and dispossession; replete with graft and corruption. . . . They must make themselves—or they must be made—dead, like many others who cross the US-Mexico border without documentation, as well as many other kinds of border crossers around the globe" (2022, 191).

28 *Tres Madres: Three Mothers Fighting for Justice*, YouTube video, accessed April 2019, www.youtube.com/watch?v=UfmXS4fzVSs.

29 John Fife, interview by author, January 24, 2018, Tucson, AZ.

30 Orozco and Anderson 2018, 6.

31 Russell-Kraft, "Edith Espinal Has Spent 18 Months Hiding."

32 "Sanctuary for Edith," Columbus Mennonite Church, accessed November 20, 2017, www.columbusmennonite.org.

33 Miller, interview by author, October 23, 2019.

34 Reverend Dr. John Lentz, meeting with Forest Hills sanctuary team, August 9, 2018, Cleveland Heights, OH.

35 "Leonor, Ohio Mom of Four, Takes Sanctuary in Ohio Church," *America's Voice*, September 12, 2017, https://americasvoice.org.

36 The "sensitive location memo" is a 2011 memorandum issued by the Obama administration that establishes ICE policy and enforcement actions that "do not occur at nor are focused on sensitive locations such as schools and churches unless (a) exigent circumstances exist, (b) other law enforcement actions have

led officers to a sensitive location as described in the '*Exceptions to the General Rule*' section of this policy memorandum, or (c) prior approval is obtained." See "Memorandum for Field Office Directors, Special Agents in Charge, Chief Counsel," US Immigration and Customs Enforcement, Department of Homeland Security, October 24, 2011, www.ice.gov.

37 In Fyodor Dostoevsky's novel *The Brothers Karamazov*, Father Zosima explains the difference between active love and love in dreams: "Active love is a harsh and fearful thing compared with the love in dreams. Love in dreams thirsts for immediate action, quickly performed, and with everyone watching. Indeed, it will go as far as the giving even of one's life, provided it does not take long but is soon over, as on stage, and everyone is looking on and praising. Whereas active love is labor and persistence, and for some people, perhaps, a whole science."

38 Harrington, interview by author, January 24, 2018.

39 Fife, interview by author, January 24, 2018.

CHAPTER 3. "¡NO ESTÁS SOLO!"

1 Sabrina Eaon, "Sen. Sherrod Brown Says He's Working to Help Immigrant Families in Sandusky-Area Raid," *Cleveland Plain Dealer*, June 6, 2018, www.cleveland.com.

2 Previous to this, the largest workplace raid was in Postville, Iowa, on May 12, 2008, when 398 employees in meatpacking industries were arrested.

3 Press conference following Corso's raid, El Centro de Servicios Sociales, June 7, 2018.

4 Bonilla describes the coloniality of disaster in the following way: "how catastrophic events like hurricanes, earthquakes, but also other forms of political and economic crisis deepen the fault-lines of long-existing racial and colonial histories" (2020, 1).

5 "Bienvenidos a Lorain County: Un guía de nuestra comunidad de Lorain," December 11, 2017.

6 Lloréns 2021, 9.

7 Lloréns writes, for example, that "the archipelago experienced the longest blackout of US history and the second longest ever recorded globally" (9). Yarimar Bonilla and Marisol LeBrón document the devastation of Hurricane María and what they refer to as the "aftershocks of disaster." See Bonilla 2020; and Bonilla and LeBrón 2019.

8 Bonilla 2020, 2.

9 Rodríguez Soto 2017.

10 Hinojosa and Meléndez 2018, 1. Estimates of Puerto Rican exodus vary widely and reflect both the difficulty of capturing outflows and different methodologies used to capture Puerto Ricans relocating throughout the diaspora. See Yarimar Bonilla, "How Puerto Ricans Fit into an Increasingly Anti-Immigrant US," *Washington Post*, January 19, 2018, www.washingtonpost.com. See also Lloréns 2018. In October 2017, Meléndez and Hinojosa estimated that the post-María exodus could be

unprecedented: "Puerto Rico will lose the same population in a span of a couple of years after Hurricane María as the island lost during *a prior decade* of economic stagnation" (1, emphasis mine).

11   Vélez-Vélez and Villarrubia-Mendoza 2018, 542–43. PROMESA is the Puerto Rico Oversight, Management and Economic Stability Act passed in 2016 that installed a fiscal review board to restructure Puerto Rico's debt. Also referred to as "la junta," PROMESA has ushered in an era of unprecedented austerity measures that have had a devastating impact on public education, public pensions, and the economic livelihood of Puerto Ricans.

12   Lloréns 2018; Bonilla 2020.

13   Lydia DePillis, "Puerto Rican Exodus Could Boost Small Town USA," *CNN Money*, October 13, 2017, http://money.cnn.com.

14   Meléndez and Hinojosa 2017, 2.

15   Alicea and Toro-Morn 2018, 548.

16   Jill Sell, "The Aftermath of Hurricane María," *Cleveland Magazine*, April 19, 2018, https://clevelandmagazine.com.

17   Bruce Walton, "From Puerto Rico to Lorain, Students Learn to Adapt," *Chronicle-Telegram*, March 4, 2018, www.chroniclet.com. See also Michael Sangiacomo, "Lorain Responds to Needs of Puerto Rican Newcomers Six Months after María," *Cleveland Plain Dealer*, March 19, 2018, www.cleveland.com.

18   "Bienvenidos a Lorain County."

19   "Puerto Ricans in Ohio, the United States and Puerto Rico, 2014," Centro: Center for Puerto Rican Studies, April 2016.

20   Michael Sangiacomo, "Northeast Ohio Needs Coordinated Effort to Help Puerto Ricans Fleeing Hurricane," *Cleveland Plain Dealer*, November 13, 2017, www.cleveland.com. The differential treatment of Puerto Ricans—US citizens—was repeatedly invoked during heated discussions about the failure of the federal government to respond appropriately to the hurricane and its aftermath and was often attributed to Puerto Rico's colonial status and racial/ethnic subordination. These invocations were reminiscent of critiques of the Bush administration's chaotic response to largely Black and poor residents of New Orleans following Hurricane Katrina in 2005.

21   José Mendiola, interview by author, October 31, 2019, Amherst, OH.

22   Sister Cathy McConnell, interview by author, January 21, 2019, Lorain, OH.

23   Rivera, interview by author, August 1, 2019.

24   Victor Leandry, interview by author, March 20, 2019, Lorain, OH.

25   Leandry, interview by author, March 20, 2019.

26   McConnell, interview by author, January 21, 2019.

27   Leandry, interview by author, March 20, 2019.

28   Zavella writes, "All reproductive justice organizations that are integrating self-care, spiritual activism, and healing justice are following Norma Wong Roshi's advice: 'Self care is foundational to our power, our resilience, our creativity, our health and our collective impact.' By encouraging self-care and spiritual activism,

reproductive justice organizations are countering the burnout engendered by social activism" (2020, 180).

29 I want to thank Yarimar Bonilla for engaging me in conversations about the complicatedness of resilience. For one powerful critique of narratives of resilience, see Yarimar Bonilla, "Why Must Puerto Ricans Always Be Resilient?," *New York Times*, October 10, 2022, www.nytimes.com. See also Hilda Lloréns's work (2021), which offers a similar and important critique of resilience, even while also acknowledging and understanding its need and value in providing support for families, communities, and people that the state—local, national, federal—has neglected and/or actively contributed to their economic, social, political, and cultural dispossession.

30 Anabel Barrón Sánchez, oral history, "A Roller Coaster Life," interview by Caide Jackson, Latina/o/x Oral Histories of Northeast Ohio, Oberlin College.

31 Barrón Sánchez, oral history.

32 "Statement on the Emerging Crisis in Puerto Rico and the Response by the Catholic Church," Diocese of Cleveland, November 2, 2017, www.dioceseofcleveland. org. See also "Letter to Congress," United States Conference of Catholic Bishops, October 12, 2017, www.usccb.org.

33 Lloréns 2021, 169.

34 Lloréns 2021, 146.

35 "Statement from Most Reverend Nelson J. Pérez, Bishop of Cleveland, on the Administration's Decision to End the Deferred Action for Childhood Arrivals (DACA) program," Department of Communications, Diocese of Cleveland, September 7, 2017.

36 "Cleveland Bishop Nelson Says, 'Churches Have No Borders'; Prays for Immigration Reform," WKSU, July 9, 2018, www.wksu.org.

37 *Parish Companion Program Handbook*, Catholic Diocese of Cleveland, updated November 6, 2018.

38 *Parish Companion Program Handbook*.

39 Indeed, Protestant, Jewish, Muslim, and other faith-based activists, workers, and religious leaders have played an indispensable and visible role during these years, in particular organizing and participating in workshops, protests, prayer vigils, and daily acts supporting immigrants. In fact, throughout Trump's presidency, an ecumenical, Protestant-led prayer vigil took place weekly outside the ICE center in Brooklyn Heights protesting the detention of migrants while also seeking to provide support for those released and their family members. Jewish organizations and synagogues like Temple Israel of Akron were also deeply involved in immigrant advocacy and organizing through organizations like the Akron Area Interfaith Council and the Akron Interfaith Immigration Advocates. I want to thank Steve Volk for drawing my attention to these efforts; his work with interfaith and Jewish organizations has provided an important bridge among different faith-based immigrant advocacy over the years.

40 Bishop Nelson Pérez, interview by author, July 10, 2018, Cleveland, OH.

41 Pérez, interview by author, July 10, 2018.

42 Jen Picciano, "Ohio Teen Looking After Young Siblings after Mother Taken by ICE during Immigration Sting," Cleveland 19 News, June 18, 2018, www.cleveland19.com.

43 In my formal interviews and conversations with people like Victor Leandry, Sarah Johnson, and Anabel Barrón Sánchez, they shared the great toll that doing this work day after day, week after week had on them and the need for capacity-building to support employees even while they recognized their limited means and resources to do so.

44 Eli Saslow, "'Are You Alone Now?': After the Raid, Immigrant Families Are Separated in the Heartland," *Washington Post*, June 30, 2018, www.washingtonpost.com.

45 Saslow, "'Are You Alone Now?'"

46 Saslow, "'Are You Alone Now?'"

47 Scholars have amply documented the extent and depth of deportation, family separation, and immigrant detention. Some excellent examples include Miranda 2017; Golash-Boza 2012; and Abrego 2014. Journalists like Sonia Nazario have been equally indefatigable in their coverage of the costs of unauthorized immigration on families and communities both in the United States and in countries of origin. For a local perspective and critique of the impact of immigrant raids and family separation, see Steven S. Volk, "Our Immigrant Neighbors Are Not Violent Criminals to Be Uprooted and Separated from Their Children," *Cleveland Plain Dealer*, June 20, 2018, www.cleveland.com.

48 Zoe Greszler, "People Are Afraid," *Norwalk Reflector*, June 6, 2018, https://advertiser-tribune.com. See also Michael Harrington, "Immigrants Are 'Real People,'" *Sandusky Register*, June 26, 2018, https://sanduskyregister.com.

49 "Outrage at Mass Immigration Raid in Ohio," *America's Voice*, June 8, 2018, https://americasvoice.org.

50 "Outrage at Mass Immigration Raid in Ohio."

51 Sister Jane Omlar, "It's a Moral Issue," *Advertiser-Tribune*, June 14, 2018, https://advertiser-tribune.com.

52 "Outrage at Mass Immigration Raid in Ohio."

53 Greszler, "People Are Afraid."

54 Harrington, "Immigrants Are 'Real People.'"

55 "Outrage at Mass Immigration Raid in Ohio."

56 Michael Harrington, "Rally for Corso's Workers," *Sandusky Register*, June 11, 2018, https://sanduskyregister.com. See also Daniel Carson, "Ohio ICE Raid: Ohio Teen Helping Children of Arrested Workers," *Fremont News Messenger*, June 7, 2018, www.thenews-messenger.com; and Victoria Idoni, "Teen Is Helping Kids Affected by Immigration Raid," WTOL11 News, June 8, 2018, www.wtol.com. The Los Niños de Corso's Facebook page also includes posts, videos, and other information about their sustained efforts beginning in June 2018.

57 Justin Wise, "Franklin Graham Criticizes Trump Policy of Separating Families at Border," *The Hill*, June 13, 2018, https://thehill.com. Franklin Graham is also the son of the late evangelical leader and preacher Billy Graham.

58 Monica Gutierrez Alonso, "Natalia Alonso Goes Down to Mississippi to Assist the Families Affected by Largest ICE Raid," YouTube video, October 2019, www.youtube.com/watch?v=m29ty2vzz40.

59 Lloréns 2021, 8.

60 Lloréns 2021, 14.

CHAPTER 4. BECOMING SANCTUARY PEOPLE

1 Hondagneu-Sotelo 2008, xi.

2 Paik 2020.

3 Roediger 2016, 224.

4 Roediger 2016, 227.

5 Kelley 2002, 12.

6 My colleagues and dear friends Meredith Gadsby, Shelley Lee, and I offered three distinct courses as part of Oberlin College's Studio OC learning community, titled "Sanctuary Practices: Race, Refuge and Immigration in America." The goal was to invite students to explore questions of sanctuary and refuge from literary, historical, and anthropological approaches as well as across the fields of Africana, Asian American, and Latina/o studies.

7 Anabel Barrón Sánchez, interview by author, August 14, 2019, Lorain, OH.

8 Barrón Sánchez, interview by author, August 14, 2019.

9 Barrón Sánchez, interview by author, August 14, 2019.

10 Barrón Sánchez, interview by author, August 14, 2019.

11 Barrón Sánchez, interview by author, August 14, 2019.

12 Barrón Sánchez, interview by author, August 14, 2019.

13 See Mitchell and Pollack 2011. This history of Latinas/os in Lorain is also captured in the exhibit *Vine Avenue: 100 Years of Latinas/os in Lorain*, which premiered September 16, 2021. See https://latinolorain.org.

14 Mendiola, interview by author, October 31, 2019.

15 Mendiola, interview by author, October 31, 2019.

16 "About Us," HOLA, n.d., www.holaohio.org.

17 Mendiola, interview by author, October 31, 2019.

18 Bautista's pathbreaking work on Latino deacons in Ohio describes cursillos as "a gendered ethno-religious experience where machista narratives are confronted and/or reinforced," and details the pivotal role of the Cursillo movement in the lives of both Latino deacons and Latina/o religious laypeople more broadly. See Bautista 2013, 25.

19 Rivera, interview by author, August 1, 2019.

20 Rivera, interview by author, August 1, 2019.

21 Rivera, interview by author, August 1, 2019.

22 Rivera, interview by author, August 1, 2019.

23 See Hobson 2016, which details the history of LGBTQ rights activist solidarity efforts with Central American solidarity movements in the 1970s and 1980s.

24 Nabhan-Warren 2021, 9.

25 John Gates, interview by author, July 31, 2019, Oberlin, OH.

26 Gates, interview by author, July 31, 2019.

27 Steve Hammond, interview by author, August 13, 2019, Oberlin, OH.

28 Steve Hammond, interview by author, August 13, 2019.

29 Nancy Finke, interview by author, July 30, 2019.

30 Finke, interview by author, July 30, 2019.

31 David T. Hill, interview by author, September 4, 2019, Oberlin, OH.

32 Finke, interview by author, July 30, 2019.

33 NISGUA (Network in Solidarity with the People of Guatemala), "About Us," n.d., https://nisgua.org.

34 NISGUA, "About Us." NISGUA continues to adapt its work while preserving the centrality of accompaniment in its practice with the creation of GAP Internacionalista in 2019, "a visionary new accompaniment program that will connect trans-territorial movements for Indigenous sovereignty and immigrant justice."

35 Sarah Johnson, interview by author, August 22, 2019.

36 2020–2021 SEPA Annual Report, www.obsepa.org.

37 The Overground Railroad refers to organized efforts of sanctuary workers in the 1980s who used a complex network of people to move migrants from Central America through Mexico and the United States and often to Canada. See González 2022.

38 Gates, interview by author, July 31, 2019. For news coverage of the decision by First Church to become a sanctuary church in 2018, see Bruce Walton, "First Church in Oberlin Unanimously Votes to Become a Sanctuary Church," *Chronicle-Telegram*, April 24, 2018.

39 Mary Hammond, interview by author, August 12, 2019.

40 Brown 1984.

41 Mary Hammond, interview by author, August 12, 2019.

42 Mary Hammond, interview by author, August 12, 2019.

43 Finke, interview by author, July 30, 2019.

44 "Martyrs for Justice," n.d., informational paper in Martyr's Chapel, Jesuit Retreat Center, Parma, OH.

45 Dorothy Kazel was an Ursuline Sister, while Ita Ford and Maura Clarke were Maryknoll Sisters.

46 "Martyrs for Justice," informational paper.

47 Margaret Swedish, "Ita, Maura, Dorothy, Jean: The Legacy of 4 Missionaries Murdered in El Salvador 40 Years Ago," *America*, December 2, 2020, www.americamagazine.org. This powerful article commemorating the fortieth anniversary provides important details and reflections on their lives.

48 Swedish, "Ita, Maura, Dorothy, Jean."

49 McConnell, interview by author, January 21, 2019.

50 *Parish Companion Program Handbook*, Catholic Diocese of Cleveland, updated December 5, 2018.

51 Mendiola, interview by author, October 31, 2019.

52 Rivera, interview by author, August 1, 2019.

53 Barrón Sánchez, interview by author, August 14, 2019.

54 Kornblith and Lasser 2018, 2.

55 Steve Hammond, interview by author, August 13, 2019.

56 Steve Hammond, interview by author, August 13, 2019.

57 In the spring of 2018, Oberlin College faculty, staff, and alumni, as well as city residents, collaborated to develop a traveling interactive exhibit titled *Courage and Compassion*, which documented the role of Oberlin City and the college in enrolling Japanese American students and providing them refuge and safety in the town and on campus during Japanese internment. This exhibit was supported by the Go For Broke National Education Center and the National Park Service. See "Courage and Compassion: Our Shared Story of the Japanese American World War II Experience," February 16, 2018, www.oberlin.edu.

58 Steve Hammond, interview by author, August 13, 2019.

59 Gates, interview by author, July 31, 2019.

60 Hill, interview by author, September 4, 2019.

61 See "Immigration Raids Ohio Restaurants, Arrest 58," Reuters, July 23, 2008, www.reuters.com; Martha Grevatt, "Ohioans Demand: Stop the Raids," *Workers World*, August 8, 2008, www.workers.org; Richard Payerchin, "Restaurant Owner Charged with Immigration Offenses," *Lorain Morning Journal*, January 22, 2010, www.morningjournal.com.

62 Hill, interview by author, September 4, 2019.

63 Kornblith and Lasser 2018, 252.

64 Finke, interview by author, July 30, 2019.

65 Rivera, interview by author, August 1, 2019.

CONCLUSION

1 Miriam Jordan and Remy Tumin, "'I Ended Up on This Little Island': Migrants Land in Political Drama," *New York Times*, September 15, 2022, www.nytimes.com.

2 Jordan and Tumin, "'I Ended Up on This Little Island.'"

3 Will Sennott, Zolan Kanno-Youngs, Eileen Sullivan, and Patricia Mazzei, "With Faraway Migrant Drop-Offs, G.O.P. Governors Are Doubling Down," *New York Times*, September 15, 2022, www.nytimes.com. Governor DeSantis's actions, however, were supported by elected officials and others in his state, with the *New York Times* reporting that in 2022 "the Florida Legislature set aside $12 million to transport migrants out of the state."

4 Sennott et al., "With Faraway Migrant Drop-Offs."

5 According to the *New York Times*, between August 9 and September 14, 2022, "the population of the main shelter system . . . [grew] by more than 5,000, from 51,000 to nearly 56,000, an increase of nearly 10 percent." In the week alone prior to their

reporting, "the shelter population has jumped by over 1,000." See Andy Newman, "Adams Wants to Reassess a Shelter System 'Nearing Its Breaking Point,'" *New York Times*, September 14, 2022, www.nytimes.com.

6 By early October 2022, the number of people in New York City's shelter system "stood at 61,379" and was poised to "break the record of 61,415 set in 2019." An emergency declaration "allows the city to open emergency relief centers more quickly by exempting them from the normal land-use and community-review process that often slows the opening of shelters." See Andy Newman and Emma G. Fitzsimmons, "New York Faces Record Homelessness as Mayor Declares Migrant Emergency," *New York Times*, October 7, 2022, www.nytimes.com.

7 Newman and Fitzsimmons report, "Even setting aside the 12,700 migrants in shelters, the population of the city's main shelter system has risen by 6 percent since mid-April—the biggest jump in that short a time since 2015." Newman and Fitzsimmons, "New York Faces Record Homelessness." See also Mihir Zaveri, "Discrimination Weakens Tool for Reducing N.Y. Homelessness, Lawsuit Says," *New York Times*, May 25, 2022, www.nytimes.com.

8 Mayor Adams made it a point to distinguish between Mayor Leeser's approach and Governor Abbott's in that Leeser was "willing to meet and 'figure out a humane way to coordinate.'" For his part, Mayor Leeser also distanced his practices from those of the governor by emphasizing his administration's coordination with local officials in receiving cities. According to a Reuters report, the mayor maintained that El Paso's program is "completely different" from the other busing efforts and that it seeks to "treat people with respect." See Ted Hesson, Paul Ratje, and Kristina Cook, "Democrat-Led Texas City Steps Up Migrant Busing to New York, Outpacing Republican Effort," Reuters, October 6, 2022, www.reuters.com.

9 Hesson, Ratje, and Cook, "Democrat-Led Texas City."

10 Patricia Mazzei, Remy Tumin, and Eliza Fawcett, "Florida Flies 2 Planeloads of Migrants to Martha's Vineyard," *New York Times*, September 14, 2022, www.nytimes.com.

11 Karen Zraik, "Migrants in New York Are Grateful for Help. But They Want to Work," *New York Times*, October 17, 2022, www.nytimes.com.

12 See Gina Pérez, "In Defense of Ohio's Sanctuary Cities," *Cleveland Plain Dealer*, February 24, 2017, www.cleveland.com.

13 Brittany Shammas, "Voters Declare Lubbock, Tex., a 'Sanctuary for the Unborn' in Effort to Ban Abortions," *Washington Post*, May 5, 2021, www.washingtonpost.com.

14 Ed Richter, "Lebanon Council Votes to Become Sanctuary City for the Unborn, Outlaws Abortion in City," *Dayton Daily News*, May 26, 2021, www.daytondailynews.com.

15 Emily Wax-Thibodeaux, "Mark Lee Dickson Paved the Way for the Texas Abortion Ban, One Small Town at a Time," *Washington Post*, September 16, 2021, www.washingtonpost.com.

16 Erika I. Ritchie and Kaitlyn Schallhorn, "After Public Outcry, San Clemente Rejects 'Anti-Abortion Sanctuary for Life' Resolution," *Orange County Register*, August 10, 2022, www.ocregister.com.

17 Kristen Hwang, "Newsom Signs Abortion Protections into Law," *CalMatters*, September 27, 2022, https://calmatters.org; Melody Gutierrez, "Bills Aimed at Creating California Abortion Sanctuary Headed for Newsom," *Los Angeles Times*, September 1, 2022, www.latimes.com.

18 "Governor Abbott Signs Second Amendment Legislation into Law," press release, June 17, 2022, https://gov.texas.gov.

19 Hatewatch Staff, "Popular among Antigovernment Extremists, 'Second Amendment Sanctuary' Resolutions Pose Risks," Southern Poverty Law Center, April 5, 2021, www.splcenter.org.

20 Paik 2020.

21 Ransby 2018.

22 See Felipe Hinojosa's remarkable book *Apostles of Change: Latino Radical Politics, Church Occupations, and the Fight to Save the Barrio* for a discussion of how Latinas/os' involvement in freedom movements in the 1960s not only blurred boundaries between politics and faith, but also offered "a bold new vision for the church and the world."

23 Danae King, "Coronavirus: Isolation Nothing New for Immigrant Edith Espinal after 2 1/2 Years in Sanctuary at Ohio Church," *Columbus Dispatch*, March 31, 2022, www.dispatch.com.

24 Fife, interview by author, January 24, 2018.

BIBLIOGRAPHY

Abrego, Leisy. 2014. *Sacrificing Families: Navigating Laws, Labor, and Love across Borders*. Stanford, CA: Stanford University Press.

Alicea, Marisa, and Maura Toro-Morn. 2018. "Puerto Rican Chicago *Dice Presente*: Preliminary Reflections on Community Responses to Hurricanes Irma and María." *Latino Studies* 16: 548–58.

Aparicio, Ana, Andrea Bolivar, Alex Chávez, Sherina Feliciano-Santos, Santiago Ivan Guerra, Gina M. Pérez, Jonathan Rosa, Gilberto Rosas, Aimee Villarreal, and Patricia Zavella. 2022. "Introduction." In *Ethnographic Refusals, Unruly Latinidades*, edited by Alex E. Chávez and Gina M. Pérez, xiii–xxxv. Albuquerque: University of New Mexico Press.

Barba, Lloyd D. 2022. "Pentecostalism's Instrumental Faith and Alternative Power: César Chávez and Reies López Tijerina among Pentecostal Farmworkers, 1954–1956." In *Faith and Power: Latino Religious Politics since 1945*, edited by Felipe Hinojosa, Maggie Elmore, and Sergio M. González, 121–44. New York: New York University Press.

Barba, Lloyd, and Tatyana Castillo-Ramos. 2019. "Sacred Resistance: The Sanctuary Movement, from Reagan to Trump." *Perspectivas*, no. 16, 11–36.

———. 2021. "Latinx Leadership and Legacies in the US Sanctuary Movement, 1980-2020." *American Religion* 3(1): 1–24.

Bau, Ignatius. 1985. *The Ground Is Holy: Church Sanctuary and Central American Refugees*. New York: Paulist Press.

Bautista, Adrian. 2013. "Vatos Sagrados: Cursillo and a Midwestern Catholic Borderlands." *Diálogo* 16(2): 19–26.

Beltrán, Cristina. 2014. "'No Papers, No Fears': DREAM Activism, New Social Media, and the Queering of Immigrant Rights." In *Contemporary Latina/o Media: Production, Circulation, Politics*, edited by Arlene Dávila and Yeidy M. Rivero, 245–66. New York: New York University Press.

Bolivar, Andrea. 2022. "Trans-Latina *Fantasías*: Creating Trans Latina Selves, Families, and Futures." In *Ethnographic Refusals, Unruly Latinidades*, edited by Alex E. Chávez and Gina M. Pérez, 115–33. Albuquerque: University of New Mexico Press.

Bonilla, Yarimar. 2020. "The Coloniality of Disaster." *Political Geography* 78: 102181.

Bonilla, Yarimar, and Marisol LeBrón, eds. 2019. *Aftershocks of Disaster: Puerto Rico before and after the Storm*. Chicago: Haymarket Books.

Brown, Robert McAfee. 1984. *Unexpected News: Reading the Bible through Third World Eyes*. Louisville, KY: Westminster John Knox Press.

Buff, Rachel I. 2019. "Sanctuary Everywhere: Some Keywords, 1945–Present." *Radical History Review*, October, 15–42.

Cacho, Lisa. 2012. *Social Death: Racialized Rightlessness and the Criminalization of the Unprotected*. New York: New York University Press.

Cadava, Gerardo. 2016. *Standing on Common Ground: The Making of a Sunbelt Borderland*. Cambridge, MA: Harvard University Press.

———. 2022. "Afterword." In *Faith and Power: Latino Religious Politics since 1945*, edited by Felipe Hinojosa, Maggie Elmore, and Sergio M. González, 299–307. New York: New York University Press.

Chávez, Alex E., and Gina M. Pérez, eds. 2022. *Ethnographic Refusals, Unruly Latinidades*. Albuquerque: University of New Mexico Press.

Chavez, Leo R. 2008. *The Latino Threat: Constructing Immigrants, Citizens, and the Nation*. Stanford: Stanford University Press.

Collingwood, Loren, and Benjamin Gonzalez O'Brien. 2019. *Sanctuary Cities: The Politics of Refuge*. New York: Oxford University Press.

Collins, Jane, Micaela di Leonardo, and Brett Williams. 2008. *New Landscapes of Inequality: Neoliberalism and the Erosion of Democracy in America*. Santa Fe: School of Advanced Research.

Coutin, Susan Bibler. 1993. *The Culture of Protest: Religious Activism and the US Sanctuary Movement*. Boulder: Westview.

Crittenden, Ann. 1988. *Sanctuary: A Story of American Conscience and the Law in Collision*. New York: Weidenfeld and Nicolson.

Cunningham, Hilary. 1995. *God and Caesar at the Rio Grande: Sanctuary and the Politics of Religion*. Minneapolis: University of Minnesota Press.

Delgadillo, Theresa. 2015. *Latina Lives in Milwaukee*. Champaign: University of Illinois Press.

Delgado, Melvin. 2018. *Sanctuary Cities, Communities, and Organizations: A Nation at a Crossroads*. New York: Oxford University Press.

Díaz-Barriga, Miguel, and Margaret Dorsey. 2020. *Fencing in Democracy: Border Walls, Necrocitizenship, and the Security State*. Durham: Duke University Press.

Diaz-Edelman, Mia. 2017. "Activist Etiquette in the Multicultural Immigrant Rights Movement." In *Religion and Progressive Activism: New Stories about Politics and Faith*, edited by Ruth Braunstein, Todd Nicholas Fuist, and Rhys H. Williams, 138–60. New York: New York University Press.

Dowland, Seth. 2015. *Family Values and the Rise of the Christian Right*. Philadelphia: University of Pennsylvania Press.

Edwards, Erica R. 2021. *The Other Side of Terror: Black Women and the Culture of US Empire*. New York: New York University Press.

Ellis, Treva. 2019. "From Sanctuary to Safe Space: Gay and Lesbian Police-Reform Activism in Los Angeles." *Radical History Review*, October, 95–118.

Escudero, Kevin. 2020. *Organizing While Undocumented: Immigrant Youth's Activism under the Law*. New York: New York University Press.

Espinosa, Gastón, Virgilio Elizondo, and Jesse Miranda, eds. 2005. *Latino Religions and Civic Activism in the United States*. New York: Oxford University Press.

Farmer, Paul. 2013. "Conversion in the Time of Cholera: A Reflection on Structural Violence and Social Change." In *In the Company of the Poor: Conversations with Dr. Paul Farmer and Fr. Gustavo Gutiérrez*, edited by Michael Griffin and Jennie Weiss Block, 95–146. New York: Orbis.

Fuist, Todd Nicholas, Ruth Braunstein, and Rhys H. Williams. 2017. "Introduction: Religion and Progressive Activism—Introducing and Mapping the Field." In *Religion and Progressive Activism: New Stories about Politics and Faith*, edited by Ruth Braunstein, Todd Nicholas Fuist, and Rhys H. Williams, 1–25. New York: New York University Press.

García, María Cristina. 2005. "'Dangerous Times Call for Risky Responses': Latino Immigration and Sanctuary." In *Latino Religions and Civic Activism in the United States*, edited by Gastón Espinosa, Virgilio Elizondo, and Jesse Miranda, 159–73. New York: Oxford University Press.

———. 2006. *Seeking Refuge: Central American Migration to Mexico, the United States, and Canada*. Berkeley: University of California Press.

Golash-Boza, Tanya Maria. 2012. *Immigration Nation: Raids, Detentions, and Deportations in Post-9/11 America*. Boulder, CO: Paradigm.

Gonzales, Alfonso. 2013. *Reform without Justice: Latino Migrant Politics and the Homeland Security State*. New York: Oxford University Press.

González, Sergio M. 2022. "Political Fellowship and the Sanctuary Movement: Central American Refugees and Practices of Religiopolitical Accompaniment, 1982–1990." In *Faith and Power: Latino Religious Politics since 1945*, edited by Felipe Hinojosa, Maggie Elmore, and Sergio M. González, 211–32. New York: New York University Press.

Griffin, Michael, and Jennie Weiss Block, eds. 2013. *In the Company of the Poor: Conversations with Dr. Paul Farmer and Fr. Gustavo Gutiérrez*. New York: Orbis.

Groody, Daniel G. 2013. "Reimagining Accompaniment: An Interview with Paul Farmer and Gustavo Gutiérrez." In *In the Company of the Poor: Conversations with Dr. Paul Farmer and Fr. Gustavo Gutiérrez*, edited by Michael Griffin and Jennie Weiss Block, 161–88. New York: Orbis.

Hansen, Helena. 2018. *Addicted to Christ: Remaking Men in Puerto Rican Pentecostal Drug Ministries*. Berkeley: University of California Press.

Hinojosa, Felipe. 2014. *Latino Mennonites: Civil Rights, Faith, and Evangelical Culture*. Baltimore: Johns Hopkins University Press.

———. 2017. "Religious Migrants: The Latina/o Mennonite Quest for Community and Civil Rights." In *The Latina/o Midwest Reader*, edited by Omar Valerio-Jiménez, Santiago Vaquera-Vásquez, and Claire F. Fox, 213–28. Urbana: University of Illinois Press.

———. 2022. *Apostles of Change: Latino Radical Politics, Church Occupations, and the Fight to Save the Barrio*. Austin: University of Texas Press.

Hinojosa, Felipe, Maggie Elmore, and Sergio M. González, eds. 2022. *Faith and Power: Latino Religious Politics since 1945*. New York: New York University Press.

Hinojosa, Jennifer, and Edwin Meléndez. 2018. "Puerto Rican Exodus: One Year since Hurricane María." Research Brief, Center for Puerto Rican Studies, September.

Hobson, Emily. 2016. *Lavender and Red: Liberation and Solidarity in the Gay and Lesbian Left*. Berkeley: University of California Press.

Hondagneu-Sotelo, Pierrette. 2008. *God's Heart Has No Borders: How Religious Activists Are Working for Immigrant Rights*. Berkeley: University of California Press.

Kelley, Robin D. G. 2002. *Freedom Dreams: The Black Radical Imagination*. Boston: Beacon.

Kornblith, Gary J., and Carol Lasser. 2018. *Elusive Utopia: The Struggle for Racial Equality in Oberlin, Ohio*. Baton Rouge: Louisiana State University Press.

LeBrón, Marisol. 2019. "Building Accountability and Secure Futures: An Interview with Mari Mari Narváez." In *Aftershocks of Disaster: Puerto Rico before and after the Storm*, edited by Yarimar Bonilla and Marisol LeBrón, 319–31. Chicago: Haymarket Books.

Lin, Tony Tian-Ren. 2020. *Prosperity Gospel Latinos and Their American Dream*. Chapel Hill: University of North Carolina Press.

Lippert, Randy K., and Sean Rehaag, eds. 2013. *Sanctuary Practices in International Perspectives: Migration, Citizenship, and Social Movements*. New York: Routledge.

Lloréns, Hilda. 2018. "Imagining Disaster: Puerto Rico through the Eye of Hurricane María." *Transforming Anthropology* 26(2).

———. 2021. *Making Livable Worlds: Afro-Puerto Rican Women Building Environmental Justice*. Seattle: University of Washington Press.

Lorentzen, Robin. 1991. *Women in the Sanctuary Movement*. Philadelphia: Temple University Press.

Martínez, Anne M. 2022. "The Spiritual Is Political: The Pilsen Via Crucis as a Path to Resistance." In *Faith and Power: Latino Religious Politics since 1945*, edited by Felipe Hinojosa, Maggie Elmore, and Sergio M. González, 253–72. New York: New York University Press.

Martínez, Juan R. 2017. "Religious Culture and Immigrant Civic Participation." In *Religion and Progressive Activism: New Stories about Politics and Faith*, edited by Ruth Braunstein, Todd Nicholas Fuist, and Rhys H. Williams, 205–24. New York: New York University Press.

Matovina, Timothy. 2012. *Latino Catholicism: Transformation in America's Largest Church*. Princeton: Princeton University Press.

Meléndez, Edwin, and Jennifer Hinojosa. 2017. "Estimates of Post-Hurricane María Exodus from Puerto Rico." *CENTRO*, October 2017.

Miranda, Almita. 2017. "Living in Legal Limbo: Migration, Citizenship, and Mexican Mixed-Status Families in the Neoliberal Era." PhD diss., Northwestern University, Evanston, IL.

Mitchell, Pablo, and Haley Pollack. 2011. "Making the 'International City' Home: Latinos in Twentieth-Century Lorain, Ohio." In *Beyond El Barrio: Everyday Life in*

Latina/o America, edited by Gina M. Pérez, Frank A. Guridy, and Adrian Burgos Jr., 149–67. New York: New York University Press.

Nabhan-Warren, Kristy. 2021. *Meatpacking America: How Migration, Work, and Faith Unite and Divide the Heartland*. Chapel Hill: University of North Carolina Press.

Nazario, Sonia. 2007. *Enrique's Journey: A Story of a Boy's Dangerous Odyssey to Reunite with His Mother*. New York: Random House.

Nepstad, Sharon Erickson. 2019. *Catholic Social Activism: Progressive Movements in the United States*. New York: New York University Press.

Orozco, Myrna, and Noel Anderson. 2018. "Sanctuary in the Age of Trump." Church World Service, January.

Orozco Flores, Edward. 2018. *"Jesus Saved an Ex-Con": Political Activism and Redemption after Incarceration*. New York: New York University Press.

Paik, Naomi. 2017. "Abolitionist Futures and the US Sanctuary Movement." *Race & Class* 59(2): 3–25.

———. 2020. *Bans, Walls, Raids, Sanctuary: Understanding US Immigration for the Twenty-First Century*. Berkeley: University of California Press.

Paik, Naomi, Jason Ruiz, and Rebecca Schreiber. 2019. "Sanctuary's Radical Networks." *Radical History Review*, October, 1–13.

Pallares, Amalia. 2015. *Family Activism: Immigrant Struggles and the Politics of Noncitizenship*. New Brunswick, NJ: Rutgers University Press.

Pallares, Amalia, and Nilda Flores-González, eds. 2010. *¡Marcha!: Latino Chicago and the Immigrant Rights Movement*. Urbana: University of Illinois Press.

Pérez, Gina M. 2015. *Citizen, Student, Soldier: Latina/o Youth, JROTC, and the American Dream*. New York: New York University Press.

———. 2022. "Becoming Sanctuary People: Latina/o Practices of Accompaniment in Northeast Ohio." In *Ethnographic Refusals, Unruly Latinidades*, edited by Alex E. Chávez and Gina M. Pérez, 153–74. Albuquerque: University of New Mexico Press.

Rabben, Linda. 2016. *Sanctuary and Asylum: A Social and Political History*. Seattle: University of Washington Press.

Ransby, Barbara. 2018. *Making All Black Lives Matter: Reimagining Freedom in the 21st Century*. Berkeley: University of California Press.

Ridgley, Jennifer. 2012. "The City as Sanctuary in the United States." In *Sanctuary Practices in International Perspectives: Migration, Citizenship, and Social Movements*, edited by Randy Lippert and Sean Rehaag, 219–31. New York: Routledge.

Rios, Victor. 2011. *Punished: Policing the Lives of Black and Latino Boys*. New York: New York University Press.

Rivera, Eugene. 2005. "La Colonia de Lorain." In *The Puerto Rican Diaspora: Historical Perspectives*, edited by Carmen Whalen, 151–73. Philadelphia: Temple University Press.

Rivera-Servera, Ramón. 2012. *Performing Queer Latinidad: Dance, Sexuality, Politics*. Ann Arbor: University of Michigan Press.

Rodríguez Soto, Isa. 2017. "Colonialism's Orchestrated Disasters in Puerto Rico." *Anthropology News*, November 27.

Rodríguez V, Jorge Juan. 2022. "Lived Religion in East Harlem: The New York Young Lords Occupy First Spanish—The People's Church." In *Faith and Power: Latino Religious Politics since 1945*, edited by Felipe Hinojosa, Maggie Elmore, and Sergio M. González, 145–65. New York: New York University Press.

Roediger, David. 2016. "Making Solidarity Uneasy: Cautions on a Keyword from Black Lives Matter to the Past." *American Quarterly* 68(2): 223–48.

Rosas, Gilberto. 2022. "Witnessing in Brown: On Making Dead to Let Live." In *Ethnographic Refusals, Unruly Latinidades*, edited by Alex E. Chávez and Gina M. Pérez, 175–94. Albuquerque: University of New Mexico Press.

Stoltz Chinchilla, Norma, Nora Hamilton, and James Loucky. 2009. "The Sanctuary Movement and Central American Activism in Los Angeles." *Latin American Perspectives* 36(6): 101–26.

Tomlinson, Barbara, and George Lipsitz. 2013. "American Studies as Accompaniment." *American Quarterly* 65(1): 1–30.

———. 2019. *Insubordinate Spaces: Improvisation and Accompaniment for Social Justice.* Philadelphia: Temple University Press.

Vargas-Ramos, Carlos, and Anthony Stevens-Arroyo, eds. 2012. *Blessing La Política: The Latino Religious Experience and Political Engagement in the United States.* New York: Praeger.

Vega, Sujey. 2015. *Latino Heartland: Of Borders and Belonging in the Midwest.* New York: New York University Press.

———. 2022. "Latina/o Mormons: Spanish-Speaking Saints Negotiating Identity in the Deseret." In *Faith and Power: Latino Religious Politics since 1945*, edited by Felipe Hinojosa, Maggie Elmore, and Sergio M. González, 94–117. New York: New York University Press.

Vélez-Vélez, Roberto, and Jaqueline Villarrubia-Mendoza. 2018. "Cambio desde abajo y desde adentro: Notes on Centros de Apoyo Mutuo in Post-Hurricane María, Puerto Rico." *Latino Studies* 16(4): 542–47.

Villarreal, Aimee. 2019. "Sanctuaryscapes in the North American Southwest." *Radical History Review*, October, 43–70.

———. 2022. "*Anthropolocura* as Homeplace Ethnography." In *Ethnographic Refusals, Unruly Latinidades*, edited by Alex E. Chávez and Gina M. Pérez, 195–218. Albuquerque: University of New Mexico Press.

———. Forthcoming. *Sanctuaryscapes in the New Mexico Borderlands: Movements and Revivals across the Secular-Religious Divide.* Chapel Hill: University of North Carolina Press.

Villarreal Sosa, Leticia, Silvia Díaz, and Rosalba Hernández. 2019. "Accompaniment in a Mexican American Community: Conceptualization and Identification of Biopsychosocial Outcomes." *Journal of Religion and Spirituality in Social Work* 38(1): 21–42.

Wilkinson, Meredith T., and Karen D'Angelo. 2019. "Community-Based Accompaniment and Social Work—A Complementary Approach to Social Action." *Journal of Community Practice* 27(2): 151–67.

Wilson, Catherine E. 2008. *The Politics of Latino Faith: Religion, Identity and Urban Community*. New York: New York University Press.

Young, Elliott. 2019. "From Sanctuary to Civil Disobedience: History and Praxis." *Radical History Review*, October, 171–80.

Yukich, Grace. 2013. *One Family under God: Immigration Politics and Progressive Religion in America*. New York: Oxford University Press.

Zavella, Patricia. 2020. *The Movement for Reproductive Justice: Empowering Women of Color through Social Activism*. New York: New York University Press.

———. 2022. "'While You Are Struggling, You Are Healing': Latinas Enact *Poder* through the Movement for Reproductive Justice." In *Ethnographic Refusals, Unruly Latinidades*, edited by Alex E. Chávez and Gina M. Pérez, 1–24. Albuquerque: University of New Mexico Press.

INDEX

accompaniment, 32, 141; a discourse that captures the ways faith-based organization articulated safety, refuge, and sanctuary, 101, 112; a disposition, a sensibility, and a pattern of behavior, 14; affinity to welcoming the stranger actions, 97, 100; a potential corrective to neoliberal hegemony, 14, 162; a principle of being and knowing within a commitment to the poor and marginalized communities, 14; articulation with human rights, 134; as a challenge to state-sanctioned terror and violence, 98; as a liberatory praxis, 6; as a process based in humility, discernment, careful listening, and proximity, 14-15; associated with pilgrimage, walking with, and solidarity, 98; Bishop Pérez, Nelson, emphasized the importance of, 96-98, 100; can encompass religio-political dimensions, 15; challenges criminalization narratives, 98; close interrelation with solidarity, 7; close relationship to sanctuary, 13, 29; concept circumvented the discourse of sanctuary, 98, 99; guides the work of many social justice activists, 15; has a long history in Catholic social teaching, 97-98; informed by liberation theology and a commitment to solidarity and fellowship, 14, 15, 96-97; legal, 30; not exclusive to Catholic social teachings, 97; part of new ontologies and epistemologies grounded in an ethic of care, sanctuary, and, 82; salient to sanctuary as advocacy, networks of protection and housing hospitality, 29, 95; secular dimensions of, 133. *See also* Santa Elena Project of Accompaniment; solidarity

Anderson, Noel: changes in sanctuary patterns, 177n2; on mobilization under the New Sanctuary Movement, 25

Angelica: granted sanctuary in a church in Mentor (Ohio), 56

Antani, Niraj (Ohio state representative): co-sponsored HB 169, with Keller, Candice, to punish municipalities and school districts that adopted sanctuary policies, 41

Arizona's SB1070 (2010): also known as show me your papers law, 25, 179n48; Supreme Court ruling allows local police to investigate migration status, 178n15

Arrellano, Elvira, 8, 52, 55; emphasis on motherhood, 26; her actions reflect new sanctuary model, 25; sought sanctuary in a Chicago church (2006), 7, 25; sought sanctuary to contest deportation, 7-8; US-born son (Saúl), 25

asylum seekers' political theater: civil society asked to address state-produced population mobility, 157; governors Abbott (Texas), Ducey (Arizona), and DeSantis (Florida) involuntarily transported asylum seekers, and deployed the concept of sanctuary, 156, 159; Leeser, Oscar (El Paso mayor) also transported asylum seekers to New York City, 156-57;

Pérez, Nelson (*cont.*)
 views the concept of accompaniment as
 rooted in the Judeo-Christian practice
 of pilgrimage, 97; welcome the stranger,
 108, 144. *See also* accompaniment
precarity: a shared experience, 2, 4, 15, 57;
 among Latina/o residents of Ohio, 2,
 4-5, 12, 15, 44, 80, 161; and sanctuary,
 44, 159; and the COVID-19 Pandemic,
 175-76n44; as a historical and structural
 condition in Puerto Rico, 94; exacerbated by Hurricane María, 82-83, 98;
 explanation of term, 173n7; in Puerto
 Rico, 83; in the aftermath of ICE workplace raid at Corso's Flower & Garden
 Center, 102; overlapping experiences
 of Central American, Mexican, and
 Puerto Rican households, 5; shared
 across communities of color, LGBTQ
 people, Muslims, Jews, and others, 5,
 21, 57; shared across Latin American
 and African American communities, 5;
 state-produced, 112
Proposition 187 (California, 1994), 28

Rabben, Linda: sanctuary a common element in religious traditions, 2, 6; sanctuary practices engage law, 9; sanctuary
 remains a morally and religious based
 strategy, 9
Ramírez, Hilda: granted sanctuary at the
 St. Andrew's Presbyterian Church in
 Austin (Texas), 48, 182n6; participated
 in the Columbus Mennonite Church
 sanctuary event (2018), 48
Ransby, Barbara, 162; importance of
 building nationally-linked political
 struggles, 9; importance of the Combahee River Collective Statement (1977),
 9, 174-75n24; importance of the long
 history of Black feminist praxis, 8; liberation and freedom struggles of Black
 queer youth, 116; metaphor for national

coalition building, 9; need for a more
 rigorous political education, 9
resilience, 117; among victims of Hurricane María, 82; Bonilla's, Yarimar,
 strong critique of the concept, 92,
 187n29; dual and opposing dimensions
 of, 82; Lloréns, Hilda critical but ac-
 cepting view of the concept of, 187n29
Rios, Victor: youth control complex, 33;
 youth control complex explained, 33
Rivera, Celestino: his activism influenced by
 the Black Power, Chicano, and the Young
 Lords movements, 126; observed the
 important role of women in social movements, 40; parishioner at Sacred Heart
 Chapel, 120, 125; police chief of Lorain,
 38; sanctuary and local police, 38-39
Rodríguez V, Jorge Juan: importance of
 religion and political actions, 11-12
Roe v Wade: Supreme Court ruling on
 abortion stimulated a rhetoric of sanctuary, 160
Romero, Óscar A. (Roman Catholic archbishop), 141: assassinated in El Salvador
 (1980), 24, 140
Ruiz, Jason: on sanctuary as based in the
 divine, 6; on the New Sanctuary Movement, 7

Sacred Heart Chapel/ La Capilla del
 Sagrado Corazon (Lorain), 39; active
 in the collection of money and items
 for *Los Niños de Corso's*, 111; Bishop
 Pérez, Nelson (Cleveland Diocese), held
 mass at, 95; Corso's raid detainees were
 parishioners of, 96; founded to meet
 the needs of the Mexican and Puerto
 Rican communities in Lorain (1952), 90;
 has played an important role in Lorain,
 89-90; hosted a fair in support of Puerto
 Rican newcomers, 90-91; participated
 in the collection of relief for victims of
 Hurricane María in Puerto Rico, 86-88;

ABOUT THE AUTHOR

GINA M. PÉREZ is Professor in the Department of Comparative American Studies at Oberlin College. She is the author of *Citizen, Student, Soldier: Latina/o Youth, JROTC, and the American Dream*, and *The Near Northwest Side Story: Migration, Displacement, and Puerto Rican Families*; co-editor (with Alex Chávez) of *Ethnographic Refusals, Unruly Latinidades*; and co-editor (with Frank Guridy and Adrian Burgos Jr.) of *Beyond El Barrio: Everyday Life in Latina/o America*.